It's Not Hysteria

It's Not Hysteria

EVERYTHING YOU NEED TO KNOW
ABOUT YOUR REPRODUCTIVE HEALTH
(BUT WERE NEVER TOLD)

Karen Tang, MD, MPH

FLATIRON
BOOKS
NEW YORK

IT'S NOT HYSTERIA. Copyright © 2024 by Karen Tang. All rights reserved. Printed in the United States of America. For information, address Flatiron Books, 120 Broadway, New York, NY 10271.

www.flatironbooks.com

Illustrations by Suzanne Hayes, MS, CMI

Library of Congress Cataloging-in-Publication Data

Names: Tang, Karen, author.
Title: It's not hysteria : everything you need to know about your reproductive health
     (but were never told) / Karen Tang, MD, MPH.
Description: First edition. | New York : Flatiron Books, [2024] | Includes bibliographical
     references and index.
Identifiers: LCCN 2023048068 | ISBN 9781250894151 (hardcover) | ISBN 9781250894182 (ebook)
Subjects: LCSH: Reproductive health.
Classification: LCC RG133 .T34 2024 | DDC 618.2—dc23/eng/20240123
LC record available at https://lccn.loc.gov/2023048068

Our books may be purchased in bulk for promotional, educational, or business use. Please contact your local bookseller or the Macmillan Corporate and Premium Sales Department at 1-800-221-7945, extension 5442, or by email at MacmillanSpecialMarkets@macmillan.com.

First Edition: 2024

10 9 8 7 6 5 4 3 2 1

To everyone whose health has suffered because of the patriarchy.

You are seen, you are believed, and you deserve change.

CONTENTS

Part III: What Are the Treatments?

It's Not
Hysteria

Introduction

This Is Your Story

I was motivated to write this book by countless stories I've heard over the years from patients in my practice, of people who have suffered enormously from a wide range of gynecologic issues: pelvic pain, menopause, abnormal periods, sexual dysfunction, infertility, and others. I realized I couldn't choose just one person's story to illustrate why gynecologic problems are problematic. Because if you're holding this book in your hands, then you likely have your own story, and I can guess it involves one of these issues:

- You've suffered with excruciating pelvic pain, horrific period bleeding, or both—probably for many years.
- Period problems or pelvic pain have affected your ability to function, go to school or work, or engage in activities you enjoy such as exercise and sex. Your life has started to revolve around your period or ovulation, when pain, bleeding, and mood swings take over everything.
- You've tried to tell family members, friends, even doctors about your experiences but have been told "That's normal," "Everyone's periods are like that," "You're just being dramatic," or "Just take birth control."

- You may have bowel issues, such as constipation, diarrhea, pain with bowel movements, bloating, and nausea, or bladder issues, such as urinary frequency and urgency. You wonder if this is all in your head.

- You may be suffering from sexual dysfunction, pelvic organ prolapse, infertility, or vulvovaginal symptoms that you are embarrassed to bring up with family or friends or even your doctor, and you're not sure what questions to ask or how to get help.

- You may be transgender or nonbinary, assigned female at birth. You may no longer be having periods because of testosterone, but somehow you're still having pelvic pain or irregular bleeding. You're not sure what could be happening, and these menstrual and pelvic issues are worsening your gender dysphoria.

Your story is more than enough. You already know why these topics are vitally important. Your experience is one of millions that are both completely individual and terribly similar.

In my career as a minimally invasive gynecologic surgeon, I've heard more of these stories than I can count—stories from people just like you who have felt frustrated, overwhelmed, unheard. People who were desperate for information and solutions to their unbearable symptoms and searching for guidance on how to find the help that they need. Often, they had already seen multiple doctors and bounced between medical offices and emergency rooms, undergoing blood draws and imaging studies but being given no answers. When patients finally find a doctor who partners with them on this path, they feel immense relief that what they've been going through is not just in their heads. It's real. Their suffering has a cause, and there are options to end that suffering.

This book is for them—it's for you. There is hope. And more than just hope, there are concrete steps that can take you from suffering to empowerment and freedom from the symptoms that have prevented you from living the life that you want and deserve. I want to give you the information that you need to be able to understand your symptoms, weigh your options for treatment, and find and communicate with healthcare professionals. I want to help you reclaim your life.

Countless books have been written about dieting, weight loss, and preventing cancer, but there are not nearly enough books about period problems, pelvic pain, sexual health, and fertility issues. These gynecologic problems affect more than half the population, but we don't talk about them. Why? Because they're stigmatized and considered embarrassing, and because women's health issues have been universally understudied and underfunded. We need to change every aspect of this status quo. People deserve resources to learn about their bodies and the options available to treat their symptoms, and right now, our education and formal medical systems are falling short. I hope this book is one step toward filling the enormous need out there for reliable and accessible gynecologic health information.

I want *It's Not Hysteria* to create a revolution for how people understand their bodies and their choices and how the medical community communicates with patients. One of my favorite comedians, Ali Wong, said, "I have suffered *enough*" when it comes to the physical and emotional challenges of pregnancy and childbirth. Just because a biological function can be painful doesn't mean that the pain is acceptable or that you must continue suffering. If you are like most people assigned female at birth, you have almost certainly suffered far more than you should have already. The injustice needs to end now, and I'm going to start by arming you with the information that will help you take control of your health.

HOW TO USE THIS BOOK

This is not a textbook. Textbooks fill a need, but it wasn't my goal to write one. Each of the topics that I will cover could fill a textbook on its own and require years of education and training for a doctor to master. This book cannot possibly cover everything about every reproductive health condition. Instead, I want to give you clear explanations of basic sex education and anatomy, an overview of common gynecologic issues, a framework to understand your symptoms and your treatment options, and a practical guide for how to seek care.

You can think of this book as a greatest-hits collection of gynecologic topics. You can read only the sections that are relevant to you, or all of them if you're interested in learning as much as possible about these conditions.

Most important, this book will show you how to take concrete steps toward changing your health. It will arm you with facts to better understand your body and weigh the options available to you.

NOTE ON GENDER-INCLUSIVE LANGUAGE

You'll notice right away that I use gender-inclusive language in this book. As a doctor who cares for transgender and nonbinary patients and as an ally to the LGBTQIA+ community, I understand that language and respect matter. I'm a gynecologist, but I don't treat only women. Transgender men, intersex, and nonbinary individuals assigned female at birth also suffer from gynecologic problems. I want everyone who may be dealing with these health problems to feel seen and included in this discussion. Using inclusive language can mean the absolute world to people who have been discriminated against or physically threatened for being themselves. My hope is that more and more doctors will put effort into being purposeful in the use of gender-inclusive and gender-neutral language. I also hope that readers who may not know much about these issues will learn.

In some medical scenarios, gender-inclusive language may actually be more precise. For example, I may refer to "people with a uterus" when discussing uterine fibroids because some women have had hysterectomies, meaning the uterus has been surgically removed, and some intersex people may identify as women but do not have a uterus.

In many parts of this book, particularly the chapter on history and sections that discuss research studies, I use the term *women* to refer to cisgender women because that's the terminology used in the reference documents. Sadly, there are almost no studies on the gynecologic experiences of transgender men and nonbinary individuals—though hopefully more research and information will be available in the future. In this book, as in my medical practice, I try to honor the experiences of women while acknowledging the diversity of our modern population—including the millions of people who do not identify as women but suffer from gynecologic problems. I thank you all for your understanding as I try to make this book a resource for everyone.

MEDICAL DISCLAIMER

This book will provide information about medical conditions, testing, and treatment; however, it cannot diagnose your personal symptoms or tell you which treatments to choose. Any health concerns you have should be discussed with a doctor who can go over risks and benefits of options and help you select the treatment that's right for you.

MESSAGE TO HEALTHCARE PROVIDERS

To my readers who are healthcare workers—doctors, nurses, nurse practitioners, physician assistants, physical therapists, medical assistants, students, and anyone who has dedicated their lives to caring for patients: I've learned from and been inspired by you, and I look forward to partnering with you to change the status quo in reproductive health.

My fellow OB-GYN and gynecologic specialists: You all know the beauty and shortcomings of our field. We chose a field of medicine with some of the highest malpractice rates and the hardest hours, one where even standard medical treatments are subject to raging political battles. We stay in this field because we love our patients and believe in the importance of the work.

Despite our individual compassion and dedication, the healthcare system is failing too many of our patients. It takes most endometriosis patients seven years and visits to three or more doctors to receive a diagnosis. Imagine suffering with debilitating pain for seven years while trying to get help from doctor after doctor. I know that this isn't because providers don't care about their patients or are misogynistic. We want to be the best caregivers and diagnosticians that we can be. That said, we are the products of our medical education system and training. Unfortunately, the lessons we learned originated in a patriarchal society that often got it wrong. Medical students are taught that women who complain about pain, bleeding, GI and bladder symptoms, migraines, and fatigue but who have normal ultrasounds are just anxious, not that those symptoms are classic signs of endometriosis. If doctors perpetuate these mistaken ideas, we've gotten it wrong, despite our best intentions.

The information in the medical sections in this book may or may not be new to healthcare providers. Even if the basics are familiar, I hope this book will still be a helpful resource for you and your patients.

The system may be broken, but we keep on striving. We know how extraordinary it feels to hear patients say their symptoms are gone, their lives have been changed, and that you made all the difference. Doctors and patients have the same goal: to succeed in alleviating symptoms, allowing people to live the healthiest and happiest lives possible. Together we can fight for that goal. I look forward to sharing this journey with you.

PART I

What's the Background?

The History of Hysteria

How did we get here? The treatment of women throughout history provides insight into why period problems, pelvic pain, and other gynecologic health issues are often minimized or overlooked today. From ancient Greek physicians to witch hunts to modern medicine, women's reproductive functions, mental and emotional health, and perceived moral character have been inextricably linked. Even though these beliefs were often inaccurate, they were so commonly viewed as facts that the difference between truth and myth is still difficult to distinguish today. Indignities, injustices, and traumas that women have suffered throughout the centuries seep into modern views of female bodies and health.

Women's bodies and medical concerns have been misunderstood, mismanaged, and outright dismissed since the beginning of recorded history. The fathers of Western medicine and philosophy, who were greatly respected for their pioneering work in some regards, put forth many theories about women's health that sound absurd today but were accepted as gospel for generations. For example, if a woman exhibited symptoms that couldn't be explained, she was said to be suffering from faulty sexual organs, sinister forces such as witchcraft, or the catchall explanation: hysteria. This word, *hysteria*, contains all the judgments and assumptions about female bodies that have existed for thousands of years. It suggests that women's distressing physical symptoms stem from a combination of anxiety, mental or neurologic weakness, and broken uteri, rather than from not-yet-understood medical conditions.

Hysteria—an idea that originated in ancient Greece—was thought to be a combination of physical, emotional, and psychological distress somehow tied to the uterus or womanhood; it was considered an actual medical affliction for hundreds of years. In modern language, the word *hysterical* implies a person is out of control, overreacting, and imagining things, but the concept of hysteria originated as a physical malady. Through the centuries, hysteria shifted from a disease of the body to one of the mind, but the connection between the supposed flaws of women's reproductive organs and their mental well-being remained.

History provides the philosophical framework of modern-day medical systems. Even if the terms are antiquated, some concepts persist as an undercurrent in how gynecologic health is perceived and managed today. Holding the fallacies and mistakes of the past up for scrutiny can illuminate the ways in which healthcare systems must change in the present.

THE WANDERING WOMB

One of the foundations of Western medicine is a body of work called the Hippocratic Corpus, a collection of theories and teachings by Greek physicians dating from the fifth century BCE. Many people have heard of the Hippocratic oath, the code of ethics recited by students upon entering medical school. But most people don't know that Hippocrates theorized that many medical problems were caused by the uterus literally moving around the body—fleeing from unpleasant sensations such as feeling cold, or running toward desirable targets like sex and pregnancy. This concept, called the wandering womb, was thought to be caused by lack of sexual activity. Healers recommended treatments such as genital massage, intercourse, and pregnancy to appease the uterus and even held honey or other sweet foods near the genitals to trick the uterus into returning to its rightful place. The Greek philosopher Plato explained the wandering womb this way:

> And in women again . . . whenever the matrix or womb as it is called—which is an indwelling creature desirous of child-bearing—remains without fruit long beyond the due season, it is vexed and takes it ill; and by straying all ways through the body and blocking up the passages of the breath and preventing respiration it casts the body into the uttermost distress, and causes, moreover, all kinds of maladies, until the desire and love of the two sexes unite them.

While no modern doctor believes that the uterus is literally zipping around the body, echoes of these ideas persist in today's treatment of certain gynecologic problems. Patients with endometriosis are sometimes told to get pregnant to treat the condition, which is hardly a sustainable long-term plan, especially for patients who don't want to be pregnant. The medical community and society in general too often presume that anyone with a working uterus must want to use it for pregnancy, even when people say that they don't want to conceive or are done having children.

Many patients who seek tubal ligation or hysterectomy (surgery to remove the uterus), some who are well into their thirties or forties and who have children already, are told by doctors that they are too young to make such a decision and will someday regret it. Even in modern times, society still assumes women will always desire fertility—they just don't realize it. It's hard to imagine a non-gynecologic medical scenario where physicians would tell competent adult patients that they don't actually know their goals and therefore can't make decisions about their health. In this regard, the historical influences of the wandering womb remain.

FROM ANCIENT GREECE TO WITCH TRIALS

The term *hysteria* is derived from the ancient Greek word for uterus, *hystera*, and the condition was considered for centuries to be a physical malady caused by the uterus, an expansion of the concept of the wandering womb. *Hysteria* covered a wide range of symptoms, including fits, seizures, strange movements, hallucinations, anxiety, insanity, and pain.

Although disturbing behaviors and madness were thought to be signs of demonic possession or witchcraft in medieval and Renaissance Europe, some doctors were still attributing these symptoms to frustrated uteri. In 1602, an English physician, Edward Jorden, published a book titled *A Briefe Discourse of a Disease Called the Suffocation of the Mother—mother* being an old-fashioned term for the womb. In this book, Jorden explained that the physical symptoms attributed to witchcraft were actually from *passio hysterica*, or "womb suffocation." Similar to the wandering womb, a suffocated uterus—one that was not fulfilling its natural needs for sex or pregnancy—could cause distressing signs in the rest of the body. Jorden argued that this was why virgins and widows were more susceptible to the fits that were interpreted as witchcraft. He gave testimony at trial on behalf of women accused of witchcraft, trying, unsuccessfully, to explain that they were not witches but simply the victims of a suffocated uterus. Jorden's book is considered to be the earliest description of hysteria in the English language. In trying to present a scientific counterpoint to witchcraft and demonic possession, Jorden fell back on the equally misinformed idea that hysteria was to blame for these women's symptoms.

Today, despite centuries of advances in other areas of medicine, many aspects of women's health are still poorly researched and lack data to guide treatment. A surprising number of professional gynecologic recommendations over the years have been based on the opinions of leaders in the field rather than on objective facts or scientific studies. For this reason, the most cutting-edge medical theories and treatments of their time have later been deemed incorrect—in some cases, after causing suffering that exceeded the original problem being treated.

THE CLITORIS AND OVARIES IN THE NINETEENTH CENTURY

The heyday of hysteria was the 1800s, when doctors attempted to understand its origins and treatment through a formal medical lens. The uterus was no longer thought to be the source of the problem, and other female sexual organs were scrutinized as possible causes. At the same time, the field of gynecology began to develop as a specialty within Western medicine.

In the mid-1800s, gynecologists experimented with the surgical removal of the clitoris (known as a clitoridectomy) or the ovaries (an oophorectomy) to treat hysteria. Isaac Baker Brown was a well-known gynecologist in England and the president of the Medical Society of London. He recommended clitoridectomy as a treatment for insanity, epilepsy, and hysteria because he hypothesized these conditions were caused by masturbation. In the United States, Dr. Robert Battey, the president of the Georgia Medical Association, was one of the first physicians to surgically remove the ovaries; at the time, oophorectomies were known as Battey's operations. Battey attributed various medical problems, including epilepsy and hysteria, to the ovaries and recommended removal of the ovaries for cases that didn't respond to other treatments. Many thousands of oophorectomies were performed in the United States in the latter part of the nineteenth century because of these mistaken beliefs.

Fortunately, "therapeutic" clitoridectomies and the removal of normal ovaries fell out of favor relatively quickly due to their surgical risks, mortality rate, and lack of effectiveness, but not before scores of women suffered the unnecessary removal of their sexual organs.

Today, doctors no longer diagnose hysteria or perform clitoridectomies or oophorectomies to relieve it. Surgeries to remove the uterus and ovaries definitely have a role in modern medicine to treat certain conditions, such as fibroids and gender dysphoria, or to decrease cancer risks.

The problem arises when people are told that they have no options except a hysterectomy or an oophorectomy, even when they want to preserve their fertility, or when they are not adequately counseled about potential risks or alternatives. I've had many patients who underwent a hysterectomy or an oophorectomy without knowing exactly why; they just say, "The doctor told me I needed it."

HYSTERIA AND THE CENTRAL NERVOUS SYSTEM

In the late nineteenth century, neurologists took their turn at managing hysteria, treating it as a disorder of the nervous system. Dr. Silas Weir Mitchell is considered one of the founders of modern neurology. While caring for injured soldiers during the Civil War, he became an expert in nerve injuries and even coined the term *phantom limb syndrome*. He observed that nerve damage could cause hysterical symptoms and developed a famous rest cure for victims of neurologic trauma that involved a combination of social isolation, bed rest, limited physical and intellectual activity, a diet of rich foods, and electrotherapy to restore the nerves. After the war ended, he started a lucrative practice applying this rest cure to white middle- and upper-class women suffering from what was diagnosed as hysteria and nervous exhaustion. Some of the patients who underwent the rest cure were intellectuals, writers, and artists, among them Virginia Woolf, Edith Wharton, and Jane Addams. While resting and eating well sounds pleasant, the women subjected to this rest cure often faced extreme physical, social, and intellectual restrictions.

Charlotte Perkins Gilman was a patient of Mitchell's, and she based her famous short story "The Yellow Wallpaper" on her experience of the rest cure. Intellectual and creative activities were thought to exhaust the nerves and sap energy from the body, so patients were isolated and kept idle. For Gilman, this caused even worse "mental agony" than the depression the cure was supposed to be treating. In "The Yellow Wallpaper," a nameless protagonist is subjected to the rest cure by her physician husband; she's kept in an infantilized state in a New England nursery and forbidden to work or write. She is driven to madness and imagines that a woman is trapped within the wallpaper. By the end of the story, she has become the woman in the wallpaper and frees herself by ripping the wallpaper off the walls.

While women are no longer literally trapped in rooms for modern gynecologic treatments, the pattern of paternalistic management of female patients lingers. Women continue to be treated as if they need to be protected from their own minds when it comes to reproductive decisions such as birth control, sterilization, and abortion. Similarly, treatments that can cause people to feel worse than their original problems do continue to be used. For example, hormonal birth control and antidepressants can be absolutely transformative for many patients, but for some, the mental and physical side effects are worse than the symptoms being treated. The problem isn't that these options are offered but rather that some healthcare providers insist that patients continue to use them even when the treatments are causing significant distress and aren't improving symptoms.

CHARCOT, FREUD, AND THE MIND

By the end of the nineteenth century, the perceived cause of hysteria had moved from the sexual organs to the nerves to, finally, the mind. Dr. Jean-Martin Charcot, a French physician, is considered one of the founders of modern neurology. He was the first to identify conditions such as multiple sclerosis, Charcot-Marie-Tooth disorder, and amyotrophic lateral sclerosis (ALS). He also gained fame for treating women diagnosed as hysterical with hypnosis; he held large public demonstrations wherein women would writhe, shriek, moan, and then alter their behavior under the influence of hypnosis. Photographs from these dramatic performances are still used as a visual representation of the concept of hysteria.

Dr. Sigmund Freud was a student of Charcot, and he also initially tried to cure hysteria with hypnosis. In the book *Studies on Hysteria*, he and his coauthor, Dr. Josef Breuer, theorized that hysteria was the physical manifestation of repressed memories. Freud developed these ideas further in his psychoanalytic theories, stating that repressed memories of childhood sexual trauma and sexual fantasies were the causes of hysteria and that getting the patient to identify the repressed memories and fantasies through talk therapy could cure physical symptoms. Charcot and Freud took the concept of hysteria from a disease of the body to one of the mind, leading to the modern perception that if a patient is suffering from disturbing symptoms but no physical cause for them can be identified, the problem must be psychological.

There is an entire category in the current edition of the *Diagnostic and Statistical Manual of Mental Disorders* (the *DSM*), a reference used by mental health professionals, called somatic symptom disorders. Patients with somatic symptom disorders suffer from bodily complaints without an identifiable medical cause that are then thought to be a result of psychosocial stresses or trauma. The vast majority of patients diagnosed with somatic symptom disorders are women, with a ten-to-one female-to-male ratio. Given that many women with medical conditions such as endometriosis and autoimmune diseases are initially told that their symptoms are all in their heads, it's likely that many people diagnosed with somatic symptom disorders actually suffer from an undiagnosed physical malady. Since gynecologic conditions such as endometriosis, pelvic floor dysfunction, and premenstrual dysphoric disorder can cause a wide range of symptoms but don't show up on imaging studies or lab tests, patients will often be told by doctor after doctor that there is nothing wrong with them and that the problem must be emotional or mental. Sadly, this is our twenty-first-century version of hysteria.

BLACK WOMEN AND BODILY AUTONOMY

In the United States, historical records and research about women's health have traditionally focused on the health of white, cisgender, heterosexual women. The experiences of people of color and those in the LGBTQIA+ community have largely been left out of the textbooks and research studies.

In recent years, we've seen clear evidence of serious racial disparities in health outcomes for Black women, most notably when it comes to maternal mortality rates compared with white women. Researchers are investigating why such major differences exist. While the causes are complex, the American College of Obstetricians and Gynecologists (ACOG) and other professional organizations within the field of OBGYN acknowledged the role that racism has played in a joint statement issued in 2020:

> Recognizing that race is a social construct, not biologically based, is important to understanding that racism, not race, impacts healthcare, health, and health outcomes. Systemic and institutional racism are pervasive in our country and in our country's health care institutions, including the fields of obstetrics and gynecology. Many examples of foundational advances in the specialty of obstetrics and gynecology are rooted in racism and oppression.

Racial biases can be traced back to the earliest days of gynecology. The physician considered the father of gynecology, James Marion Sims, founded the first hospital for women in the United States and invented the modern version of the speculum used for examining the vagina by bending a pewter spoon. He pioneered surgical techniques for the repair of vaginal fistulas, which are injuries between the vagina and the bladder or rectum caused by obstructed childbirth. He was president of the American Medical Association, and he became one of the most famous physicians in the country, with numerous statues and memorials erected to honor him. Until recently, the medical community and the general public didn't know that he had developed several of his surgical techniques by operating on unanesthetized, enslaved Black women. Sims's records suggest there were perhaps a dozen women in total, but we know the names of only three of the women: Anarcha, Betsey, and Lucy. Anarcha alone endured thirty experimental surgical procedures. Sims conducted his experiments in the 1840s, when anesthesia for surgery was not yet widely utilized, and per Sims's own notes, the women suffered terribly during these operations. In that time, it was widely believed that Black people were less sensitive than white people to pain, both in terms of the hardships endured in slavery and the pain from accidents and surgical procedures. While Sims might not have declared this belief outright, it is notable that he did not perform fistula repair surgeries on white women until several years later, when he had perfected his techniques and used anesthesia.

Several recent studies have demonstrated that unconscious biases still exist in the treatment of Black patients, particularly Black women. Black patients are consistently undertreated for pain; they receive less pain medication than white patients do for objectively painful conditions such as broken bones and appendicitis. Black patients are less likely to be offered minimally invasive surgery for the treatment of fibroids and they experience higher rates of complications from surgery. A 2016 study showed that half of the medical students and residents polled believed that Black people had less sensitive nerve endings, thicker skin, and lower perception of pain than white people, which has no basis in scientific fact.

Black women also endure markedly elevated rates of maternal mortality. In the United States, they are three times more likely than white women to die in pregnancy or childbirth, even after accounting for factors such as income, education level, insurance coverage, and prenatal care. This statistic goes up in the UK to four times more likely. A large study conducted by the National Bureau of Economic Research that looked at birth records from California over a ten-year period showed that the maternal mortality rate for the richest Black women (top quintile in income) was similar to that of the poorest white women (lowest quintile). Therefore, the differences in outcomes are not simply because of resources, nutrition, or access to quality healthcare. There is likely a complex combination of factors at play, including potential implicit biases that may lead healthcare providers to take complaints of pain or symptoms that suggest preeclampsia or blood clots less seriously. Some researchers suggest that the chronic stress of discrimination and being in a constant fight-or-flight state, which causes high cortisol and epinephrine levels, results in adverse effects or weathering of the body, worsening blood pressure, increasing the risk of heart disease, and even changing the DNA itself. The weathering hypothesis can potentially explain why people of all races who are subject to chronic social stress experience poorer health, but this phenomenon has been studied most often in the context of health disparities facing Black communities. Research has shown that Black people experience more social stressors, such as discrimination, than white people, even after adjusting for socioeconomic status, and there is a clear relationship between life stressors and poor health.

Systemic racial biases can also affect health in unexpected ways, even through something as seemingly innocuous as hairstyle. In a study by Duke University School of Business in which participants were given different photos of potential job candidates with identical qualifications, Black women with natural hair were given lower scores for professionalism and were recommended less often for interviews than Black women with straightened hair or white women with straight or curly hair. These biases put pressure on Black women to alter their hair to fit Eurocentric standards of beauty by using relaxers and hair straighteners. Unfortunately, some chemical relaxers have been shown to increase the risk of both fibroids and uterine cancer. This is one mechanism through which racism can cause serious health disparities.

RESEARCH AND REPRESENTATION

The modern medical system prides itself on being evidence-based and using well-conducted research studies and clinical trials to guide treatment, but bias and gender inequality even seep into scientific research methods. The National Institutes of Health (NIH) is one of the largest sources of funding for medical research in the world, and yet some of the biggest multicenter clinical trials funded by the NIH in the twentieth century excluded women altogether, and it wasn't until 1993 that President Clinton signed an act mandating that NIH-funded human research projects must include women and racial minorities. That was the same year that the U.S. Food and Drug Administration (FDA) finally eliminated a policy from 1977 that actively excluded women of childbearing potential from early-phase drug trials because the medications might cause birth defects. That meant that all reproductive-age women were barred from participation in these studies, even if they were not sexually active, were using contraception, or were in same-sex partnerships. Due to these decades of excluding women from research trials, data about everything from heart disease to medication efficacy do not include information about the effects on women or potential gender differences in results.

Further, there has been very little funding for research on gynecologic conditions and diseases that disproportionately affect women. In the late 1980s, less than 15 percent of the NIH budget was allocated for the study of diseases "unique to or more prevalent or serious in women," including breast and gynecologic cancers, osteoporosis, autoimmune diseases, and other common conditions. Research studies on non-gynecologic diseases that affect the same number of people, or even far fewer, receive significantly more funding than common gynecologic conditions. In 2022, the NIH allocated $37 million for research on smallpox, a disease that was completely eradicated from the United States in 1949. Compare this with the $27 million budgeted for endometriosis, which affects at least 10 percent of women, or the $15 million for fibroids, which affect 70 percent of white women and 80 percent of Black women.

Lack of adequate funding and research means that doctors don't know the basic causes of many gynecologic conditions, much less have options for early diagnosis or effective treatment. For many non-gynecological chronic medical conditions, such as hypertension, diabetes, and asthma, there are multiple different treatment options that target biological causes. However, since the causes of many gynecological conditions, such as endometriosis, fibroids, and polycystic ovarian syndrome, aren't actually known, treatments are limited to managing symptoms or surgically removing organs after the disease has developed. This leads to frustratingly persistent symptoms and repeated procedures and surgeries without a guarantee of lasting relief. In many parts of the world, people who suffer from a litany of gynecologic conditions are offered only birth control or a hysterectomy, without much discussion of alternatives, often because there are no other accessible options. And despite the widespread use of hormonal birth control, there are very few studies comparing different brands and formulations in terms of side effects, tolerability, and effectiveness. The choice of which birth control to use is usually determined by patient preference and trial and error, whereas the type of medications used to treat non-gynecologic conditions such as hypertension and diabetes is based on studies and research.

MEDICAL SYSTEMS AND ACCESS TO CARE

Broken healthcare systems can make it difficult, and sometimes virtually impossible, for people to get adequate gynecologic care. In many OB-GYN practices, low insurance reimbursements, physician shortages, and provider burnout are the norm. Overwhelmed doctors see large numbers of patients in the office each day; some doctors across the United States and the United Kingdom routinely see forty or fifty patients per day. When providers have only ten to thirty minutes allotted per patient, complex health issues or pain concerns cannot be adequately addressed.

Outside of major metropolitan areas, there are shortages of specialists who provide gender-affirming care and treat endometriosis, infertility, pelvic floor dysfunction, and sexual dysfunction, which can lead to patients traveling for hours, paying out of pocket, or waiting many months (in some parts of the world, more than a year) for specialty care. Some people simply have no access to treatment at all. Insurance often does not cover certain services, such as infertility care, which can put these treatments completely out of reach for many patients.

There are also clear gender inequalities in how both private and government insurance plans reimburse women's health services versus how they reimburse services used by men or performed by providers in male-dominated specialties. Gynecologic procedures are reimbursed at significantly lower rates than procedures in any other surgical field, including urology, which treats the male reproductive organs. Compensation for biopsies of the uterus or vulva is much lower than compensation for biopsies of the prostate or scrotum. Extremely difficult and lengthy surgeries that treat endometriosis and fibroids are considered by insurance companies to be worth significantly less than non-gynecologic surgeries that take the same amount of time, or even less, to perform.

Poor insurance payments combined with high malpractice costs, the stress of dealing with life-and-death scenarios, and legislative attacks on reproductive rights have led to an epidemic of physician burnout. In the United States, 40 to 75 percent of OB-GYN physicians report feeling burned out, and many are leaving the practice of medicine altogether. This exodus of OB-GYN specialists is exacerbating the lack of access to care, especially in rural areas, and patients are the ones who will suffer.

WHERE DO WE GO FROM HERE?

In order for physicians to provide high-quality gynecologic care for all patients, a revolution in our existing medical systems must occur. Research and funding for reproductive health needs to increase significantly. Underrepresented minority populations require access to equitable health resources. More extensive training and education for healthcare providers should be implemented. Insurance coverage for OB-GYN care must increase, and medical systems need to invest in more comprehensive reproductive and sexual health programs. Finally, basic health education for the public must be widely accessible so that people can better understand their own bodies.

Advocates for awareness of gynecological conditions such as fibroids, endometriosis, and PCOS work tirelessly to raise awareness and lobby lawmakers to increase federal support for research because they're frustrated with the lack of resources and response from the medical community. However, it cannot be the sole responsibility of people affected by these medical problems to change the system. Healthcare providers, medical administrators, insurance companies, government leaders, and educators all have a part to play. Women and people dealing with gynecologic issues have suffered for thousands of years too long, and it's time to break the cycle. It's not hysteria, and it never was.

Anatomy and Sex Ed

My husband is an ethicist, and he used to teach a college sexual ethics class. Every semester, he would begin by giving his students a quiz about male and female reproductive anatomy and sexual education basics. The idea was that if you don't actually understand how reproduction works, you can't discuss the ethics of it. Every semester, the results were startling, to say the least. Most students couldn't identify the parts of the female and male anatomy in diagrams. When students were asked to draw basic reproductive organs on their own, ovaries were drawn connected to the vagina and the tubes and uterus were left out altogether. Very few people produced an accurate picture.

Again, these were college students. Statistically, more than 90 percent of college students are sexually active, according to the U.S. Health Resources and Services Administration. They were legal adults who had gone through secondary school and had never learned the basics of their own bodies from sex ed teachers, parents, or any other source.

To be clear, I don't fault the students. We all start out not knowing these simple health facts. The system and society are at fault. Sex and reproduction are considered so taboo that people who are old enough to vote, get married, and become parents themselves may not have basic knowledge of their own body parts.

When I see surgical patients in the office, I always draw the pelvic anatomy for them. Always. I don't care if I'm talking to another doctor, a nurse, an astrophysicist, or a high-school student. I start from scratch because everyone deserves the same foundation of knowledge. Similarly, when I teach medical students who are on rotation with me, I always say they need to know what normal is before they can understand what it means for something to be abnormal.

Before exploring problems such as endometriosis and PCOS, it's essential to discuss the basics of pelvic anatomy, the menstrual cycle, and conception in order to understand how the female reproductive system typically works. I will also discuss the parts of the gastrointestinal and urinary systems that are located in the pelvis, because they are close to the reproductive organs, and it is common to have bowel or bladder symptoms with gynecologic conditions.

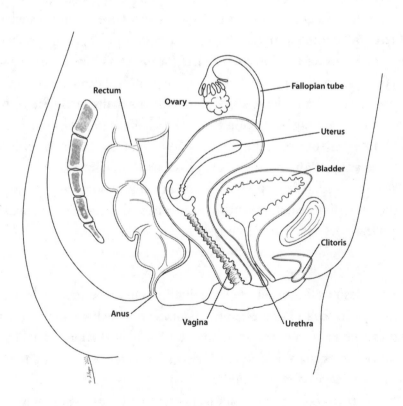

GYNECOLOGIC INTERNAL ORGANS

Reproductive anatomy includes internal organs and external genitalia. Female internal reproductive organs consist of the ovaries, fallopian tubes, uterus, and vagina.

OVARIES

There are two ovaries, and their functions are to release eggs and produce hormones. Each ovary is a few centimeters long, and they are each attached to the uterus and to the ovarian blood vessels that anchor them to the wall of the pelvis.

Eggs / Follicles

People assigned female at birth are born with all the eggs, called *oocytes* or *ova*, in their ovaries that they will ever have. Unlike testicles, which can continue producing sperm for a person's lifetime, the ovaries do not make new oocytes. During a menstrual cycle, an egg—usually just one—is released, a process called ovulation. Eggs in the ovaries that are not released will eventually break down and be reabsorbed by the body, and the quality of the remaining eggs degrades over time. As someone ages, fertility decreases and the risk of miscarriage and certain genetic conditions, such as Down syndrome, in a fetus increases. The ovaries start out with approximately one to two million eggs, but that number drops quickly, and on average, a woman will release only a few hundred eggs in her lifetime.

Hormone Production

The ovaries produce what are typically thought of as the female hormones: estrogen and progesterone. *Follicles* are structures in the ovary that consist of an oocyte surrounded by fluid and a ring of cells that produce the hormones. Some of these cells secrete estrogen, and after the egg is released during ovulation, those same cells transform into the *corpus luteum*, a cystlike structure that releases progesterone.

Progesterone helps control the growth of the *endometrium*, which is the tissue that lines the cavity of the uterus and comes out as period blood. As the corpus luteum breaks down, progesterone levels drop, which triggers a period to start. The rise and fall of progesterone is what drives period regularity. If a period is happening like clockwork once a month, then you can thank the corpus luteum, because it's hard at work in a very uniform and predictable way. If someone gets pregnant, the corpus luteum and the progesterone that it releases support the pregnancy while it is implanting in the uterus.

The follicular cells also secrete *androgens*, like testosterone, which are commonly thought of as male hormones. Many people think that androgens are made only by testes and don't realize that ovaries actually produce androgens too. Both estrogen and testosterone may play a role in libido and sexual desire. Certain birth control pills and menopause can decrease the amount of estrogen and testosterone released by the ovaries, which may cause a drop in libido.

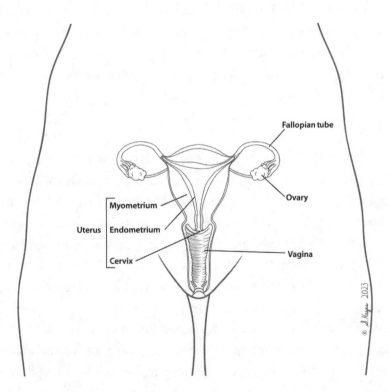

FALLOPIAN TUBES AND CONCEPTION

Fallopian tubes function as corridors from the ovaries to the uterus. They aren't directly attached to the ovaries; the feathery end of each tube, called the *fimbria*, rests on or near the ovary. During ovulation, the egg is pulled into the fimbriated end of the tube. Many people are surprised to learn that the fertilization of an egg by sperm happens in the tube, not the uterus. They're also shocked to hear that after ovulation, the fertile window during which an egg can be fertilized is only twelve to twenty-four hours because the egg is viable for only that short time.

If a sperm cell successfully fertilizes an egg, the developing embryo travels down the rest of the tube and implants in the uterus about five to six days after fertilization. An embryo exists for almost a week before it implants in the uterus or produces any detectable pregnancy hormones. Interestingly, an egg released from one ovary can actually be picked up by the tube on the opposite side. This is important for people who have a tube removed because of damage from, say, an ectopic pregnancy. The remaining tube can pick up eggs from both ovaries because the ovaries are actually quite close together and the fimbriated end of one tube can pull in eggs from the opposite ovary.

UTERUS

The *uterus* is a muscular organ that holds a developing pregnancy. During reproductive years, the average uterus is about the size of a human fist, but it can expand to hold a full-term fetus or fill an entire abdomen if it develops large fibroids. Relative to its size, the uterus can cause an absurd amount of suffering in terms of period problems, pain, abnormal bleeding, and fertility issues.

The shape of the uterus is similar to that of a pear, and the uterine anatomy can be thought of as parts of a pear. The skin of the pear would be the *serosa*, or outer surface of the uterus. The flesh of the pear would be the muscular walls of the uterus, called the *myometrium*. Most fibroids originate from the myometrium, since they are tumors made of myometrial cells. The pear's core is the cavity of the uterus. This is the space where a pregnancy implants and grows. The tissue that lines the cavity is the endometrium, and this loose, glandular tissue grows anew every month to prepare for pregnancy. When pregnancy does occur, the embryo will implant in the endometrium, and the placenta will develop and attach to the endometrial tissue in order to support the growing fetus. If pregnancy doesn't occur that month, the endometrium will shed and come out as menstrual blood. Normally, the endometrium and myometrium exist as separate layers. *Adenomyosis* is a condition where endometrial tissue, or cells that are very similar to endometrial tissue, grows into the myometrium, and there may no longer be a separation between the layers.

Finally, the tapered end of the pear would represent the *cervix*, which is the opening of the uterus that leads into the vagina. The cervix dilates, or opens, to allow a fetus to come down into the vagina during childbirth. Pap smears—Pap is short for Papanicolaou, the name of the scientist who developed them—are tests to screen for cervical pre-cancer or cancer. They're performed during pelvic exams with a small brush that picks up cells from the cervix.

The uterus is connected to the ovaries by short blood vessels. It is also loosely attached to the bladder with a layer of connective tissue. Many people are surprised to hear that the uterus and bladder are connected to each other and not floating separately. When doctors perform surgeries on the uterus, such as C-sections or hysterectomies, the connective tissue holding the bladder and uterus together is cut so that the bladder can be safely pushed away before work on the uterus begins. More of this connective tissue, called the *broad ligament*, sandwiches the uterus front and back and attaches it to the pelvic walls. Two additional types of ligaments, the *round ligaments* and the *uterosacral ligaments*, connect the uterus to the abdominal wall and to the back, respectively, and help prevent the uterus from dropping down into the vagina. The uterosacrals are a common spot for endometriosis to grow, and since they extend to the sacrum at the base of the spine, endometriosis of the uterosacral ligaments can cause lower back pain.

VAGINA

The *vagina* is a canal that leads from the cervix to the outside of the body. It serves a role in sexual intercourse, release of menstrual blood, and childbirth and is made up of a mucus membrane inner layer and a muscular outer layer. The inner walls of the vagina during reproductive years are pleated in folds called *rugae* that allow the vagina to stretch and expand during intercourse or childbirth. The vaginal walls have receptors that respond to estrogen, which helps the vagina maintain lubrication, collagen development, and elasticity.

The vagina contains a fascinating ecosystem called a *microbiome*, which consists of normal bacteria that live in the vagina to help keep it healthy. *Lactobacillus* species are the most common vaginal flora; they produce lactic acid and hydrogen peroxide, which give the vagina its normal acidic pH. This acidic environment helps prevent the growth of disease-causing bacteria and yeast. Gynecologists advise that douching is unnecessary and actually harmful, as it wipes out the good bacteria that is essential for normal vaginal health.

The *Grafenberg spot*, commonly called the *G-spot*, is a somewhat controversial concept. It's a sensitive erogenous area that may feel like a rough patch on the lower front wall of the vagina. There is no consensus in the medical literature regarding whether or not the G-spot exists as a physical structure or, if it does exist, what type of tissue it consists of. But in a review of studies, the majority of women polled reported having a G-spot that could be felt on self-exam. Some people state that stimulation of the G-spot can cause intense pleasurable sensations or orgasm, and there are women who are able to achieve orgasm only with G-spot stimulation. Other women find the sensation unpleasant or feel they don't have a G-spot.

LOWER URINARY TRACT

The urinary tract is the organ system through which urine is created and passed out of the body. The lower urinary tract consists of the parts of the system that are located in the pelvis: the bladder, ureters, and urethra.

BLADDER

The *bladder* is the organ that holds urine. The muscle that makes up the wall of the bladder is called the *detrusor muscle*, and this muscle contracts to empty the bladder. Sometimes the muscle can spasm or contract too much, and that can cause overactive bladder (OAB) symptoms of urinary urgency, frequency, leaking, or incontinence.

The inner lining of the bladder is called the *mucosa*. This lining can become inflamed or irritated and cause *interstitial cystitis* (IC), which in turn can cause chronic bladder discomfort as well as pelvic pain. Usually, when someone gets a urinary tract infection (UTI), it's an infection of the bladder, the urethra, or both.

URETHRA

The *urethra* is the tube through which urine exits the bladder and then the body. The opening of the urethra is located in front of the opening of the vagina. When people say that "women have three openings down there," they're referring to the urethra, the vagina, and the anus. *Urethral sphincters*, or muscles that wrap around the urethra, help prevent urine from leaking. Kegel exercises, which cut off the stream of urine, tense the urethral sphincter and the vaginal muscles of the pelvic floor.

URETERS

The *ureters* are the tubes through which urine travels between the kidneys and the bladder. They pass along the walls of the pelvis and enter the back wall of the bladder, which is close to the cervix and uterus.

These structures are important in gynecologic surgery for several reasons. It's common for endometriosis to grow on the pelvic walls where the ureters are located. Severe endometriosis can scar or block off the ureters, causing a backup of urine that can put so much pressure on that kidney that it leads to kidney failure. The ureters can be injured in gynecologic surgeries for endometriosis or hysterectomies, so gynecologists will frequently check their location while operating by looking for the movement of urine within them. The ureters are located just under the surface of the pelvic walls, and the flow of urine can actually be seen visually during surgery as a ripple passing along the ureter.

LOWER GASTROINTESTINAL TRACT

Food travels through the gastrointestinal tract, which includes the stomach, small intestine, large intestine (or colon), rectum, and anus. The colon, rectum, and anus, also known as the lower GI tract, pass through the pelvis and sit right next to the female internal organs. This proximity is the reason that gynecologic conditions such as endometriosis and fibroids can cause bothersome bowel symptoms.

SIGMOID COLON

The *sigmoid colon* is the end portion of the colon. Also known as the descending colon, it is located on the left side of the pelvis; when it passes behind the uterus, it becomes the rectum. When people are severely constipated or have other colon issues such as diverticulitis they may experience severe left pelvic pain, which can be mistaken for gynecologic problems. It's not uncommon for someone to think she feels pain in her left ovary when the cause is actually a gastrointestinal issue, such as a large amount of hard stool in the sigmoid colon.

RECTUM

The *rectum* is the very end of the colon, the part that holds stool before it leaves the body through the anus. It is located behind the uterus and vagina. The connective tissue between the uterus and the rectum is called the *posterior cul-de-sac*. The uterus and rectum rest right on top of each other. Gynecologic conditions such as endometriosis, adenomyosis, and fibroids that grow in the cul-de-sac or the uterus can inflame or compress the rectum, causing bothersome bowel symptoms. Endometriosis and adenomyosis can cause diarrhea, constipation, pain with bowel movements, or blood in the stool, and large fibroids can push against the rectum, causing severe constipation. In its most severe form, endometriosis can actually grow into the colon or rectum and cause the uterus and rectum to fuse together.

ANUS

The *anus* is the opening through which stool leaves the rectum and exits the body. There are also *anal sphincters*, muscles that wrap around the anus just like urethral sphincters do around the urethra. *Hemorrhoids* are swollen veins located in the lower rectum (called internal hemorrhoids) or underneath the skin of the anus (external hemorrhoids). These can be caused by chronic straining from constipation or from increased pressure on the veins in pregnancy.

EXTERNAL GENITALIA

The female external genitalia, collectively known as the *vulva*, is composed of the labia minora, labia majora, mons pubis, and the clitoral complex. The vulva and vagina are often confused with each other, but the vulva is external and the vagina is internal.

LABIA MINORA

The *labia minora* are the lips of tissue just outside the opening of the vagina. The labia can be different lengths and colors. Some people are self-conscious about the appearance of their labia, perhaps because a partner has suggested that they are too dark, too pink, too light, or a strange shape. In reality, there is a huge variation in labia, and unless someone has pain, discomfort with sex or exercise, or lesions, the labia are almost certainly normal. If the labia are not changing in appearance or causing symptoms, then they're exactly as they should be, regardless of partners' comments or societal pressures.

LABIA MAJORA

The fleshy areas of the vulva located on the sides of the labia minora are the *labia majora*. The labia majora are essentially the folds of skin and tissue between the labia minora and the creases of the groin and inner thigh. They contain sweat and lubricating glands and become engorged with blood during sexual arousal.

MONS PUBIS

The *mons pubis* is the mound of fatty tissue just above the clitoris and clitoral hood. Most pubic hair arises from the mons.

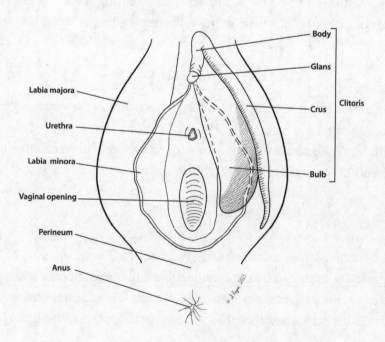

CLITORIS

Most people think of the small buttonlike object as the *clitoris*, but this is actually only the *glans*, or tip, of it. The clitoris is a much larger structure that consists of several parts. The glans contains thousands of nerve endings and is extremely sensitive to the touch. It is covered by a fold of vulvar skin called the clitoral hood. The glans extends underneath the surface to become the body of the clitoris, which splits into two arms, or crura. The body and crura are made up of erectile tissue which is similar to the shaft of a penis. The crura extend for quite a distance underneath the skin, up to four inches along the sides of the vagina and urethra. The vestibular bulbs of the clitoris are paired erectile structures that extend down toward the vaginal wall and can swell to double their usual size during arousal. The vast majority of the clitoris is not visible from the outside, and the whole system is much more extensive than many people realize.

THE MENSTRUAL CYCLE

The *menstrual cycle* is a complex interaction between the brain, ovaries, and uterus that prepares the body for possible pregnancy every month. From someone's first period in puberty until the last period in menopause, the reproductive system prepares the body for conception, and if pregnancy doesn't occur that month, the process starts all over again.

During the menstrual cycle, an egg from the pool of follicles matures and is released in a process called ovulation. The endometrial tissue in the uterine cavity thickens in preparation for the implantation of an embryo. If the egg is not fertilized, the endometrium sloughs off and comes out of the body mixed with blood, and this is called a period, menses, or menstruation.

This cycle is controlled by a pattern of hormone signals that travel between the brain, the ovaries, and the uterus. Each signal must be carefully calibrated in order to trigger the next step in the process. *Gonadotropin-*

releasing hormone (GnRH) is released in pulses by the hypothalamus in the brain. These GnRH pulses are received by the pituitary, which is another part of the brain that controls many of the hormone functions of the rest of the body. The pituitary then releases *follicle-stimulating hormone* (FSH), which stimulates development of follicles in the ovary, and a dominant follicle begins to grow. The follicles produce estrogen, which thickens the endometrial tissue lining the cavity of the uterus. *Luteinizing hormone* (LH) from the pituitary also increases, causing the follicle to become mature, and a surge of LH in the middle of the cycle leads to ovulation twenty-four to forty-eight hours later.

Many people may not realize that ovulation predictor kits, which are urine test strips used to help time intercourse for trying to conceive, actually detect the LH surge and not ovulation itself. Therefore, a positive ovulation test happens before ovulation occurs. Also, an LH surge sometimes happens without ovulation taking place afterward, so a positive ovulation test doesn't guarantee that ovulation will happen. This said, ovulation predictor kits are useful for people trying to get pregnant because the LH surge is the best time in the cycle to have intercourse for conception. Sperm require a day or two to travel through the body and reach the egg and need to be present in the body before the egg is released. If intercourse happens on the day of ovulation itself, the egg will actually start to degrade by the time the sperm reach it, and the fertile window will likely be missed.

After ovulation, the follicular cells of the ovary develop into the corpus luteum, which secretes progesterone. If pregnancy doesn't occur that month, the corpus luteum will break down, and progesterone levels fall. This drop in progesterone is actually the trigger that causes menstrual bleeding to start. Once the old endometrial tissue has been completely shed, the whole process resets and starts again.

Progesterone also helps to control the growth of endometrial tissue and keeps it from growing excessively. Without progesterone, the endometrium can thicken too much and form polyps (benign fleshy masses that can bleed heavily) or even develop into precancer or cancer. Progesterone plays a crucial role in many conditions such as

PCOS, miscarriage, and uterine cancer, as well in medications such as birth control and hormone replacement therapy after menopause.

THE PERIOD: WHAT IS NORMAL?

When someone is wondering if their periods are normal, cycle length, cycle duration, and volume of blood flow are the factors that should be considered.

Cycle length is the number of days from the first day of full-flow bleeding (not just spotting) to the first day of full-flow bleeding in the next cycle. If your doctor asks, "How long are your cycles?" they're asking about cycle length, not the number of days that you bleed, which would be called the duration of flow. The average cycle is twenty-eight days but normal cycles can range from twenty-one to forty-five days. Some variation in cycle length from month to month is normal, and few people have perfect twenty-eight-day cycles every single month unless they're on birth control.

Cycle duration is the number of days of active bleeding, not including light spotting. The normal range for cycle duration is two to seven days.

Flow is the volume of blood loss. The average person isn't aware of the amount they're bleeding in ounces or milliliters, so gynecologists get a sense of the amount of blood flow by asking how many pads or tampons they use each day or how often they change a soaked pad or tampon. Changing a soaked pad or tampon every hour, having to double up on pads and tampons to prevent leaking, or filling a menstrual cup multiple times a day is considered a high quantity of flow. A menstrual cup can hold much more liquid than a tampon or pad, so it doesn't need to be changed as frequently.

CONCEPTION: GETTING PREGNANT

All too often, information about conception and pregnancy is not taught at school or at home. These facts are essential if you want to become pregnant or if you want to prevent pregnancy. Understanding how fertilization and early pregnancy normally proceed is also necessary in order to discuss topics such as infertility, miscarriage, ectopic pregnancies, and contraception.

Ovulation usually occurs around the midpoint of the cycle, on average about fourteen days before the next period for a typical twenty-eight-day cycle. The mature egg is released from the ovary, drawn into the fallopian tube, and moves toward the uterus. Following intercourse, sperm travel through the vagina, cervical mucus, and uterus, then meet the egg in the fallopian tube, where fertilization occurs. Sperm can live up to five days in the vagina and uterus, so someone can get pregnant if they had sex almost a week before ovulation. Sperm can also be present in pre-ejaculate fluid that leaves the tip of the penis before ejaculation takes place, so pregnancy can occur even if a partner uses the pullout method and doesn't ejaculate inside the vagina.

The process of fertilization starts when the head of a single sperm binds to the egg. The sperm and egg each contain twenty-three chromosomes, which are the small structures inside of cells that contain genetic material. When a sperm and egg combine, the resulting embryo has a complete set of forty-six chromosomes. This includes two sex chromosomes—one from each parent. The fertilized egg begins to divide, forming new cells as it travels through the tube toward the uterus.

It takes five or six days for the fertilized egg to reach the uterus and implant. At this point, it has developed into a ball of cells called a *blastocyst*, which embeds into the endometrium. Part of the blastocyst forms the embryo, which will develop into a baby; part forms the *placenta*, a disklike organ through which oxygen and nutrients are transferred between the uterus and the embryo; and part forms the *amniotic sac*, a fluid-filled membrane that surrounds the embryo. If the pregnancy implants anywhere other than the endometrium, it is called an *ectopic pregnancy*. Ectopics occur most often in the fallopian tube, but they can also occur in the muscle of the uterus, the cervix, C-section scars, the ovary, the intestines, and other organs of the abdomen.

Pregnancy involves a complex sequence of events that need to occur flawlessly. Sadly, this is the reason miscarriages, ectopic pregnancies, and infertility are so common. But knowing the facts about menstrual cycles and pregnancy is important to understand if something is going wrong and provides a foundation for discussing these issues with your healthcare provider.

3

Self-Assessment and Communicating
with Your Healthcare Provider

When you're struggling with gynecologic problems, it can feel over-whelming to put the experience into words. People know that something is wrong but may have difficulty pinpointing specific issues and communicating them to their doctors. The first challenge is figuring out whether something you're feeling is actually abnormal. If you have had certain experiences with your periods for as long as you can remember, you may not know if those symptoms are typical period effects or signs of a possible medical condition. Countless patients suffer from severely painful periods, heavy bleeding, or bowel issues for years, even decades, because they think these symptoms are normal—often because they were told this by society or healthcare providers.

Symptoms may be common, but they don't need to be tolerated if they are affecting your quality of life. The most important question to ask yourself as you reflect on your health is whether your experience is causing suffering or distress. Does it prevent you from being able to work or go to school, participate in activities like sex and exercise, or otherwise affect your emotional or physical well-being?

Labs, imaging studies, and surgeries may confirm diagnoses, but your story provides your doctor with the road map to understand-ing your health. Before meeting with your healthcare provider, try to identify and organize your concerns so you can communicate them effectively. Keep a log of the symptoms you feel, as well as the characteristics of your periods. You can use a period tracker or calendar apps, the Notes feature on your phone, or a physical journal.

Periods are an indicator of not only gynecologic health but also overall health and well-being. Identifying patterns in the menstrual cycle and issues such as heavy bleeding or symptoms connected to periods can provide essential information for you and your healthcare providers.

If you're experiencing pain, the location, quality, and triggers for the pain often help determine the cause. Keep a diary of pain symptoms; if you have pain, note how severe the pain is on a scale of one to ten (one being minimal pain and ten being the most severe possible), what you ate and drank that day, what activities you engaged in, any associated symptoms, and where you were in your menstrual cycle.

You can answer the questions in this chapter to prepare for appointments and as a jumping-off point for your own understanding. This is not a comprehensive list; I've included symptoms that gynecologists encounter most often, but if you're experiencing anything not mentioned here, please jot it down and discuss with your doctor. Categories that don't appear at first glance to be related to gynecologic health, such as bowel symptoms and mental health issues, are also included here because gynecologic conditions often affect other body systems and can cause symptoms that extend far beyond the uterus.

In many medical practices, appointments may be short, sometimes only fifteen to twenty minutes. Part of the reason that many health conditions go undiagnosed for so long is that doctors may not have enough time to fully explore complex problems. It may be helpful to ask how long you will have with the doctor when you book an appointment. It is important to know that annual wellness visits provided at no cost with insurance plans are usually very brief. They focus on preventive care, such as Pap smears and breast cancer screening, and they're not intended to cover more than the most basic problems. When scheduling, make sure the office knows that you are looking for a problem visit or a surgical consult, which offer longer appointments.

Even if your appointment will be short, organizing your thoughts so you can describe your symptoms quickly will help you and your provider make the most of the time that you have. Patients who have complicated histories or many issues to discuss may need to make additional appointments to complete the evaluation and counseling. If this is the case for you, then tell your doctor your most pressing concerns and your primary focus at the first appointment.

MENSTRUAL HISTORY

- How old were you when your periods started?
- When was your last menstrual period (LMP)? (This is the first day of full flow during your most recent period.)
- What is your cycle length? (This is the number of days between the first day of a period to the first day of the next period.)
  - Is your cycle length regular from month to month or does it vary?
  - Do you skip periods? If so, how long is the longest that you've gone between periods?
- What is the duration of your period? (This is the number of days that you bleed.)
- How heavy is the flow? (This is estimated by the number of saturated pads, tampons, or menstrual cups changed per day on the heaviest days.)
  - What type of menstrual product do you use? Is it a regular absorbency, super-, ultra-, or overnight-size?
  - Are you passing blood clots? How big are they? Are they the size of a quarter, a plum, or larger?
  - Is the period blood leaking through a pad or tampon? Is this affecting your ability to go to work or exercise?
  - Do you feel weak or lightheaded during your periods? Have you been diagnosed with anemia or iron deficiency?

- Do you experience bleeding between periods?
- Do you have other issues with your health during your period or in the week leading up to your period? These issues could include pain, changes in mood or mental health, or bowel or bladder symptoms.

PAIN

- When did your pain start? Was there an inciting incident that caused the pain? Did you experience pain from the time your periods began or did it seem to develop after an injury, surgery, pregnancy, or childbirth?
- How often does the pain occur? How long does it last?
- What triggers the pain or makes it worse? This is important to know, because if running, lifting, or prolonged standing worsens pain but the pain does not change at all with periods, there may be a muscular cause rather than a gynecologic one.
- What does the pain feel like? Is it sharp, stabbing, shooting, pulling, burning, dull, or aching?
- Does the pain affect your quality of life or your ability to go to work or school, exercise, or have sex?
- What treatments have you tried to relieve the pain, and did they work? (This can include over-the-counter pain medication, heating pads, rest, stretching, and dietary changes.)

GASTROINTESTINAL (GI) SYMPTOMS

- Are you experiencing diarrhea, constipation, pain with bowel movements, bloating, nausea, vomiting, blood in your stool, or changes in appetite or weight?
- Do you notice worsened GI symptoms with certain dietary triggers or with your period?

GENITOURINARY (GU) SYMPTOMS

- Are you having urinary urgency or frequency, pain with urination, trouble completely emptying your bladder, or leaking of urine?
- Do you notice worsened urinary symptoms with certain dietary triggers or with your periods?
- If you leak urine, does the leaking occur when the bladder is stressed (such as with coughing, exercise, straining), or when you feel the urge to urinate? Do you leak constantly?

VULVOVAGINAL SYMPTOMS

- Do you have skin irritation or any bumps, sores, or changes in the appearance of the vulva? (You may need to use a hand mirror to inspect the vulva.)
- Do you have any pain with sex or touching the vulva? What part of the vulva or vagina seems to hurt?
- Does your vagina feel dry or do the vaginal walls feel irritated?
- Do you have vaginal discharge? If so, what does the discharge look like and is there an odor, itching, or burning?
- Are you waxing or shaving? Do you use feminine washes, douches, panty liners, or soap or lotion with fragrance or dyes?

MOOD SYMPTOMS

- Do you feel symptoms such as depression, anxiety, mood swings, irritability, or anger? If so, how often, and do they affect your quality of life or relationships?
- Do these symptoms get worse in the week before or during your period?
- Have you ever felt severe mood symptoms such as hopelessness or thoughts of suicide or self-harm?

SEXUAL HEALTH

- Do you have any sexual health concerns, such as pain with sex, low libido, difficulty becoming aroused, insufficient vaginal lubrication, or inability to achieve orgasm? If so, are these bothersome to you or affecting your relationships?

- If you are having pain with sex, when does the pain occur? Do you experience pain with becoming aroused, touching the genitals, initial penetration, deep penetration, or orgasm? Do you have pain after sex?

- Do you have problems during partnered sexual activity, masturbation, or both?

- Do you need birth control to prevent pregnancy? Have you tried any birth control methods before, and if you have, what was your experience with them?

FERTILITY

- Do you want to become pregnant? If yes, when?

- If you never want to become pregnant, what type of birth control or sterilization methods would you consider?

- If you are currently trying to conceive, how long have you been trying? Have you tried ovulation predictor kits or fertility awareness methods to help time intercourse, and have you undergone fertility treatments?

- Have you been pregnant before? If so, what were the outcomes? Did you have a miscarriage or an abortion? Did you give birth?

REFLECTION

- What are your greatest concerns and priorities? If you have several issues, which one or two topics would you like to focus on first?

- What do you need from your healthcare provider? (These needs could include a diagnosis, options for treatment, education and information about a medical condition, or reassurance that your experience is normal.)

• What are your personal goals for your health?

As you read the following chapters on various gynecologic conditions, you may realize that you have classic symptoms of endometriosis, PCOS, PMDD, or another condition. While it's not possible to diagnose your medical issue from a description in a book, recognizing yourself in these pages may provide an important starting point.

PART II

What's the Situation?

4

Fibroids

Fibroids are extremely common tumors of the uterine muscle that the majority of people with a uterus will eventually develop in their lifetimes. Luckily, they are benign, meaning they are noncancerous. Up to 80 percent of Black women and 70 percent of white women have fibroids by age fifty. Though not everyone with fibroids will have symptoms, up to half will experience distressing problems such as severe pain, heavy or persistent bleeding, bloating, pelvic pressure, infertility, or miscarriage.

FIBROID BASICS

Also known as *leiomyomas* or *myomas*, fibroids form when cells in the muscular wall of the uterus start to multiply rapidly. Interestingly, all the cells in a fibroid are genetically identical clones of each other. Fibroids are stimulated by estrogen and progesterone from the ovaries, usually begin growing when people are in their twenties and thirties, and can continue growing until menopause. After menopause, they often shrink in size, but they may not completely disappear.

SYMPTOMS

Fibroid symptoms generally depend on the size, number, and location of the tumors in the uterus. People with larger or more numerous fibroids tend to have more severe symptoms, but this is not always the case. Someone can have very large tumors and not experience any problems, and another person can have tiny fibroids that cause severe bleeding and pain.

Fibroid symptoms are divided into three categories: bulk, bleeding, and pain.

Bulk Symptoms

When fibroids grow, they can press on the bladder, rectum, and bowel, causing symptoms similar to those felt during pregnancy. These are called bulk symptoms and can include a sensation of bloating or abdominal fullness, urinary frequency or incontinence, and constipation. Sometimes, fibroids become so large that women look like they are pregnant.

Large tumors can block the ureters, the tubes that carry urine from the kidneys to the bladder; if a ureter is completely obstructed, it can cause kidney failure. Fibroids can also compress the pelvic veins, leading to the formation of a dangerous type of blood clot called a *deep venous thrombosis* (*DVT*). These situations are rare, but if they occur, they may require urgent surgical management to remove fibroids and treat the condition.

Bleeding

Fibroids can cause very heavy or prolonged periods, persistent bleeding, or bleeding between periods. The amount of bleeding can be truly frightening; it is not uncommon for people with fibroids to pass large clots or soak a pad or tampon in mere minutes. They can end up in the emergency room with hemorrhaging and require blood transfusions because of extremely low levels of iron and red blood cells.

Pain

Fibroids can cause severe pain with periods, but they can cause pain at other points of the menstrual cycle as well. If the fibroids are large or pushing down into the vagina, sex can be painful. Fibroids sometimes outgrow their own blood supply, causing some of the fibroid cells to die. This is called *degeneration*, and it can be extremely painful. Degeneration may occur when someone is pregnant, because estrogen and progesterone levels increase in pregnancy, which can lead to rapid fibroid growth.

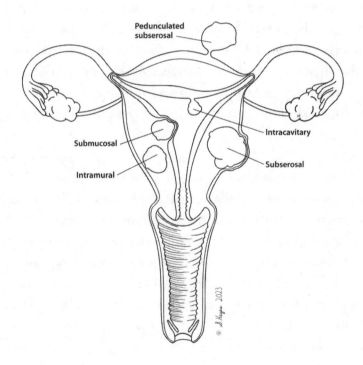

FIBROID ANATOMY

The location of a fibroid in the uterus generally determines what symptoms it causes. For example, if fibroids push into the uterine cavity, they can cause severe bleeding or miscarriage, whereas fibroids that project off the outer surface of the uterus can cause bulk symptoms or pain but they don't typically cause heavy bleeding or fertility issues. In this next section, I'll discuss fibroid anatomy and explain more about how location affects what patients feel and what treatment options they have.

Gynecologists categorize fibroids by the part of the uterus they are located in: the cavity, the muscle, or the outer surface.

Submucosal or Intracavitary

Fibroids that push into the cavity of the uterus are called *submucosal fibroids*. If the entire fibroid is inside the cavity, it's called an *intracavitary fibroid*. Sometimes a fibroid grows on a little stalk like a mushroom, and this is called a *pedunculated intracavitary fibroid*. Submucosal and intracavitary fibroids can cause heavy bleeding even if they're extremely small because they affect the endometrial tissue that is shed with menstruation. Fibroids that block or distort the cavity can cause infertility by preventing embryos from implanting; they can also increase the risk of miscarriage if there isn't enough room for pregnancies to grow.

Intramural

Fibroids growing in the muscular wall of the uterus are said to be *intramural*, or "within the wall." Intramural fibroids can cause bulk, bleeding, and pain symptoms, and if they grow large enough to compress or distort the uterine cavity or fallopian tubes, they can increase the risk of infertility and miscarriage. Very small intramural fibroids are hard to locate surgically because they're fully hidden within the wall and not visible from either the outer surface of the uterus or the inside of the endometrial cavity.

Subserosal

Subserosal fibroids are located directly underneath the outer surface of the uterus. Similar to intramural fibroids, subserosal fibroids can cause pain or bulk symptoms by pushing on adjacent organs. These tumors don't typically cause bleeding or fertility problems because they aren't in contact with the endometrium unless they are very large and extend through the entire wall of the uterus. Some subserosal fibroids can also be pedunculated, growing off the surface of the uterus on a stalk, and these are called *pedunculated subserosal fibroids*.

LEIOMYOSARCOMA

Fibroids are benign, but there are some very rare cancerous uterine tumors called *leiomyosarcomas* that look very similar to fibroids on imaging studies and during surgery. Fibroids cannot be reliably biopsied before surgery, and there is no way to clearly distinguish benign fibroids from leiomyosarcomas on ultrasound, though MRIs will sometimes detect features that are more concerning for cancer. Leiomyosarcomas are therefore usually found unexpectedly when someone undergoes surgery for fibroids, and cancer is seen in the pathology specimen.

Fortunately, these are extremely rare cancers. They are found in less than 0.1 percent of patients receiving treatment for fibroids, though they become slightly more common with age, and among patients in their sixties and seventies, the rate may be as high as 6 to 7 percent. Therefore, postmenopausal women with growing fibroids or patients with any abnormal features on imaging may be referred to a gynecologic oncologist. Fortunately, the vast majority of people just have benign fibroids, especially if they are younger.

DIAGNOSIS

Unless they're fairly large, fibroids are not usually found on routine pelvic exams. When patients have symptoms of fibroids, such as pelvic pain or heavy period bleeding, their gynecologists should order imaging studies that can diagnose and evaluate fibroids. Pelvic ultrasounds and MRIs are two types of imaging studies that can be used.

PELVIC ULTRASOUND

Ultrasounds use sound waves projected through handheld probes to create an image of the internal organs. *Pelvic ultrasounds* are usually the first imaging study done for gynecologic problems because they're commonly available, inexpensive, don't involve radiation exposure, and provide very good views of the uterus and ovaries. Pelvic ultrasounds typically involve both an abdominal portion, with a probe held against the abdominal wall, and a vaginal portion, performed by inserting a narrow probe into the vagina. Transvaginal ultrasounds provide a detailed view of the uterus and ovaries, but some large fibroids may be closer to the surface of the abdomen. This is why a pelvic ultrasound will usually be performed through both the abdomen and vagina to get the most comprehensive set of views possible.

For most patients, a transvaginal ultrasound feels like pressure and isn't painful, even if someone has never been sexually active. People who have significant pain or anxiety with pelvic exams may wish to discuss the study and expectations with their doctors in advance. Ultimately, if people do not feel comfortable proceeding with the transvaginal portion of the ultrasound, they have the right to decline it, though they should be counseled that an abdominal ultrasound may not provide as accurate an assessment of the pelvic organs.

MAGNETIC RESONANCE IMAGING (MRI)

A *pelvic MRI* uses magnets and radio waves to create images of the body. MRIs offer a much more detailed view of fibroids than ultrasounds, but there are downsides. They are much more expensive, may not be as readily available as ultrasounds, and usually require placing an IV in the arm to give contrast dye. Plus, getting an MRI can be anxiety-inducing for people who are claustrophobic because the patient must lie still in a very narrow tube while the study is done.

An MRI may be ordered when a doctor is considering surgical options to remove or destroy fibroids because it provides very precise mapping of fibroid locations. An MRI may also be performed when there is concern for cancerous uterine tumors.

RISK FACTORS

There are several factors that increase the risk of having fibroids. While people can avoid some risk factors, this may not prevent fibroid growth, and fibroids often appear in patients with no significant risk factors. Their development is never the patient's fault.

RACE

The incidence of fibroids is up to three times higher for Black patients and two times higher for Hispanic patients than it is for white patients. Asian patients develop fibroids as well, though there is limited information about fibroids and the Asian population in English-language studies.

Black women are more likely to have larger and faster-growing fibroids, more severe symptoms, and an earlier age of onset, averaging ten to fifteen years earlier than white patients. Racial disparities in fibroid prevalence are likely due to a complex interaction of family history and genetics, environmental exposures, diet, and psychosocial factors such as stress. There are some differences in specific genes that have been discovered in fibroid cells, but there is no known genetic explanation for why fibroids are more common in Black people.

FAMILY HISTORY

A family history of fibroids significantly increases the risk of developing fibroids, and social patterns can occur when fibroids are more common within a family. For example, in a family that includes many women who have fibroids with associated heavy and painful periods, members of that family may believe that heavy and painful periods are normal. Countless patients have told me that they thought hemorrhaging, soaking through pads and clothes, and having severe pain with periods was normal because their mothers, grandmothers, and sisters had the same experience. This may lead to a delay in diagnosis and treatment because people may not recognize that something is wrong until they end up in the ER with hemorrhaging or debilitating pain. If you have serious period problems, ask your family members to describe their periods. It's likely that they quietly suffer from the same issues and either don't realize it is a problem or think it is too embarrassing to discuss. As a society, we must destigmatize period discussions so everyone can get the earliest possible diagnosis and treatment. Starting these conversations at home can make a huge difference.

EARLY MENARCHE

Earlier age of onset of periods, *menarche*, is associated with an increased risk of fibroids. This may be due to increased lifetime exposure to estrogen and progesterone. Black and Hispanic adolescents have an earlier average age of menarche, and this may contribute to their increased risk of fibroids.

DIET

Several dietary factors are associated with a higher risk of fibroids, with vitamin D deficiency being one of the most well studied of these factors. People with adequate levels of vitamin D have a lower risk of fibroids than those who are deficient. Vitamin D deficiency is more common in Black people because melanin, the pigment that gives skin its color, absorbs UV rays from sunlight, which is necessary for vitamin D production. In lab experiments, vitamin D seems to inhibit the growth of tumor cells, including fibroid cells. Studies with a limited number of participants have suggested that vitamin D supplementation may slightly shrink fibroid size. This remains an area for further research, but consider asking your doctor to test for vitamin D levels and discuss supplements if levels are low, since there are other health benefits to having normal vitamin D levels.

Obesity, alcohol (particularly beer) consumption, high red-meat intake, and lower consumption of vegetables and fruits also increase fibroid risk. It's unclear whether making dietary changes causes fibroids to shrink, but because there are many benefits to having a balanced and healthy diet, these factors are worth discussing with your doctor.

STRESS

Increased chronic stress is associated with a higher risk of fibroids, particularly among non-Hispanic Black patients. There are no studies explaining why stress is associated with fibroid growth, but in theory, it may be related to the influence of hormones such as cortisol and adrenaline.

ENVIRONMENTAL EXPOSURES

Chemicals such as phthalates and bisphenol A (BPA) may lead to an increased risk of fibroids. Phthalates are used to increase the durability of plastics and stabilize perfumes, cosmetics, and shampoos. BPA, found in some plastics such as water bottles, can leach into food or liquids that are stored in these containers. Some phthalates and BPA are endocrine or hormone disruptors because they bind to and activate estrogen receptors. This is potentially the mechanism by which they increase the risk of fibroid growth.

Studies suggest that products such as hair relaxers (some of which contain phthalates) are also associated with increased likelihood of developing fibroids and uterine cancer. These products can cause sores in the scalp, which may increase absorption into the body. The use of chemical hair straighteners might be yet another risk factor for the development of fibroids in Black women, who are more likely to use hair-straightening products than white, Asian, and Hispanic women.

TREATMENT

Treatment options for benign fibroids are divided into two categories: medications, used to control bleeding or pain, and procedures or surgeries to shrink or remove the fibroids or uterus. There is no one-size-fits-all approach to fibroid treatment, so it often becomes a matter of trial and error. Decisions about treatment should take into consideration symptoms, future fertility plans, and patient perspectives on medications and surgeries. Unfortunately, some patients may be offered only birth control or a hysterectomy for fibroids. It's never the case that there's only one option, although there may be one choice that is most fitting given a patient's anatomy or symptoms. If you feel your doctor isn't listening to your perspective or isn't able to meet your treatment needs, you should seek a second opinion with a fibroid specialist.

MEDICATIONS

Bleeding and pain from fibroids can be treated with medications. There are two types of medicines used for fibroid treatment: pain medications and prescription drugs that contain hormones or adjust hormone levels.

Over-the-Counter Pain Medication

Nonsteroidal anti-inflammatory drugs (NSAIDs) such as ibuprofen (Motrin or Advil) and naproxen (Aleve) are the most effective over-the-counter medications for uterine pain. NSAIDs increase bleeding elsewhere in the body but actually decrease menstrual bleeding. In fact, NSAIDs are almost as effective as birth control methods in lightening uterine bleeding. Acetaminophen (Tylenol) may also improve pain but usually to a lesser extent than NSAIDs, and it does not have the same beneficial impact on bleeding.

Hormonal Medications

Even though estrogen and progesterone from the ovaries stimulate fibroids, medicines containing these hormones actually lessen menstrual bleeding and painful periods by suppressing the amount of hormones released by the ovaries. Therefore, hormonal methods like birth control and noncontraceptive progesterone tablets are usually first-line treatments for fibroid symptoms. They are commonly available and usually affordable with insurance, and many reproductive-age patients may want to be on birth control to prevent pregnancy anyway.

The impact of birth control on fibroid size is not clear; some studies with small numbers of participants suggest fibroids may increase slightly in size with birth control, whereas other studies actually show that the risk of fibroid development or progression is lower with hormonal birth control.

Progesterone intrauterine devices, or IUDs, are another option for period suppression for those who want to minimize systemic hormones. Unfortunately, fibroids sometimes block or distort the shape of the uterine cavity, which can prevent IUD insertion.

Tranexamic Acid

Tranexamic acid (Lysteda) blocks the breakdown of blood clots and therefore slows or stops bleeding. It is a pill that is taken only as needed when heavy bleeding occurs. People may choose this method if they want an option that lightens blood loss but doesn't need to be taken every day or if they want to avoid hormones. Tranexamic acid does not affect the size of fibroids or improve pain or bulk symptoms.

Gonadotropin-Releasing Hormone (GnRH) Agonists and Antagonists

These medications suppress the ovaries and lighten or stop periods. They work by shutting down or blocking the GnRH-signaling system in the brain that controls the menstrual cycle. This leads to lower estrogen levels and decreased period bleeding. GnRH medications can be given as injections or oral pills. Leuprolide (Lupron) and goserelin (Zoladex) are injections. Elagolix (Oriahnn) and relugolix (Myfembree) are oral pills that also include a small amount of estrogen and progesterone to minimize the risk of developing side effects like hot flashes. Of note, this is the only category of medications that can decrease the size of fibroids. Other medications help only with bleeding and pain. Unfortunately, their duration of use is limited to a year or two because of the potential for side effects like bone thinning from low estrogen levels. Also, the shrinkage effect is not permanent; any decrease in fibroid size reverses after the medication is stopped. GnRH agonists or antagonists can be helpful when used prior to surgery, to control symptoms temporarily if surgery is not an option, or to bridge patients to their own natural menopause if they're close to menopausal age.

PROCEDURES AND SURGERIES

Medications help relieve symptoms, but procedures and surgeries can destroy or remove fibroids. Procedures that destroy fibroids include uterine fibroid embolization and radiofrequency ablation; surgeries that remove fibroids are myomectomies and hysterectomies.

Uterine Fibroid Embolization (UFE)

This procedure is performed by interventional radiologists (IRs), not gynecologists. In UFE, a catheter is threaded through a vein in the wrist or groin and passed under X-ray guidance to the blood vessels that feed the fibroids. Tiny particles are injected to block the vessels and deprive the fibroids of their blood supply. This decreases bleeding and causes the fibroids to shrink. On average, they decrease fibroid volume about 50 percent. It provides a minimally invasive option that allows the uterus to be preserved and has a relatively fast recovery time compared with surgery.

UFE is not recommended for patients who want to preserve their fertility because blocking blood flow to parts of the uterus may affect the growth of a future fetus, and the particles may also affect blood flow to the ovaries. Some fibroids are better managed with surgical removal, especially any fibroids with a stalk, because the stalk can break down after embolization and the fibroid can actually detach from the uterus.

Dying fibroid tissue can sometimes cause a malodorous vaginal discharge after UFE.

If you are interested in the option of UFE, make an appointment with an IR doctor to discuss the procedure. Gynecologists can make recommendations or referrals for interventional radiologists, and they may order an MRI to map the locations of the fibroids before your appointment.

Myomectomy

A surgical procedure to remove fibroids from the uterus is called a *myomectomy*. This is the gold standard of treatment for patients who want to preserve their fertility because it has been studied for much longer than other procedures and therefore has more data on safety in future pregnancies.

There are several different ways to perform a myomectomy, depending on the location, size, and number of fibroids.

Hysteroscopic Myomectomy

Submucosal or intracavitary fibroids, which are found in the cavity of the uterus, are removed using a *hysteroscope*, a narrow camera inserted through the vagina and cervix and into the uterus. The cavity of the uterus is then filled with saline, and a hysteroscope containing a spinning blade or an electrified metal loop is used to shave the fibroids down so they can be removed in fragments. Hysteroscopic myomectomies offer a very quick recovery, no abdominal incisions, and sometimes can even be performed in the doctor's office if the fibroids are small. This is only an option for fibroids that are within the cavity. Also, the equipment is very small, so it may require multiple treatments to fully remove larger fibroids; it isn't possible to remove extremely large fibroids in this way.

Laparoscopic or Robotic Myomectomy

Intramural or subserosal fibroids are removed through the abdomen rather than the vagina. These types of myomectomies are performed under general anesthesia, meaning the patient is fully asleep and unaware of the surgery. Fibroids are cut out of the uterine wall, which is then repaired using dissolvable stitches.

This type of myomectomy can be done with laparoscopy, which is a minimally invasive type of surgery where small incisions are made in the abdominal wall, the abdomen is filled with carbon dioxide gas, and a camera and narrow instruments are inserted into the abdomen for the operation. Laparoscopic surgery may also be performed using a surgical robot. In robotic surgeries, mechanical arms are attached to the camera and instruments; the surgeon sits at a console several feet away from the patient and moves the robotic arms with finger controls and foot pedals. Some surgeons may prefer robotics because it makes certain procedures, such as laparoscopic suturing, easier to perform, but ultimately the robot is simply a tool controlled by the surgeon, not a different or superior type of surgery.

The small incisions of laparoscopic or robotic surgery allow for faster recovery and lower risk of complications when compared to surgeries with a large incision. Unfortunately, this option may not be feasible for patients with very large or numerous fibroids, which would need to be cut into pieces to be removed through the tiny laparoscopic incisions, and not every gynecologist is trained to perform minimally invasive myomectomy.

Open Myomectomy

Abdominal myomectomies can also be performed through traditional open surgery via a large incision in the abdominal wall. Open myomectomy may involve an incision across the lower abdomen similar to a C-section or an up-and-down incision in the middle of the abdomen that goes up to or past the belly button. Open surgery is usually faster than laparoscopic surgery. It requires less time under anesthesia and it is easier for the surgeon to identify and remove very small fibroids that cannot be felt during laparoscopic surgery. But a larger incision comes with a longer recovery and more risks of complications. The decision about the type of surgery is highly individualized and will depend on the expertise of the doctor, the health of the patient, and the characteristics of the fibroids.

Risks of Myomectomy

There are certain surgical risks that are common to both laparoscopic and open myomectomies. Because fibroids have blood vessels that can bleed heavily when cut, patients must give consent for a possible blood transfusion before undergoing a laparoscopic or open myomectomy. Surgeries that require a substantial incision into the uterine wall can also pose a risk of that weakened area of the muscle tearing open in future pregnancies. This is called a uterine rupture, and it can be extremely dangerous for both the pregnant person and the fetus. Therefore, if a deep cut is made in the wall of the uterus during a myomectomy, the patient will be counseled to deliver future babies by C-section rather than going through labor, because contractions could cause the uterus to rupture. Hysteroscopic myomectomies do not carry these risks because the uterine muscle and blood vessels are not cut in a substantial way.

For any myomectomy that affects the uterine cavity, there's a possibility that scar tissue can form in the cavity, and this may affect future fertility.

It is important to know that fibroids can grow back after surgical removal, and up to half of women who undergo a myomectomy may eventually need another surgery for treatment.

Ultrasound-Guided Radiofrequency Ablation (RFA)

Two newer surgeries, the Acessa and Sonata procedures, use radiofrequency energy to ablate—meaning destroy—fibroids. The patient is placed under anesthesia, and an ultrasound is used to guide the insertion of needle-like probes into each tumor to deliver waves of energy to heat and destroy the fibroids. The Acessa is performed through the abdomen using laparoscopy, and Sonata is performed through the vagina via hysteroscopy. Over several months, the body reabsorbs some of the dead tissue, causing the fibroids to shrink. These methods can treat bleeding, pain, and bulk symptoms of fibroids while preserving the uterus.

Radiofrequency ablation procedures have much lower surgical risks than myomectomies, including significantly less bleeding and less time under anesthesia. RFA devices do have limitations in the size of fibroids that can be destroyed, and they are not currently approved for use in those who want to become pregnant in the future because there is not yet enough information on pregnancy outcomes. Also, because there are not many gynecologists who are trained in these procedures, the Acessa and Sonata are not widely available at this time. But RFA treatments are a promising option for those who want to preserve the uterus, and more surgeons are beginning to offer them each year.

Focused Ultrasound

When ultrasound waves are concentrated in one area, they can heat tissue. *Focused ultrasound* under MRI guidance has been used to destroy fibroids. This is another procedure performed by interventional radiologists. Unfortunately, it is offered only in a very limited number of locations and may not even be available in major cities, so most people will not have access to this option.

Hysterectomy

Hysterectomy is considered the definitive therapy for fibroids, meaning it is the only treatment that ensures that fibroids will never return. With every other method, the uterus is preserved, so existing fibroids can continue to grow or new ones can appear. This potential for regrowth continues until menopause.

Some gynecologists may tell patients with many fibroids or large fibroids that a hysterectomy is their only option. This is often because the doctor feels that a myomectomy or other procedure that preserves the uterus has too high a risk of fibroid recurrence or surgical complications such as bleeding. In reality, a hysterectomy is never required unless there is concern for cancer. If a doctor offers only a hysterectomy and does not discuss any other options, a second opinion with another gynecologic surgeon should be considered—especially if you want to preserve your fertility. No one should be told to have an organ removed if they do not feel comfortable with this option.

HOLISTIC OPTIONS

Beyond traditional treatments such as medications and surgeries, there are ways of improving overall health and well-being by considering the whole person, both mind and body. This is known as a *holistic approach* to medical care, and it can include factors such as nutrition, mental health care, stress relief, exercise, acupuncture, and dietary supplements to complement traditional medical treatments. Because healthy diet, exercise, and mental health care are always beneficial, healthcare providers will generally encourage these lifestyle modifications.

Herbal Supplements

There is minimal research on herbal and dietary supplements, so caution must be exercised in weighing their potential risks versus benefits. Companies may attempt to profit off the desire for a more natural approach by selling supplements that promise to magically melt away fibroids with herbs or vitamins. Most herbal supplements have not been studied in terms of safety or efficacy, and they may be expensive, with no guarantee of results.

There are supplements made from chasteberry, the fruit of the vitex plant, that are promoted for the treatment of fibroids and heavy or painful periods. There is no high-quality evidence that these are effective, but some women report that they feel better when taking them.

Dietary Changes

The natural treatment that has the most supporting research is vitamin D supplementation for women who are deficient. There is evidence that restoring normal levels may stabilize or even slightly decrease fibroid size. Vitamin D is found naturally in beef liver, fatty fish like salmon, and products like milk and cereals that are fortified with additional vitamins. People with vitamin D deficiency are usually given prescription or over-the-counter supplements because it can be difficult to get enough vitamin D from diet or sunlight exposure alone.

Other dietary changes may also be beneficial. Some studies have shown that women who consume several servings of fruits and vegetables per day seem to have a lower likelihood of developing fibroids. This effect seems to be strongest for citrus fruits and cruciferous vegetables such as broccoli, kale, and cabbage.

Stress Relief

Chronic stress can increase the risk of developing fibroids. Reducing stress won't cause fibroids to shrink or disappear, but it might improve symptoms and minimize fibroid growth.

TAKE-HOME POINTS

- Fibroids are benign tumors of the uterus that affect up to 80 percent of Black women and 70 percent of white women.
- In a fibroid, all the cells are identical clones of each other.
- Risk factors for fibroid growth include BPA exposure, use of hair relaxers, low vitamin D levels, and chronic stress.
- New surgical treatment options use radiofrequency energy to heat and destroy fibroids.
- Hysterectomies guarantee that fibroids are gone and won't return, but they are never the only option.

Endometriosis and Adenomyosis

Endometriosis and adenomyosis can feel like invisible conditions—there are no lab tests or imaging studies that can definitively diagnose them, so patients are often initially told that there's nothing wrong. People with endometriosis and adenomyosis often undergo multiple ultrasounds, CT scans, blood tests, and ER visits with perfectly normal results. Meanwhile, endometriosis can affect essentially every organ system in the abdomen and pelvis, causing debilitating pain and problems with the bowel, bladder, nerves, and muscles. The experience of receiving normal test results but having extensive and far-ranging symptoms leads patients to suffer not just physical pain but also the anguish of being told by doctors that their symptoms might be in their heads. Medical professionals tend to depend on measurable, objective data such as lab results, vital signs, and EKGs. It's hard to identify a condition that causes a wide number of symptoms but can't be detected by standard diagnostic tests. For these reasons, it takes seven years on average for an endometriosis patient to finally get the correct diagnosis, and often people with endometriosis see multiple specialists before being diagnosed.

For many of the conditions discussed in this book, patients have led the push for research, funding, and public education. Endometriosis advocates have to fight tooth and nail just to receive the right diagnosis and often struggle for access to specialists and effective treatment. Frustrated by a broken system, they have formed online communities such as Nancy's Nook, where they share educational resources and recommendations for specialists. They've championed this fight and successfully lobbied for increased government funding for endometriosis awareness and research.

ENDOMETRIOSIS AND ADENOMYOSIS BASICS

When endometrium-like tissue grows outside of the uterine cavity, it causes endometriosis and adenomyosis. Endometriosis and adenomyosis have many similarities, can cause overlapping symptoms, and are managed in similar ways, but they occur in different places. In endometriosis, the tissue grows outside of the uterus, commonly between the uterus and rectum, on the surface of the bladder or bowels, on the walls of the pelvis or abdomen, in the ovaries, on the diaphragm, or even in the belly button, surgical scars, or in the thorax. In

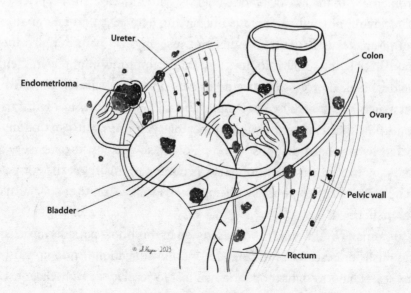

Endometriosis

Adenomyosis

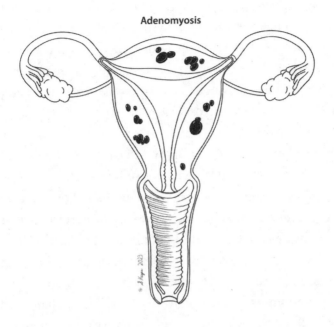

adenomyosis, the tissue grows within the myometrium, the muscular wall of the uterus.

Both of these conditions are extremely common. Endometriosis affects at least one in ten women and up to half of women who experience infertility. Almost everyone knows someone who has endometriosis. Adenomyosis is more difficult to track, as it usually requires a hysterectomy to diagnose, but it has been found in up to a third of hysterectomy specimens. The true numbers of those with endometriosis and adenomyosis are almost certainly significantly underestimated since they must be diagnosed surgically, and many people experience symptoms but never undergo surgery.

As is the case with fibroids, the causes of endometriosis and adenomyosis are unknown. There is likely some sort of genetic link that is not yet understood, since endometriosis can run in families. There are several theories about the origins of endometriosis. It may come from the structures that later form the uterus in early embryologic development. There may be other cell types that transform into endometrium-like cells, or there may be tissues or a biological signal that travels through the lymphatic system or bloodstream that triggers the growth of endometrial tissue. Adenomyosis is more common in patients who have had a cesarean section or other uterine surgery, so it is possible that it can be spread when the wall of the uterus is cut, but many patients with adenomyosis have had no prior surgeries.

One of the earliest theories about endometriosis was Sampson's theory of retrograde menstruation, which suggested that actual endometrial tissue from the uterine cavity spilled backward through the fallopian tubes during periods and then implanted on pelvic surfaces. Sampson's theory doesn't explain how endometriosis can grow in places like the belly button and inside the chest or how endometriosis can grow after a hysterectomy. Cisgender men can even get endometriosis; there are case reports of endometriosis found in men complaining of abdominal pain, usually men with higher-than-usual levels of estrogen. Retrograde menstruation clearly isn't the primary way that endometriosis forms, but this outdated theory is still sometimes propagated by healthcare providers. For instance, many doctors tell patients that a hysterectomy will cure endometriosis because they believe that it cannot return if there is no uterus; however, endometriosis can and does recur in women who have had a hysterectomy. While there are many theories, there is no definite answer as to the origin of endometriosis and adenomyosis. It is possible there may be more than one pathway, and endometriosis that grows in men or outside of the pelvis might have slightly different causes. Further research is essential so we can create more targeted treatments and find methods to prevent these conditions from developing in the first place. Like fibroids, endometriosis and adenomyosis have no known cause, so we are limited to removing the disease or giving medications to suppress symptoms.

SYMPTOMS

Endometriosis and adenomyosis cause pain and other symptoms by inflaming surrounding structures. Since the uterus and ovaries are located near several other pelvic organs, endometriosis and adenomyosis can cause a wide range of symptoms depending on what parts of the body are affected. The organs and structures that can be affected by endometriosis and adenomyosis are the uterus, bowel and rectum, bladder and ureters, muscles, and nerves.

UTERUS

Adenomyosis can cause severe and persistent uterine bleeding, similar to fibroids. To a lesser extent, endometriosis can also cause bleeding symptoms, including heavy periods or irregular spotting.

BOWEL AND RECTUM

Some of the most common symptoms of endometriosis are bowel-related, because many people will have disease that is right next to the rectum and colon. In fact, many patients are initially misdiagnosed with irritable bowel syndrome because they have persistent constipation, diarrhea, pain with bowel movements, bloating, nausea, or rectal bleeding. It isn't uncommon for people to see their primary care doctor or a gastrointestinal specialist before their gynecologist because their GI symptoms are so severe. If someone's irritable bowel symptoms seem to become much worse around ovulation and periods, that is very suggestive of possible endometriosis.

Adenomyosis can also cause bowel symptoms, but they are much more common with endometriosis, and the severity of diarrhea, constipation, pain, and bloating is usually much worse with endometriosis.

BLADDER AND URETERS

Although bladder issues are less common than bowel symptoms in endometriosis and adenomyosis, both can cause urinary urgency, frequency, burning, or blood in the urine. People might feel like they're having recurrent UTIs but the urine will not show any bacteria. In severe cases, endometriosis can grow into the bladder or ureters.

MUSCLE

Muscles of the pelvic floor surround the bladder, vagina, and rectum, and they connect to the legs, hips, and lower back. These muscles can become inflamed by endometriosis or adenomyosis, leading to pain with sex or exercise or aching pains radiating down the legs. Muscle spasms can make it difficult to control bodily functions like having bowel movements or urinating, leading to constipation or a feeling that the bladder is not completely empty after going to the bathroom.

NERVES

Nerves run through the pelvis and down into the legs, and if they are inflamed due to endometriosis or adenomyosis, they can cause burning or shooting pains in the lower back, buttocks, and legs. In severe cases, there may even be lower extremity numbness or weakness.

SYSTEMIC SYMPTOMS

Systemic symptoms affect multiple organ systems or the entire body rather than just one part. Patients with endometriosis or adenomyosis can experience systemic symptoms that are not felt in the pelvis. For example, endometriosis can cause severe fatigue or migraines. These symptoms are harder to explain than pelvic symptoms, which occur because the endometriosis or adenomyosis directly inflame nearby organs. It's possible that there may be a link between endometriosis and adenomyosis and more systemic inflammation that affects the rest of the body.

Endometriosis and adenomyosis can also worsen mood. The physical symptoms may be so distressing that they cause depression or anxiety, which in turn worsen pain and bowel and muscle symptoms, resulting in a terrible cycle of physical and emotional suffering.

TIMING OF SYMPTOMS

Endometriosis and adenomyosis are thought to be stimulated by hormones from the ovaries, especially estrogen, so pain and symptoms tend to worsen during the hormone surges that occur with ovulation and menstrual periods. Symptoms usually resolve after menopause, when hormones drop, but it's important to know that some people continue to have problems after menopause because there is still some estrogen production from the ovaries, fat cells in the rest of the body, and even the endometriosis itself. Transgender men can suffer from endometriosis for the same reasons, even if they're on testosterone and no longer have periods.

RISK FACTORS

There are several possible risk factors for developing endometriosis, including menstrual history, uterine anatomy, and family history of endometriosis. It isn't caused by a person's actions—it's not the patient's fault, and in many cases, endometriosis appears in people with no risk factors. Less is known about risk factors for adenomyosis, but it is associated with prior uterine surgeries.

ESTROGEN EXPOSURE

Several risk factors for endometriosis are related to having a higher lifetime exposure to estrogen from the ovaries. These include getting a first period at an earlier age and experiencing menopause at a later age.

FAMILY HISTORY

Endometriosis tends to run in families, and having relatives with endometriosis is a risk factor for having it yourself. Older female family members might not actually have been diagnosed with endometriosis, but they may have a history of severe pain with periods, infertility, or miscarriage that suggests endometriosis.

PELVIC DISORDERS

People with disorders of the pelvic anatomy, such as a wall (septum) in the middle of the vagina or uterine cavity or a heart-shaped (bicornuate) or duplicated (didelphys) uterus, also have a higher risk of endometriosis.

PREGNANCY AND SURGERY

There is a higher risk of adenomyosis in women who have had multiple children or who have had uterine surgeries such as C-sections or dilation and curettages (D and Cs). It is possible that pregnancy and surgery may disrupt the border between the endometrium and myometrium in the uterus, allowing adenomyosis to grow.

FERTILITY

Endometriosis can increase the risk of infertility and miscarriage. Adenomyosis may also affect fertility and miscarriage rates, but there are fewer studies about adenomyosis and pregnancy. Up to half of patients assigned female at birth who are dealing with infertility have endometriosis, so there is a very close connection between endometriosis and fertility struggles. It can cause scarring of the fallopian tubes, which may lead to problems conceiving or an increased risk of ectopic pregnancy. Inflammatory fluid or trapped menstrual blood can fill scarred tubes. These swollen tubes are called *hydrosalpinges*, and studies of in vitro fertilization have shown that the presence of a hydrosalpinx decreases embryo implantation rates and increases miscarriage risk. This is thought to be due to the presence of inflammatory factors in the tubal fluid, which flows backward into the uterine cavity and may affect the function of the endometrium.

Beyond tubal causes of infertility, both endometriosis and adenomyosis are associated with decreased implantation rates with IVF and increased overall risk of miscarriage—in theory due to inflammation of the endometrium or worsening of egg quality, though the actual mechanisms are not known. Later in pregnancy, endometriosis and adenomyosis are associated with higher risks of preterm labor, and patients with endometriosis also have higher rates of preeclampsia and C-section delivery for unclear reasons. Surgical treatment of endometriosis and adenomyosis may decrease some of these risks.

Some people dealing with infertility may have already been diagnosed with endometriosis because of severe pain or other bothersome symptoms. Others will be surprised to learn that they have endometriosis after their workup for trouble conceiving or staying pregnant. That is because it is possible to have severe endometriosis with pelvic scarring and tubal damage without having significant symptoms. The first hint that something is wrong may be discovering that the tubes are blocked during fertility testing.

Finding out that you have endometriosis while dealing with infertility can be emotionally distressing. On the one hand, a diagnosis may finally provide a long-sought answer to fertility issues and offer options for treatment that might improve the chances of conceiving and staying pregnant. On the other hand, dealing with a chronic condition that can be challenging to treat may be another source of frustration and confusion in an already very stressful and emotionally painful process. Fortunately, many fertility doctors have some expertise in endometriosis, and even if they don't surgically treat the endometriosis themselves, they should be able to refer patients to an endometriosis specialist if one is needed.

DIAGNOSIS

Since there is no simple lab test or imaging study that can definitively identify endometriosis or adenomyosis, these conditions must be surgically diagnosed. A gynecologist needs to operate and remove tissue that is then examined under a microscope. If cells that look like endometrium are seen in the surgical specimens, that confirms whether endometriosis or adenomyosis had been present.

Before having surgery to diagnose endometriosis, patients must first consult with a primary care provider or a gynecologist, who will likely recommend basic testing such as a pelvic exam and imaging studies. Doctors can discuss options for management, including laparoscopic surgery for diagnosis and treatment, or refer patients to an endometriosis specialist if they don't perform the surgery themselves.

IMAGING: ULTRASOUND AND MRI

If a patient has pelvic pain, abnormal bleeding, or fertility issues, the gynecologist will likely order a pelvic ultrasound to assess the uterus and ovaries. Ultrasounds may not show any abnormalities in people who have endometriosis because the disease usually starts as small flat spots on the surfaces of the pelvic walls or organs, almost like dots drawn on a sheet of paper; they are too small to be detected by imaging studies.

As endometriosis progresses, it may form cysts in the ovaries or nodules of dense tissue that grow into the walls of the pelvis, vagina, or other nearby organs; this is called *deep infiltrating endometriosis*. Radiologists or gynecologists who specialize in endometriosis care may be able to identify subtle findings on an ultrasound, such as thickening of the vaginal or rectal walls, that suggest possible deep infiltrating endometriosis.

Endometriosis cysts, known as *endometriomas*, are visible on ultrasound as fluid collections within the ovaries. Endometriomas are filled with a thick brown fluid that looks similar to blood on ultrasound.

MRI is a more accurate imaging test that can better assess surrounding structures such as the bowel. Severe endometriosis can be visible on MRI as areas of inflammation or small masses in the walls of the vagina, bowel, or bladder. Endometriosis can cause organs such as the uterus and bowel to become stuck together with scar tissue, and this scarring may also be seen on MRI.

Adenomyosis may appear on ultrasound or MRI as *heterogeneous myometrium*—which is uneven or blotchy-appearing muscle—small collections of blood in the uterine wall, or blurring of the border between the endometrium and myometrium.

MRI is more accurate than ultrasound at detecting adenomyosis and subtle endometriosis, but even MRIs may miss many cases.

LABORATORY TESTS

Researchers are looking for biomarkers of endometriosis so that the condition can be diagnosed through blood work or a biopsy of the endometrial tissue inside the uterus. These tests are not yet available to the general public, but they're a promising diagnostic testing frontier.

TREATMENT

For endometriosis and adenomyosis, treatment options can be thought of in two categories: surgery to remove the tissue and medication to help manage symptoms. Surgery is the only method to confirm a diagnosis and the only way to completely remove the disease. This doesn't mean that every patient will need to undergo an operation. The goal of endometriosis and adenomyosis treatment is to optimize someone's quality of life, and for some people, medications such as birth control might be enough to completely relieve their pain and other symptoms.

Surgical treatment for endometriosis is more straightforward than surgery for adenomyosis. In many cases, adenomyosis is found throughout the uterine wall, so surgical removal often requires a hysterectomy, and not every patient with adenomyosis is ready or willing to have the uterus removed.

SURGERY FOR ENDOMETRIOSIS

The gold standard for endometriosis diagnosis and removal is *excision*, which is cutting out the tissue where the endometriosis is growing. Most endometriosis surgery is done laparoscopically or robotically. Endometriosis can also involve other parts of the body, such as the belly button or C-section scars, and in these cases the disease is cut out by simply opening the skin with a scalpel and removing affected fat and tissue from under the skin while the patient is under anesthesia.

Because most endometriosis is found in the pelvis and abdomen, the primary type of surgery is laparoscopic. A straightforward laparoscopy for endometriosis is a minimally invasive, same-day surgery with a relatively fast recovery period. Patients can usually return to work or resume exercise within a few days to up to four weeks, depending on how they're feeling and how extensive the surgery was.

Laparoscopic Excision of Endometriosis

The *peritoneum* is a clear connective tissue layer that coats surfaces in the pelvis. This is tissue that is usually excised in laparoscopic treatment of endometriosis, sometimes along with the fat underneath this surface layer. Endometriosis can have many different appearances: clear blisters; white, red, black, or brown lesions; breaks in the peritoneum; or nodules of fat and scar tissue. These lesions can be very small spots on the walls of the pelvis or pelvic organs, or they can be large areas causing inflammation of the entire pelvis. It can be very difficult for even expert surgeons to tell if a lesion is endometriosis just by the way it looks during laparoscopy. Not every blister, white, or pigmented spot is definitely endometriosis, so most specialists will excise as much of the abnormal-appearing tissue as possible for accuracy and completeness. Endometriosis lesions can be extremely tiny, as small as one millimeter or less, and these spots can be virtually impossible to see with the naked eye. This is why laparoscopy is the preferred surgical approach. A narrow laparoscope or camera is inserted into the abdomen to look closely at the tissue in the pelvis. If a possible endometriosis lesion is seen, it is cut out with tiny laparoscopic scissors, a focused laser beam, or other long, narrow surgical instruments that are inserted through small incisions in the abdomen.

Another approach to laparoscopic treatment of endometriosis is ablation. This means destroying the tissue instead of cutting it out. Ablation of endometriosis is usually performed with electrified instruments that destroy the tissue using heat. For mild disease, there may be no difference in postoperative improvement in symptoms or likelihood of recurrence with ablation compared with excision. There aren't many studies on surgical outcomes, so much of the approach to endometriosis is based on the expertise of endometriosis surgeons.

Most endometriosis specialists will excise whenever possible for several reasons. If all lesions are burned instead of excised, there won't be any samples to confirm the diagnosis of endometriosis. Also, ablation runs the risk of injuring nearby structures, such as the bowel or ureters, because the instruments generate heat that can spread to adjacent tissue. Another reason specialists prefer to excise is that ablating the surface doesn't treat disease growing in the deeper tissue, so ablation has more potential to leave much of the endometriosis behind.

Severe Endometriosis

As the disease progresses, endometriosis can involve other organs, such as the ovaries. Endometriosis cysts grow inside of the normal ovarian tissue. They can be very inflammatory, leading to scarring of the ovary to the bowel, uterus, tubes, or walls of the pelvis. Having a large endometrioma is strongly associated with having other severe disease in the pelvis, and surgeries to remove endometriomas can be challenging to perform.

In severe cases, endometriosis can also spread to the bowel, appendix, bladder, ureters, or diaphragm, and excision may require a multidisciplinary team of colorectal, urologic, and thoracic surgeons in order to remove all the disease. These can be extremely complex surgeries, which is why it is important to diagnose and remove endometriosis as early as possible. Fortunately, most cases of endometriosis surgery are much simpler for both patient and surgeon, especially if the disease is caught early.

Robotic Excision of Endometriosis

Some gynecologists use robotic surgery for the treatment of endometriosis. There is some research into using an intravenous fluorescent dye that makes endometriosis lesions glow green when viewed using a special infrared light during robotic surgery. Theoretically, this helps to identify and remove endometriosis lesions that would be missed by the naked eye. However, studies have not shown robotic surgery to be significantly better or worse than traditional laparoscopy for endometriosis treatment. This technology, and robotic surgical devices in general, are expensive and may not be widely available. The equipment itself is not as important as the expertise and skill of the doctor performing the surgery.

Endometriosis Staging

When people say they have a certain stage of endometriosis, they're referring to the severity of their disease. The classic staging system was developed by the American Society of Reproductive Medicine (ASRM), the professional society for fertility specialists. ASRM staging is a point system based on the appearance of disease during surgery, and it ranges from stage 1 (very small amounts of superficial disease) to stage 4 (the most severe disease, with large endometriosis cysts or dense scar tissue between organs).

Endometriosis staging is very different from cancer staging. Cancer treatment decisions and prognoses are determined by stage, but the endometriosis staging system was developed to standardize the extent of disease for research study purposes and to predict the likelihood of having issues with fertility, not to guide treatment decisions. The general strategy of managing endometriosis remains the same, regardless of stage.

Furthermore, stage doesn't determine symptom severity. In fact, studies show that on average, patients with the worst pain and symptoms are more likely to have mild disease, and patients with the most extensive disease tend to have less severe symptoms. The reason for this is unknown, but it's possible that people who experience severe pain will seek treatment early on and the endometriosis will be caught when it is more limited, whereas the disease can progress silently in those who are not as bothered by it, and surgery might not be performed until after the endometriosis becomes advanced.

Finding an Endometriosis Specialist

It's easy to say that laparoscopic excision is the definitive treatment for endometriosis, but unfortunately, actually getting the surgery done may be extremely difficult. In many places, general OB-GYNs manage endometriosis but may not have the training or resources to handle the most severe disease. Sometimes, patients wind up undergoing multiple surgeries because their initial surgeon does not feel comfortable removing all the disease and leaves some of it behind.

General OB-GYN physicians may refer patients to minimally invasive gynecologic surgeons for management. These specialists also usually have expertise in evaluation and management of chronic pelvic pain from other sources, including the muscles, bowel, bladder, and nerves. Because endometriosis treatment can be difficult—from identifying subtle lesions and managing challenging surgeries to diagnosing other associated causes of pain such as pelvic floor dysfunction—seeing a specialist can optimize someone's chances of having complete symptom relief. But for many patients who live outside major metropolitan areas, finding an endometriosis expert can be difficult or even impossible and may involve traveling long distances or paying out of pocket for care. This is one of the most serious frustrations that many endometriosis patients face.

Endometriosis support groups, such as Nancy's Nook, publish lists of expert endometriosis surgeons, but we need far more endometriosis experts to be trained, and healthcare systems need to improve coverage for endometriosis and adenomyosis care so that everyone can access the care that they deserve.

SURGERY FOR ADENOMYOSIS

Adenomyosis presents a different type of challenge for treatment. A hysterectomy is required to fully remove all disease. This can be great news for those who are not interested in fertility, since adenomyosis can't grow back again once there is no longer a uterus. However, the lack of other treatment options is problematic for patients eager to preserve their fertility or who do not want a hysterectomy.

There are some cases where patients have adenomyosis concentrated in one part of the uterus. This is called an *adenomyoma*. On imaging, this may appear similar to a fibroid but with more indistinct borders. It is possible for adenomyomas to be surgically excised from the uterus, but they are often more challenging to remove than fibroids because there might not be a clear border between adenomyomas and the normal uterine wall.

Another surgical approach, called *presacral neurectomy*, involves cutting out a bundle of nerve fibers from the surface of the sacrum at the bottom of the spine. This may help with pain felt in the midline of the pelvis, including uterine pain from adenomyosis. There are some risks, including injury of the nearby blood vessels or ureters and functional problems such as constipation or urinary urgency. Also, presacral neurectomy is a very specialized surgery, and few gynecologists are trained to perform this procedure.

HYSTERECTOMY AND OOPHORECTOMY

Since hysterectomy is a definitive treatment for adenomyosis, not endometriosis, most specialists will offer hysterectomy only if they suspect a presence of adenomyosis or there is known endometriosis involving the surface or attachments of the uterus. For instance, if the uterus is severely stuck to the rectum with deep endometriosis growing between the two organs, a hysterectomy might be offered. A gynecologist may also discuss hysterectomy if someone is experiencing severe bleeding that is difficult to control with other methods, but a hysterectomy is never mandatory for endometriosis—especially for someone who wants to preserve fertility. As is the case with fibroids, people may be told that a hysterectomy is their only treatment option for endometriosis, and that is not true.

The same applies for *bilateral oophorectomy*, or removal of the ovaries, which triggers surgical menopause. Oophorectomy would likely resolve symptoms and may be considered for someone who has very severe endometriosis that has recurred despite multiple surgeries, but it can lead to serious health issues, including cardiovascular disease, osteoporosis, and menopausal symptoms such as vaginal dryness, hot flashes, and mood swings. Removal of the ovaries should really be an option of last resort in the most severe cases of endometriosis that have not responded to other treatments.

MEDICATION

The nonsurgical treatments for endometriosis and adenomyosis usually involve over-the-counter and prescription medications for pain control and hormonal methods such as birth control. Unfortunately, there are no medications that will actually eliminate or remove endometriosis or adenomyosis—they can only suppress or improve symptoms.

Over-the-Counter Pain Medication

Because endometriosis and adenomyosis are inflammatory conditions, nonsteroidal anti-inflammatory drugs such as ibuprofen and naproxen are usually the pain medications recommended. Acetaminophen (Tylenol) may help, but the NSAIDs are generally more effective for pain control.

Hormonal Medications

Hormonal birth control and progesterone pills often improve pain, heavy bleeding, and other symptoms. At a minimum, hormonal medications can suppress ovulation and periods, when endometriosis and adenomyosis symptoms tend to be the worst. Progesterone IUDs placed in the uterus may help with painful or heavy periods, but they don't prevent ovulation or endometriosis cysts of the ovaries.

There is some debate about whether taking hormonal medications after surgical removal of endometriosis can help prevent recurrence. Every endometriosis surgeon, regardless of level of expertise, will have patients who experience recurrence of disease or only partial resolution of symptoms. Therefore, some people may choose to continue hormonal methods after surgery to control remaining symptoms or if they simply need birth control.

Gonadotropin-Releasing Hormone (GnRH) Agonists and Antagonists

Endometriosis and adenomyosis are stimulated by estrogen, so GnRH agonists and antagonists are effective for endometriosis and adenomyosis pain because they lower estrogen levels. Since they can cause bone thinning over time, they're typically prescribed for six to twenty-four months at most.

HOLISTIC OPTIONS

Because endometriosis and, to a lesser extent, adenomyosis can affect so many different organs, many patients do not experience complete relief from symptoms with surgery or medication alone. They may require physical therapy to treat inflamed muscles or dietary changes to help with bowel symptoms. The good news is that a holistic approach to wellness often gives these patients excellent chances of controlling all their symptoms.

Dietary Changes

Studies have demonstrated that some nutritional changes might improve endometriosis symptoms, but these studies were small and data is limited, so there are no clear guidelines in terms of dietary interventions. Vitamin D supplementation was shown to improve pain scores in a randomized control trial, but the placebo group experienced almost the same improvement in pain as those who received the vitamin D.

Some endometriosis patients subjectively report improvement in symptoms with taking turmeric. There have been several studies showing that curcumin, the main active agent in turmeric, has anti-inflammatory and antioxidant activity, which in theory may address some of endometriosis pain and symptoms. Unfortunately, there are no direct studies on the use of turmeric for endometriosis.

Many people with endometriosis or adenomyosis also report subjective improvement in pain and bowel problems with avoidance of inflammatory foods such as dairy, red meat, gluten, and sugar. There are no studies confirming that dietary changes are truly effective in decreasing endometriosis and adenomyosis symptoms, but since limiting these foods or consuming them in moderation can have other health benefits, they're worth considering. Keeping a journal may help identify dietary triggers. Track symptoms every day, including pain on a scale of one to ten, and write down all food and beverages consumed as well as any activities done that day. This may help identify factors that are exacerbating pain, bowel, or bladder symptoms.

Pelvic Floor Physical Therapy

Many endometriosis patients suffer from inflammation or spasm of the muscles of the pelvic floor and therefore may benefit from pelvic floor physical therapy (PT). Pelvic physical therapists are experts in treating muscular causes of chronic pain as well as the bowel and bladder dysfunction that can result from pelvic inflammation. Even if a surgeon does an extremely thorough surgical removal of endometriosis, if a patient has tight and painful muscles, they may continue to cause pain and difficulty with bowel movements, urinating, or sex until treated with physical therapy. PT is a wonderful treatment option that is very effective and has minimal risks.

Medical Marijuana and CBD

A few studies have shown improvement in endometriosis pain and symptoms with medical marijuana. Medical marijuana must be prescribed by a licensed healthcare professional, as there are risks to use, including nausea, vomiting, and mood symptoms. Some people use cannabidiol, or CBD, to treat endometriosis pain. CBD is a chemical compound found in marijuana that does not produce a high. Research is limited by the fact that CBD products are not federally regulated and can vary significantly in concentration and formulation.

Mental Health

Since pain and distressing symptoms of endometriosis and adenomyosis can directly affect someone's mood and emotional well-being, mental health interventions are an important part of the healing process. Caring for one's mental wellness is always important, but anxiety and depression have been shown to worsen pain, bowel symptoms, and muscle tension, so managing mood symptoms can also help break the cycle of pain experienced by so many people with endometriosis and adenomyosis. The good news is that some studies have shown that *cognitive behavioral therapy* (talk therapy to identify patterns of thinking, improve coping skills, and relieve emotional distress) and practices such as mindfulness and meditation may improve endometriosis symptoms. Cognitive behavioral therapy in particular has been found to be effective in the management of several medical conditions that have a mind-body connection, including endometriosis. Anyone feeling significant depression, anxiety, or other mood symptoms should see a licensed mental health professional. Good mental health care should be prioritized as much as surgery or medication.

TAKE-HOME POINTS

- Endometriosis is tissue that resembles the tissue from inside the cavity of the uterus found outside the uterus. Adenomyosis is a similar condition but the tissue grows in the walls of the uterus.

- One in ten women has endometriosis.

- Endometriosis affects up to half of women with infertility.

- On average, it takes seven years to be diagnosed with endometriosis.

- A combination of surgery and pelvic floor PT can help relieve the pain, bowel, bladder, and nerve symptoms of endometriosis and adenomyosis.

Polycystic Ovarian Syndrome

On the surface, almost nothing about PCOS (polycystic ovarian syndrome) appears to make sense: it can cause periods to disappear for months on end, or it can cause persistent heavy bleeding. Lack of regular periods is one of the most common symptoms, but physicians sometimes treat PCOS by giving hormonal birth control, which can make periods lighter or make then disappear entirely. Even the name itself is contradictory, because people don't actually have to have polycystic ovaries to be diagnosed with PCOS if they have other symptoms, such as irregular periods, acne, or facial hair, that fit the syndrome.

The most common endocrine (hormone-related) disorder among women of reproductive age, PCOS affects 10 percent or more of those assigned female at birth. There are far more questions than answers when it comes to PCOS, and this causes enormous frustration for those who suffer from it. PCOS can affect every aspect of someone's life: appearance, weight, overall health, fertility, and mood. Like other common gynecologic conditions, such as endometriosis and fibroids, the exact causes are not known and there is no cure, but symptoms and associated health problems can be managed. Some studies are looking into possible biological causes, and hopefully, as more is understood about PCOS, there will be more targeted prevention and treatment options in the future.

PCOS BASICS

PCOS is an imbalance in the hormones that normally regulate ovulation and periods. It is a syndrome, which means that it is a group of associated signs and symptoms rather than a specific disease caused by a known biological source. The constellation of problems can include menstrual abnormalities, infertility, mood disorders like depression and anxiety, skin changes such as acne and *hirsutism* (increased facial or body hair), and metabolic issues such as high blood pressure, high cholesterol, insulin resistance, diabetes, and obesity.

The symptoms and features of PCOS can differ widely among patients. Sometimes, PCOS patients have different symptoms at different points in their lives as they age or as their weight changes. There are also ethnic and regional differences in how PCOS presents. People from Middle Eastern, Hispanic, and Mediterranean backgrounds can have more significant facial or body hair growth; there are higher rates of metabolic health issues for those from Southeast Asia and Africa; and patients from East Asian backgrounds are less likely to be overweight and may have milder hair growth. Because people with PCOS can have such varying experiences, there may actually be several underlying conditions that are currently bundled under the umbrella of PCOS.

DIAGNOSIS

Because PCOS is a syndrome rather than a disease with a known cause, there is no lab test specifically for PCOS; it is diagnosed based on a combination of symptoms and physical findings. The definition of PCOS has changed and expanded throughout the years. What we currently call PCOS was first described in 1935 by gynecologists Irving Stein and Michael Leventhal, but Stein and Leventhal discussed only a combination of missing periods and polycystic ovaries. Since then, several different definitions have been suggested, incorporating associated symptoms of high testosterone and chronic medical issues. In 2003, experts from the European Society for Human Reproduction and Embryology and the American Society for Reproductive Medicine met in Rotterdam, Netherlands, and came to a consensus about the definition of PCOS. The current diagnostic features of PCOS are therefore called the Rotterdam criteria, and someone is diagnosed with PCOS if they meet at least two out of these three criteria:

1. Oligo-Ovulation or Anovulation:

People with PCOS may not ovulate regularly, so they might skip periods for several months or even years. *Oligo-ovulation* means someone doesn't ovulate as often as they should. *Anovulation* means they're not ovulating for many months at a time. Since most people don't know when they're ovulating, the symptom to watch out for is missed periods. PCOS patients may have *oligomenorrhea*, when periods occur thirty-five days to three months apart, or *amenorrhea*, meaning that they have no periods at all for three or more months.

2. Clinical or Biochemical Signs of Hyperandrogenism

Everyone has testosterone, including people assigned female at birth. But patients with PCOS often have symptoms of higher than normal testosterone, such as significant acne or excess facial or body hair, and lab tests may show higher levels of testosterone than are usually seen in cisgender women. The presence of acne or excess body hair symptoms is enough to meet this criterion, even if testosterone levels are normal. It's important to note that other medical conditions, such as adrenal disorders and tumors, can cause elevated testosterone, and extremely high levels of testosterone may suggest one of these other endocrine conditions. Symptoms of more severe masculinization, such as male-pattern balding, voice deepening, and enlargement of the clitoris, are not typical of PCOS, so if patients are experiencing these symptoms and they are not taking testosterone, their doctors should check for other causes.

3. Polycystic Ovaries

The cysts of PCOS are follicles, which are very small fluid pockets that each contain an egg. To be considered *polycystic*, ovaries must have a certain number of follicles seen on an ultrasound (twenty or more, according to the most recent guidelines) or be larger than normal. The cysts look like a string of tiny pearls on an ultrasound, with follicles lined up just underneath the surface of the ovary.

Ovaries can appear polycystic even if someone doesn't have PCOS. Polycystic ovaries can be normal when found without the presence of other hormone and metabolic symptoms of PCOS. Conversely, plenty of people have PCOS without having polycystic ovaries because they meet the other two Rotterdam criteria.

DIAGNOSTIC TESTING

During an evaluation for PCOS, patients should expect to be asked about their menstrual cycles and symptoms such as acne or facial hair. Their medical team will draw blood to check hormone levels. If the diagnosis is questionable, a pelvic ultrasound is done to check the ovaries for cysts. The ultrasound can show other causes of unusual bleeding as well, which is important because many people with PCOS also have irregular and sometimes heavy periods.

The doctor will order labs to check testosterone levels and thyroid function, and some doctors also screen for diabetes and high cholesterol. Doctors may order check levels of other hormones, such as luteinizing hormone and follicle-stimulating hormone. This lab work is part of fertility testing for patients experiencing difficulty getting pregnant, and LH and FSH levels can also help distinguish PCOS from early menopause and ovarian failure.

RISK FACTORS

There is an increased risk of PCOS with being overweight or obese. Body fat, called *adipose tissue,* may contribute to the hormone imbalances of PCOS, but having PCOS is also associated with weight gain and difficulty losing weight. It's a chicken-or-the-egg situation in that it's unclear which comes first, the PCOS or the extra weight, or if it's a cycle. For people with PCOS who are overweight, losing weight can lead to resolution or improvement of symptoms. However, there are many people with what is called lean PCOS, meaning they have normal or low body weight but suffer from PCOS symptoms.

People with insulin resistance or diabetes have a higher risk of PCOS, and up to 70 percent of patients with PCOS will have insulin resistance. Insulin resistance, also known as prediabetes, means that the body doesn't respond normally to insulin, a hormone that lowers blood sugar levels. If a person's blood sugar is frequently high, the pancreas produces more and more insulin. Insulin itself might be part of the cause of PCOS symptoms—it increases testosterone release from the ovaries, stimulates appetite, causes the body to hold on to fat, and may contribute to weight gain.

In PCOS, as with many other gynecologic issues, family history is a risk factor, so people with a mother or sister with PCOS have a higher likelihood of having it.

HEALTH RISKS

People with PCOS have a higher risk of chronic medical conditions, abnormal period bleeding, uterine precancer or cancer, infertility, depression, and anxiety. For these reasons, people with PCOS should see their gynecologists, primary care doctors, and perhaps an endocrinologist on a regular basis to monitor their health closely.

METABOLIC SYNDROME

In addition to having a higher risk of insulin resistance and diabetes, someone with PCOS can develop high blood pressure and cholesterol. This cluster of medical conditions is called *metabolic syndrome*.

Most people don't get blood sugar or cholesterol testing done in their teens or twenties unless they have a strong family history of these issues, but patients with PCOS will usually have testing recommended because it isn't unusual for them to have insulin resistance and high cholesterol despite being young with no other risk factors.

PCOS patients will continue to have a higher risk of metabolic syndrome well into perimenopause or menopause, even after the other menstrual and hormonal abnormalities have resolved.

ABNORMAL UTERINE BLEEDING AND UTERINE CANCER

When PCOS patients are not having regular periods, they can develop excessive buildup of endometrial tissue in the uterus. This can lead to very abnormal bleeding patterns or even health risks like uterine pre-cancer or cancer. Progesterone, which is released after ovulation, helps control the growth of endometrium in the uterus; irregular ovulation means less progesterone production, so endometrial cells can grow unchecked. If periods don't occur, the tissue builds up over time instead of being flushed out during the monthly flow, which can lead to the growth of endometrial polyps or precancerous and cancerous cells.

This buildup of tissue also causes the excessive or prolonged bleeding that PCOS patients often experience. If a woman doesn't have a period for four to six months, when she finally starts to bleed, the body may try to flush out four to six months' worth of endometrium, and bleeding can last for weeks or even months. People with PCOS often alternate between having no periods at all and bleeding uncontrollably. When gynecologists recommend that they take hormonal birth control or medications, part of the rationale is to protect the uterus from cancer—progesterone is given to keep endometrial tissue from building up and to prevent abnormal bleeding and the development of cancerous cells.

INFERTILITY

PCOS is associated with infertility. If ovulation doesn't occur, conception cannot take place, and people with PCOS may ovulate only a few times a year. Up to 80 percent of people with PCOS may experience trouble conceiving, and it is one of the most common causes of infertility.

DEPRESSION AND ANXIETY

People with PCOS have an increased likelihood of depression and anxiety. There's a significant emotional, physical, and social toll in coping with the symptoms of PCOS, and the condition itself may increase the risk of mood disturbances.

TREATMENT

Unfortunately, there is currently no direct treatment for PCOS because the root cause of this syndrome is unknown. Treatment of PCOS mostly involves addressing the symptoms that patients are experiencing. Management of PCOS involves an entire team of health providers—gynecologists, endocrinologists, fertility specialists, nutritionists, mental health professionals—and a multidisciplinary approach that includes medications, lifestyle modifications, and sometimes surgeries or procedures.

MEDICATIONS

Different types of medications can be used to address the various symptoms of PCOS. A combination of hormonal methods, fertility treatments, dermatologic treatments, and diabetes medications can be tailored to fit each person's individual needs.

Hormonal Medications

Medicines with progesterone, including birth control methods and noncontraceptive progesterone pills, help prevent irregular or heavy bleeding and decrease the chances of a patient developing polyps or uterine cancer. The goal is not necessarily to induce periods but to prevent the endometrium from building up excessively. In fact, many of these medications suppress endometrial growth so much that periods may actually disappear altogether, because there is little to no tissue left to shed. This can be very confusing for people with PCOS who alternate between missing periods and too much bleeding and think that treatment should bring back monthly menses.

If experiencing a regular period is personally important to patients, they should discuss this preference with their doctors, as it may influence choice of treatment. But it isn't medically necessary for patients to experience period bleeding if they are on progesterone medications that protect the uterus from overgrowth of cells.

Treatments for Acne and Hirsutism

Dermatologists can treat acne and hirsutism if patients are bothered by these symptoms. A diuretic medication called spironolactone treats acne and excess hair by decreasing testosterone, but it has some risk of causing electrolyte abnormalities and low blood pressure. Other options to treat acne are medications such as retinoids and antibiotics.

While some people with PCOS don't feel the need to change their hair-growth patterns and embrace it as part of their identity, other patients prefer treatment, which includes shaving, waxing, laser hair removal, electrolysis, and depilatory creams.

Birth control that contains estrogen can also improve acne and facial and body hair, because estrogen suppresses testosterone levels. Dermatologists often send patients to gynecologists to discuss birth control as a treatment for severe acne for this reason. Some birth control pills contain types of progesterone (drospirenone and cyproterone) that directly block the effects of testosterone, so pills containing these hormones are often offered to PCOS patients.

Medications for Ovulation Induction

If patients with PCOS are having difficulty conceiving, medications for *ovulation induction* can be prescribed to stimulate ovulation. Reproductive endocrinology and infertility specialists (REIs) are gynecologists who manage fertility issues, and they can prescribe these medications. Some general OB-GYN providers may also prescribe ovulation induction medications, but they'll refer to an REI if the patient does not get pregnant after a few attempted cycles.

The treatments most commonly used to induce ovulation for PCOS patients are clomiphene (Clomid) and letrozole (Femara). Both are oral pills that work by causing the pituitary to release more FSH and LH to stimulate follicle development and trigger ovulation. Letrozole has been shown to be the most effective method in terms of successfully increasing the chances of pregnancy in PCOS patients, so it's considered by many specialists to be the first-line option for people with PCOS who need fertility treatment.

Patients who do not successfully conceive with oral medications may be offered gonadotropins, which are FSH and LH in injectable form. Usually, these are given by REI specialists as part of other treatments, such as insemination or IVF.

Treatments for Insulin Resistance and Diabetes

Lowering high blood sugar will decrease insulin levels, which may improve PCOS symptoms. In the past, the oral diabetes medication metformin was used to induce ovulation for PCOS patients. We now know that metformin is less effective than ovulation induction medications, so it's recommended only for PCOS patients who have insulin resistance or diabetes.

Newer generations of diabetes medications such as semaglutide (Ozempic, Wegovy) also seem to help with weight loss, and achieving or maintaining a healthy weight can improve PCOS symptoms. Metformin and semaglutide can cause side effects such as nausea, vomiting, and stomach pain, and they should be taken only as part of a broader plan focusing on healthy diet and physical activity.

Inositol, a type of sugar that is found in brown rice, whole grains, almonds, walnuts, and certain fruits and beans, can also be prescribed in supplement form by endocrinologists as part of PCOS treatment. Inositol may be involved in insulin signaling, and treatment with these supplements has been shown to decrease testosterone levels and improve ovulation and pregnancy rates in some people with PCOS.

SURGERIES

Most PCOS patients don't need surgery for treatment, but there are a few surgical procedures that can help patients who have not been able to achieve their health goals with medication and lifestyle modifications.

Bariatric surgery can be an option for obese patients to accelerate weight loss and help manage conditions such as diabetes, high blood pressure, and sleep apnea. Bariatric surgeries, such as laparoscopic banding and gastric bypass, work by restricting the stomach's capacity to hold food, decreasing absorption, and suppressing appetite. These surgeries are done only after very careful counseling about benefits versus risks and the dietary and lifestyle changes necessary to maintain nutrition while losing weight safely.

Another surgery, called *ovarian drilling*, is almost exactly what it sounds like. Using laparoscopy, a surgeon creates several tiny holes in each ovary. Ovarian drilling can restore ovulation in up to 80 percent of patients; it's almost as effective as fertility medications, and the improved ovulation can last for several years. It's unclear why drilling works, and there is no standard surgical protocol for drilling procedures. It isn't performed often these days because there are less invasive options for inducing ovulation, but it's a good second-line option for patients willing to undergo surgery when standard treatments have failed.

HOLISTIC OPTIONS

Much of PCOS care actually takes place at home rather than in a doctor's office. Nutritious diet, exercise, and stress relief are important for everyone, but they are especially important for people with PCOS because of their increased risk of metabolic problems such as diabetes and high cholesterol.

For people with PCOS who are overweight or obese, the loss of 5 to 10 percent of body weight can reverse symptoms, restore ovulation, and normalize testosterone levels. This does not mean that the goal of PCOS management should be a patient losing a certain number of pounds. In fact, crash diets can be dangerous, and they are not sustainable. The overall priority should be optimizing health, and this includes developing sustainable exercise habits and balanced nutritional goals. Registered dieticians and primary care doctors are essential members of the treatment team to help guide healthy weight management as well as maintenance of blood sugar, cholesterol, and blood pressure levels.

Regular exercise, sleep, and stress management also help decrease insulin and blood sugar levels. They may also reduce the amount of stress hormones like cortisol, which can cause hunger and weight gain.

Optimizing nutrition, maintaining regular exercise and sleep habits, and getting regular checkups can help people with PCOS take back control of their health and reverse some of the effects of the condition.

TAKE-HOME POINTS

- PCOS is a condition in which hormone imbalances cause symptoms such as missing periods, infertility, acne, and increased facial hair, and it increases the risk of high blood pressure and diabetes.

- It's the most common endocrine disorder among reproductive-age women.

- A patient can have PCOS without having polycystic ovaries.

- Up to 70 percent of people with PCOS have prediabetes.

- Nutrition, exercise, and stress management can help prevent health problems associated with PCOS such as high cholesterol and diabetes.

Ovarian Cysts

Ovarian cysts are incredibly common. If you do an imaging study on a person with functioning ovaries, chances are that you'll find cysts. They're the most common red herring when it comes to pelvic pain because they are seen on ultrasound so often. Patients may worry when they hear they have cysts, but oftentimes their gynecologists will explain that the small cyst seen on the ultrasound is a normal finding, is almost certainly not causing their pain, and will likely go away within a few weeks.

But sometimes a cyst is actually the source of the pain—cysts can rupture, causing a sudden and severe pain. Cysts can also become large and heavy, sometimes so heavy that the ovary twists and cuts off its own blood supply; this is a surgical emergency called *ovarian torsion*. Certain types of ovarian cysts, such as endometriomas, are notorious for causing severe pain. It can be difficult to tell the difference between cysts that are normal and cysts that require close monitoring or surgical treatment, but knowledge is power, so let's start demystifying.

NORMAL CYSTS

The majority of ovarian cysts are innocent bystanders. In the course of making hormones and releasing eggs, the ovary often creates *physiologic cysts*, also called functional cysts, which are fluid-filled structures that develop as part of the ovary's normal functioning. Common physiologic cysts include *follicular cysts*, which are large follicles filled with fluid; *corpus luteum cysts*, which occur after ovulation; and *hemorrhagic cysts*, which form when ovarian tissue bleeds after ovulation. All these cysts are extremely common and considered normal findings. They almost always are reabsorbed and disappear on their own without treatment, and they usually don't cause any sort of pain or symptoms. In fact, gynecologists may not even mention these types of cysts when reviewing imaging studies with patients because they're considered a normal part of healthy reproductive-age ovaries.

When physiologic cysts become large, they can cause pain, pressure, or discomfort, or they can rupture. If a patient is having bothersome symptoms from physiologic cysts that keep recurring, birth control pills may be prescribed; these help prevent cyst development because they block follicle growth and ovulation. Unfortunately, it's a myth that birth control can treat or shrink existing cysts; they have to be reabsorbed on their own.

ABNORMAL CYSTS

There are some types of cysts that don't resolve on their own or that commonly cause severe pain. These abnormal cysts may need to be surgically removed if they're causing symptoms or pose other health risks.

ENDOMETRIOMAS

Endometriomas are ovarian cysts filled with old blood and endometriosis tissue. The fluid inside of endometriomas looks like chocolate syrup, so they're commonly referred to as chocolate cysts. Endometriosis cysts can cause severe pain even if they are small. Endometriomas look very similar to hemorrhagic cysts on ultrasounds and MRIs, since they're both filled with what looks like old blood. However, hemorrhagic cysts usually go away on their own, whereas endometriomas either stay the same size or grow larger. When it's unclear if a cyst is hemorrhagic or an endometrioma, gynecologists may recommend waiting a few weeks or months and repeating an ultrasound to see if the cyst remains.

DERMOIDS

Dermoid cysts, also known as mature or benign *teratomas*, are without a doubt some of the strangest things that can possibly grow in the human body. Dermoids develop from germ cells, which have the potential to turn into other types of tissue; they're usually filled with hair, teeth, and an oily liquid, and they sometimes even contain skin, bone, thyroid, or brain tissue. No one knows why they develop.

Having an ovary filled with hair and teeth can be very painful. Dermoids can become quite heavy, which poses a risk for ovarian torsion. Small dermoids that don't cause pain can be monitored with ultrasounds to ensure they don't grow. Surgery may be recommended if they are causing pain or if the cyst is large. If a dermoid cyst ruptures, either spontaneously or during surgery, it can cause very severe inflammation of the abdomen and pelvis. Surgery for dermoid cyst removal must be performed extremely carefully to avoid spilling cyst material.

CYSTADENOMAS

These are benign fluid-filled cysts that form from cells on the surface of the ovary. *Serous cystadenomas* contain clear, watery straw-colored liquid called serous fluid. *Mucinous cystadenomas* are filled with a mucus-like fluid, and they're unique because they can grow to an enormous size. They can fill an entire abdomen and contain many liters of fluid, causing severe pressure, pain, and bloating. Because of their size, mucinous cysts may initially be alarming for both patients and doctors, though patients will be relieved to hear that most cases end up being benign and noncancerous.

BORDERLINE TUMORS

Borderline ovarian tumors are also known as tumors of low malignant potential. These are rare tumors that are not cancerous, as they grow more slowly than cancers and don't usually invade nearby tissues as cancer does, but they do have the potential to spread or become cancerous, so they're treated with caution. If there's concern for possible borderline cyst or ovarian cancer, a general gynecologist will refer the patient to a gynecologic oncologist for counseling and surgical management.

CYST EMERGENCIES

Ovarian cysts can sometimes pose a serious risk to someone's health, in which case they must be evaluated immediately. Emergency situations include ruptured or hemorrhaging cysts and ovarian torsion.

OVARIAN CYST RUPTURE

All types of ovarian cysts can potentially rupture, or burst, causing a sudden sharp pain. If a patient goes to the emergency department with this type of acute pain, the doctor will likely order an ultrasound. Signs of a possible ruptured cyst include fluid around the ovary or in the pelvis and a residual cyst with some fluid remaining inside.

Most ruptured cysts don't need treatment, as the ovary will usually heal itself and the fluid will be reabsorbed. The pain usually improves on its own within a few days. Doctors may prescribe pain medication such as ibuprofen or acetaminophen for discomfort during healing while they monitor for signs of internal bleeding. Surgery is necessary only if there is concern for active bleeding that isn't stopping, if pain is severe and not improving, or if there's a possibility that another type of emergency such as torsion may be occurring.

OVARIAN TORSION

Torsion is one of the few true surgical emergencies in gynecology. Surgery must be done immediately because torsion can cut off blood supply and lead to death of the ovary. Imagine a ball hanging on a string. In this analogy, the ovary is the ball, and the blood vessels that feed the ovary are the string. If the ball rotates, it twists the string each time it turns. If a blood vessel becomes twisted in this way, eventually blood will no longer flow to or from the ovary, and ovarian tissue will die if blood flow is not restored quickly.

This can cause excruciating pain that resembles the level of pain from kidney stones, and people experiencing torsion may be seen writhing in bed in the emergency department (ED). The pain can come and go as the ovary twists and untwists. In addition to sudden severe pain, torsion causes nausea and vomiting.

An ultrasound may show a large ovary with or without a cyst, and there may be a lack of blood flow to the ovary. Since torsion can come and go, it can't be ruled out even if blood flow appears normal on ultrasound. If there is suspicion for torsion, emergency laparoscopic surgery is needed immediately to untwist the ovary, restore blood flow, and remove the cyst so that the ovary doesn't twist again. For this reason, anyone having sudden severe pelvic pain, especially with nausea and vomiting, should seek emergency medical care, and gynecologists will take patients for urgent surgery if they have signs of possible torsion.

DIAGNOSIS

Most of the time, a pelvic ultrasound is all that is needed to assess the type of cyst and guide decisions about management. But if there is uncertainty about the type of cyst or concern that the cyst might be cancerous, an MRI or blood tests for what are called *tumor markers* may be ordered to provide additional information.

IMAGING

Pelvic ultrasounds are very good studies for ovarian cysts and can clearly identify functional cysts, endometriomas, and dermoids. If the radiologists can't determine the type of cyst or need more information, they may recommend an MRI.

Computerized tomography (CT) scans, which are often used in the ED for evaluation of abdominal pain, are good at visualizing bowel abnormalities or kidney stones, but they're actually very poor at evaluating the gynecologic organs. If a CT shows something in the uterus or ovaries, gynecologists will recommend a pelvic ultrasound for more accurate assessment. It's not uncommon for an ultrasound ordered to evaluate a cyst seen on a CT scan to show no evidence of a cyst.

TUMOR MARKERS

Tumor markers are proteins produced by cancer cells, and they're sometimes used to help determine if a cyst is cancerous. The most well-known ovarian cancer tumor marker is cancer antigen 125 (CA-125). Tumor markers do not tell you whether someone has cancer or not, and some patients who have ovarian cancer have perfectly normal tumor markers. Many benign conditions, such as endometriosis and fibroids, and even non-gynecologic inflammatory diseases, such as tuberculosis, can cause very elevated levels of CA-125. For these reasons, experts don't recommend checking CA-125 blood levels in premenopausal patients with an average risk of ovarian cancer.

CA-125 is used to screen people who have a high risk of ovarian cancer, particularly women with mutations in the *BRCA1* and *BRCA2* genes, which significantly increase the likelihood of developing breast and ovarian cancer (*BRCA* is an acronym for BReast CAncer). It can also be helpful in evaluating whether an ovarian cyst or tumor is concerning for cancer in postmenopausal patients.

Lab work for other tumor markers for ovarian cancer may be ordered for premenopausal patients depending on the imaging. Panels combining multiple tumor markers can increase the accuracy of assessing malignancy, though these specialized tests are often unavailable outside of major metropolitan areas.

Ultimately, tumor markers are one part of a broader evaluation that includes imaging studies, physical exam, age, and family history. Doctors use them to help decide whether someone should be referred to a gynecologic oncologist and to monitor treatment response for those who do have cancer.

SURGERIES

When someone is diagnosed with a cyst, their first questions are usually "How is this treated, and do I need surgery?" Physiologic cysts often resolve on their own, so they can be monitored until they go away, but endometriomas and dermoids stay put unless removed surgically. This does not mean that someone with these cysts must have surgery; when discussing treatment options, a gynecologist considers factors such as pain severity, cyst size, the risk of torsion, impact on fertility, and possibility of cancer.

There are two options for surgical treatment of cysts. One is *cystectomy*, which is the removal of the cyst but not the ovary, and the other is *oophorectomy*, which is removal of the entire ovary. Cystectomies and oophorectomies can be performed with laparoscopy or laparotomy (open surgery), depending on the size of the cyst and whether there is a concern about cancer or spillage of the contents. As with any surgery, the smaller the incisions are, the faster the recovery and lower the risk of complications.

OVARIAN CYSTECTOMY

Cysts grow inside normal ovarian tissue. Picture a water balloon inside of another balloon. The normal ovary is the outer balloon, and the inner balloon is the cyst wall, filled with fluid or material such as the hair and teeth of a dermoid. To remove the cyst, the surgeon cuts into the ovary, and the normal ovarian tissue will be peeled off the cyst, similar to peeling a grape. Usually, cysts are not drained, because if you simply drain the fluid but don't fully remove the cyst, it can fill with fluid again.

In a laparoscopic cystectomy, once the cyst has been removed from the ovary, it is put in a plastic bag, and the bag is pulled out through the belly button. The ovary doesn't need to be stitched back together after a cystectomy; it seals itself up on its own.

Because the ovary has to be cut to remove the cyst, some follicles will be lost. Since ovaries cannot regenerate eggs—people are born with all the eggs they will have in their lifetime—a cystectomy can decrease the pool of available eggs, known as the *ovarian reserve*. When a surgeon is deciding whether a cyst needs to be removed, the potential effect on ovarian reserve is weighed against the risks of leaving the cyst in the ovary.

The default treatment is to remove the cyst and preserve the ovary, especially if the patient is concerned about future fertility. The downside of a cystectomy, as opposed to an oophorectomy, is that an ovary that has created a cyst once can do it again, so other surgeries may be needed down the line. Also, if there is a concern that the cyst may be cancerous, spillage of the contents during removal may spread abnormal cells. For these reasons, ovary removal may be preferable in a postmenopausal patient or anyone who has a high risk of cancer.

OOPHORECTOMY

To remove an ovary, the blood vessels that supply it are sealed and cut. Usually, the connected fallopian tube is removed with the ovary; this is called a *salpingo-oophorectomy* (removal of the tube and ovary). The gynecologist will usually try to preserve the other ovary in order to maintain normal hormone levels unless there is cancer or a high risk of ovarian cancer, as in the case of *BRCA* gene mutations. Removal of one ovary doesn't usually significantly change overall hormone levels, since a single ovary can maintain hormone levels on its own, but even patients who have just one ovary removed may have higher rates of depression and neurologic issues.

The removal of both ovaries can have significant adverse effects. Premenopausal women who have had both ovaries removed have higher risks of cardiovascular disease and a higher overall risk of death. The ovaries continue making some hormones even after menopause, which is important for cardiac and other health benefits. In the past, gynecologists sometimes removed both ovaries even if only one was abnormal. Today it is rare for a gynecologist to take out both ovaries in a patient under fifty unless they have cancer or a high risk of getting cancer.

TAKE-HOME POINTS

- Most women of reproductive age have ovarian cysts. The majority of cysts are normal, will go away on their own, and don't usually cause pain.

- Dermoids are a rare type of cyst filled with hair, teeth, or other types of tissue like bone.

- Pelvic ultrasounds are the go-to diagnostic method for cysts.

Pelvic Floor Dysfunction

Pelvic muscle spasm and pelvic dysfunction are extremely common causes of pain and bowel and bladder symptoms, but they are often missed because they don't show up on imaging or lab work, and they require a specialized pelvic exam to diagnose. I used to care for patients part-time at a Veterans Administration hospital, and I discovered that almost all the female military veterans who were referred with chronic pain had pelvic muscle issues. Very often, this was caused by a strenuous exercise and work regimen or a physical injury in the past.

Pelvic floor problems are common, and pelvic physical therapy helps prevent pain and distressing vaginal and urinary symptoms. In many people, pain with sex, leaking of urine, difficulty controlling the bladder, or chronic constipation is caused by spasm or dysfunction of the pelvic muscles, and this can be treated with physical therapy. Endometriosis patients commonly have pelvic muscle issues because the endometriosis inflames nearby muscles and nerves. And most people who have given birth have experienced damage to the pelvic floor from the stresses of pregnancy or labor. For this reason, some European countries, such as France, provide pelvic physical therapy for all women postpartum to aid in recovery and prevent symptoms such as urinary incontinence.

PELVIC FLOOR ANATOMY

The simplest way to understand the pelvic floor is to imagine the pelvis as a bowl made up of muscles. Some of these muscles connect to the lower back, hips, and legs. Patients are often shocked to learn that pains that they're feeling in their lower abdomen, buttocks, hips, upper thighs, or back are from pelvic muscles, because they didn't know that the pelvic muscles extended to those parts of the body.

The pelvic floor muscles are usually in a state of contraction, meaning they are somewhat tensed. This muscle tone helps prevent the uterus, rectum, bladder, and vagina from prolapsing (dropping). These muscles are also connected to the urethral and anal sphincters and help control the release of urine and feces.

A muscle called the *levator ani* wraps around the vagina, urethra, and rectum and functions almost like a sling to support the pelvic organs and prevent *incontinence* (leaking of urine or stool). The *obturator muscles* are located in the front of the pelvis and rotate and stabilize the hip. A small muscle called the *coccygeus* attaches to the tailbone (also called the coccyx) and can be injured in a fall or with childbirth. Another small muscle next to the coccygeus is the *piriformis*,

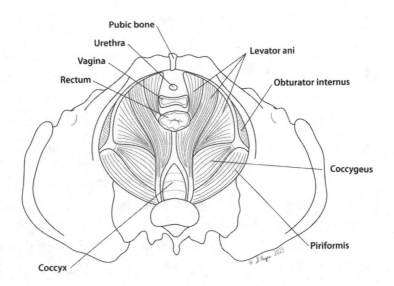

which connects the *sacrum* (lower part of the spine) with the femur bone in the upper leg, and *piriformis syndrome* may occur when the nearby *sciatic nerve* gets compressed or inflamed by the piriformis muscle. This can cause *sciatica*, which is pain or numbness of the buttock or leg. *Psoas muscles*, which aren't typically considered part of the pelvic floor, pass through the pelvis. These large muscles connect the vertebrae in your lower spine to your femurs, and their primary function is to lift the legs.

The *perineal muscles* are not usually included in the pelvic floor muscles, but they help support the vagina and pelvic organs. They are tiny muscles directly underneath the skin of the vulva and between the legs, and they extend from the pubic bone in front to the coccyx in a triangular shape. Nerve fibers and the erectile tissue of the clitoris pass through this area. Several perineal muscles converge into the *perineal body*, which is a meeting of the muscles between the vagina and the anus. The anal sphincter connects to this perineal body, and the entire complex supports the vagina and rectum. Some of the muscles and connective tissue of the perineum and pelvic floor can be stretched or torn during pregnancy and childbirth, leading to pelvic organ prolapse or incontinence.

SYMPTOMS

Dysfunction of the pelvic floor muscles can cause a wide range of bothersome issues. Just as the muscles of your back, neck, arms, and legs can spasm and become painful, spasming pelvic muscles can cause severe pain. Because they are closely connected to the vagina, rectum, and bladder, spasms in these muscles can also cause functional problems, such as pain with sex, constipation, and incontinence.

Pelvic floor muscle spasm and pelvic dysfunction can occur randomly or can be triggered by injury, infection, or inflammation. Possible triggers are sudden injury of the legs, back, pelvis, or vagina and chronic stresses such as intense exercise or heavy lifting. Runners, dancers, people with very physically strenuous jobs, people who have suffered sexual trauma, and people who have been in car accidents or had other physical injuries are all at risk of developing pelvic floor dysfunction. The pelvic muscles can spasm and become tight and painful, or they can fail to contract normally, leading to difficulty emptying the bladder or having bowel movements.

A surprising cause of pelvic floor dysfunction is hovering over public toilets instead of sitting on the seat. Hovering causes the pelvic floor muscles to tense unnaturally, leading to difficulty relaxing the muscles when trying to urinate or have bowel movements. Pelvic physical therapists recommend that people sit directly on the toilet (with a seat cover if desired) or, even better, use a Squatty Potty, which positions the muscles at the proper angle. Squat toilets, which are common in Asia, Africa, and the Middle East, are toilets located in the floor itself, and users squat over the opening to urinate or defecate. Squat toilets also allow the pelvic muscles to relax in a more natural way while going to the bathroom.

The muscles and nerves of the pelvis and pelvic organs are all interconnected, so multiple issues tend to arise simultaneously. For instance, someone may have symptoms of difficulty urinating, constipation, pain with sex, and chronic pain of the pelvis, lower back, legs, and hips.

PAIN

Pelvic floor spasms can feel like aching or cramping, pressure, or burning, and associated nerve pain, such as sciatica, can feel sharp and shooting and radiate down the legs or to the back. It can start suddenly when triggered by exercise or intercourse, or it can be chronic and persist daily.

In *myofascial pelvic pain*, the muscles become tight, causing particularly painful spots, called trigger points, to develop. When these trigger points are pushed or touched—for example, during intercourse, tampon insertion, or pelvic exams—they can cause severe pain, which sometimes radiates out to other parts of the body. Trigger points might be the cause of pain with sex that occurs only in certain positions.

Vaginismus is a condition where the pelvic muscles spasm involuntarily during vaginal penetration, causing severe pain with sex. In recent years, the definition of vaginismus has been expanded, and now it is considered part of a larger category of female genito-pelvic pain disorder. People with these conditions often have severe pain and muscle spasms when they have intercourse, insert tampons, or get a pelvic exam. Because the pain can be so distressing, people with vaginismus may develop severe anxiety or fear that is provoked by even the thought of vaginal penetration. This anxiety further conditions the body to respond by tensing the muscles when penetration is attempted, leading to a cycle of worsening symptoms.

BLADDER SYMPTOMS

Pelvic floor muscle dysfunction can cause bladder symptoms, such as an urgent or frequent need to urinate, difficulty fully emptying the bladder, and leaking of urine. The muscles of the pelvic floor and bladder can be either too weak or too tense, and both can cause problems with bladder control.

Interstitial cystitis (IC), also known as painful bladder syndrome, is strongly associated with pelvic floor dysfunction. People with IC can have bladder pain and urinary frequency, and IC symptoms can be mistaken for the symptoms of a UTI; however, urine tests will not show any sign of bacteria. Treatment of pelvic floor dysfunction is an important part of IC symptom management.

BOWEL SYMPTOMS

Tight pelvic floor muscles can cause severe constipation, straining, and pain with bowel movements. Pelvic floor or anal sphincter spasms can cause sudden, sharp rectal pain, called *proctalgia fugax*. Colorectal surgeons and gastroenterologists may refer patients with constipation, rectal pain, or fecal incontinence to pelvic floor physical therapy. If you are experiencing any of these issues, you may want to request a referral to a pelvic physical therapist in addition to the routine gastrointestinal tests and treatments.

DIAGNOSIS

Pelvic floor disorders are diagnosed with a combination of symptom evaluation and an exam of muscle strength, tone, and tenderness. Patients should expect doctors and physical therapists to ask about pain and triggers. They'll be asked what alleviates the pain, what type of pain it is, and whether they have issues with exercise, sex, or bladder or bowel function. Often, the answers to these questions will point to pelvic floor dysfunction as the likely diagnoses before a physical exam is even done.

Patients may feel anxious about the pelvic floor exam, and knowing what to expect ahead of time can help ease that anxiety. Whether the exam is done by a gynecologist, a colorectal surgeon, or a pelvic physical therapist, it is usually a combination of an internal vaginal and, possibly, rectal exam and external inspection of the vulva, perineum, and anus. The specialists should tell the patients what to expect and what they're looking for, which allows patients to feel safe and comfortable throughout the process. The version of this exam that many gynecologists do can be quite quick—simply using a single finger or two to gently push on the muscles of the vulva and vagina to check for pain, spasm, and weakness and assess whether pelvic physical therapy is needed.

Pelvic floor physical therapists are physical therapists who have done additional formal training focusing on the pelvic floor and problems related to pelvic or sexual pain and bowel and bladder symptoms. The physical therapist will perform a detailed examination of the pelvic muscles and the nerves, joints, and muscles of the legs, hips, back, and abdomen.

TREATMENT

The main treatment for pelvic floor dysfunction is physical therapy guided by licensed pelvic floor physical therapists. Medications can be used as an adjunct to PT to help relax the muscles or make them less painful.

PELVIC FLOOR PHYSICAL THERAPY

Many people have heard of Kegel exercises, which involve tightening the pelvic floor muscles for several seconds multiple times throughout the day; this can prevent or limit urinary incontinence. However, pelvic floor physical therapy is far more complex than that. In fact, sometimes doing Kegels can make pelvic floor dysfunction worse because it causes further spasm of the muscles. Pelvic PT is always customized for each individual patient and can include a combination of stretching and releasing tight muscles or trigger points, strengthening weak muscles, retraining the bladder and muscles in normal functioning and relaxation, and coordinating the activity of the muscles.

Physical therapists may guide patients in exercises to control and strengthen the muscles. They may use biofeedback, a technique in which small sensors are placed in the vagina or anus or on the skin around the anus. When the muscles are tightened and relaxed, the pressures achieved are conveyed as a visual display on a monitor or as auditory cues; this helps the patient target the correct muscles and assess improvement in strength and control. Other tools that may be used to help strengthen weak pelvic muscles are electrical stimulation (where a gentle electrical current is used to help activate and contract the muscles) and small plastic or silicone weights, which are held in the vagina to help engage the muscles.

Physical therapists may manually release tight muscles, sometimes using small curved silicone or plastic wands to reach particularly painful or tight spots. If a patient is experiencing vaginismus or uncomfortable vaginal tightening due to menopause or testosterone use, they may also use vaginal dilators. Dilators are narrow, tube-shaped devices that come in different sizes and gently stretch and relax the vaginal walls and pelvic muscles. Starting with the narrowest size, the physical therapist or the patient inserts the dilator in the vagina. Once patients are comfortable with a dilator size, they will move to the next larger size, and hopefully, over time, they will be able to insert tampons or have intercourse without pain. Most physical therapists will teach patients how to use dilators so they can continue their exercises at home.

Many people feel anxious or confused about what they might experience during pelvic PT. Pelvic physical therapists understand that patients may be nervous, and they know that many people who have pelvic floor issues have experienced sexual trauma or feel uncomfortable with vaginal exams. They will work within each patient's comfort level and pace, allowing the patient to feel safe and centered in the experience.

MEDICATIONS

Sometimes pelvic PT can be augmented with certain medications; they don't take the place of PT but they can help make PT more comfortable or effective. There is very little research about medications for the treatment of pelvic floor dysfunction—their use is often based on findings extrapolated from other types of chronic pain or muscle spasms. In fact, all the following medications are technically off-label for use in treating pelvic pain, meaning that they are not officially approved by the FDA for the treatment of these symptoms. Because some people do find them helpful for pelvic floor issues, they may be worth discussing with your doctor.

Oral Medications

Gabapentin (Neurontin) is an antiseizure medication that is used for the treatment of nerve-related pain. Certain types of antidepressants, such as amitriptyline, can actually improve pain as well as bladder and bowel symptoms, so they are sometimes used for IC or irritable bowel syndrome. Muscle relaxants such as cyclobenzaprine can also temporarily relieve pelvic muscle spasm. All these medications can cause side effects such as sedation and dizziness, and people sometimes stop using them because they find the side effects bothersome.

Vaginal Suppositories and Creams

It is possible for the above medications to be made into vaginal suppositories, which have fewer side effects than pills. Vaginal suppositories come in different shapes, are small, and can fit comfortably inside the vagina. Another medication that can be used in this way is diazepam (Valium), which is commonly used to treat anxiety. The data is conflicting on whether vaginal diazepam has a significant effect on pelvic floor spasm. Some studies show it improves pain scores and patients can feel a difference in their pelvic floor symptoms.

Vaginal suppositories are prescribed for people to insert at home if they experience pain or to use around the days that they will undergo PT. A limitation in their use is that they must be created by compounding pharmacies, as they are not available from traditional commercial pharmacies.

Injections

For patients with painful trigger points, another treatment option is trigger point injections. A combination of a local anesthetic to numb pain and a steroid to decrease inflammation are injected into the trigger point. These injections can also treat nerve conditions such as sciatica and piriformis syndrome.

Pelvic floor botulinum toxin (Botox) injections may help with severe muscle spasm, and when injected into the bladder wall, they can improve symptoms of urinary frequency or urgency. This is an expensive treatment that may not be covered by insurance.

Trigger point and botulinum toxin injections are usually administered in the doctor's office by urogynecologists. Though the injections are given with a local anesthetic to numb the area, it's possible to feel some initial pain when they are administered, and some patients prefer to have them performed when they're under sedation. Several treatments over weeks or months may be necessary to provide sufficient pain and symptom relief.

TAKE-HOME POINTS

- Pelvic floor muscle spasm can cause pain in other parts of the body, like the lower back, abdomen, hips, buttocks, and legs.
- A surprising cause of pelvic floor dysfunction is hovering over public toilets instead of sitting directly on the seat.
- Tight and dysfunctional pelvic muscles can cause severe constipation and sharp rectal pains.
- Pelvic floor physical therapists specialize in the pelvic floor, sexual and pelvic pain, and problems with bladder and bowel function.
- Kegel exercises can worsen pelvic floor dysfunction and pain.

Pelvic Organ Prolapse

Pregnancy, childbirth, and changes of menopause can weaken pelvic muscles and the support structures, such as ligaments and connective tissue, that keep the uterus, bladder, and rectum in place. When these structures weaken or tear, *pelvic organ prolapse* (POP) can occur—the dropping of the pelvic organs into the vagina or out of the body through the vagina. Though many people in the general public are not familiar with this condition, it is actually extremely common, and around two hundred thousand surgical procedures to treat pelvic organ prolapse are performed in the United States every year.

There is an entire subspecialty of medicine that deals with these conditions: urogynecology, also known as female pelvic medicine and reconstructive surgery (FPMRS). Urogynecologists are urologists or gynecologists who specialize in the management of prolapse, incontinence, and other bladder problems such as pain, difficulty emptying the bladder, or urinary infections. People who are dealing with incontinence or prolapse can ask their primary care doctors or gynecologists for a referral to a urogynecologist to discuss their options for treatment.

RISK FACTORS

Risk factors for developing prolapse and incontinence include any stressors that damage or weaken the muscles, ligaments, and fascia that surround the pelvic organs. The most common stressors are pregnancy, childbirth, and menopause. Other risk factors include aging; obesity; family history; connective tissue disorders, such as Ehlers-Danlos syndrome, which weaken the vaginal walls and ligaments of the body; chronic cough; and straining from constipation. High-intensity exercise and heavy lifting during strength training or with physically strenuous jobs can also weaken the pelvis over time and increase risk of prolapse.

PELVIC ORGAN PROLAPSE BASICS

Prolapse can be thought of as hernias of the pelvis. Similar to hernias of the belly button, groin, and abdomen, there is normally a strength layer that keeps organs in place, but if there is a weak area, the organs underneath that strength layer can bulge through. For pelvic organ prolapse, the weaknesses are in the vaginal walls or the support structures that keep the uterus in place. When weak areas develop, bulges can form in the vaginal walls, allowing the bladder, urethra, rectum, intestines, or uterus to push into the vaginal canal.

In early stages of prolapse, this may simply feel like a sensation of fullness in the vagina; some people describe it as feeling like they're sitting on a ball. As the prolapse worsens, the vaginal walls or uterus can begin to be seen or felt outside the body as a flesh-colored bulge at the opening of the vagina. In the most severe form of prolapse, called *complete procidentia*, the entire uterus or vagina can hang outside the body as a large tubular bulge.

Even mild prolapse can cause vaginal pressure or pain, and patients with more severe prolapse can experience difficulty having sex or exercising, irritation of the tissue from rubbing against clothing, or the inability to entirely empty the bladder or bowels because urine or feces get trapped in the bulge.

DIAGNOSIS

During an evaluation for prolapse, the doctor will conduct a pelvic exam that is done first while patients are lying down with their feet in stirrups and then while they're standing up. The pelvic exam is done in two positions because standing up causes the organs to drop more significantly. Patients are asked to strain or bear down like they're having a bowel movement, then the doctor will measure the distance in centimeters that the front and back walls of the vagina, uterus, and cervix come down with pressure. They'll also measure the diameter of the opening of the vagina and the perineum, because a widened vaginal opening and a shortened perineum indicate weakening of the pelvic supports.

The type of prolapse is based on the organ that is bulging into the vaginal wall. A *cystocele* is the prolapse of the bladder, a *rectocele* is the prolapse of the rectum, and an *enterocele* is the prolapse of a small loop of the intestines. The uterus can also prolapse, and the top of the vagina can prolapse if the uterus has been removed.

Examination for prolapse is combined with tests of bladder function, pelvic muscle strength, and vulvovaginal sensation to get a sense of the person's general pelvic health.

TREATMENT

Treatment for POP is necessary only if the prolapse is causing pain or discomfort or affecting someone's ability to urinate, have bowel movements, or engage in sexual activity. If there are risk factors for prolapse that can be managed, such as chronic constipation or cough, minimizing that strain on the pelvic support structures can prevent further worsening of prolapse.

If someone requires treatment, the choice of treatment option depends on several factors: age and overall health, prolapse severity and type, whether the person is sexually active, and desire for fertility. Doctors tend to recommend starting with pelvic PT or a vaginal pessary (discussed further below), then considering surgical repair if symptoms don't improve.

PELVIC FLOOR PHYSICAL THERAPY

Pelvic floor physical therapy can decrease prolapse and prevent progression by strengthening and training the pelvic muscles. On average, pelvic PT reduces the prolapse by only about one to two centimeters, so it isn't likely to effectively treat severe POP.

PESSARIES

Pessaries are silicone or plastic devices of varying shapes (disks, rings, cubes, doughnuts) that are placed in the vagina to help lift and support the pelvic organs and reduce the prolapse. Different pessary shapes provide varying degrees of pelvic support, but rings and disks are most commonly used.

These devices need to be removed and washed with soap and water periodically. The flexible rings and disks can be removed and reinserted by the users themselves; they are similar to a contraceptive diaphragm and are washed once a week. For people who are older, who are not sexually active, or who have more severe prolapse, more rigid pessaries are used, and they're removed and cleaned by a healthcare provider every three months. Cleaning and routine examination prevents infection, discharge, and erosions into the vaginal wall.

Pessaries are a good option for people who prefer to avoid surgery, but they may not be ideal for a patient who is unable to keep up with washing the device or can't come into the doctor's office regularly for cleaning.

SURGERIES

Surgery to treat POP involves fixing the weakened areas of the vaginal walls and supporting the vagina, bladder, rectum, uterus or cervix, and upper vagina to restore the normal anatomy as best possible. It can be performed vaginally or through the abdomen and usually involves suturing weakened areas of the vagina or placing stitches between the vagina and ligaments in the pelvis to lift the vaginal walls. A hysterectomy may be considered for a prolapsing uterus, and as urinary incontinence is often associated with POP, a repair procedure for incontinence may be done at the same time. Doctors tend to recommend that patients wait to have this surgery until they are done having children, because pregnancy and birth can weaken the surgical repairs.

Surgical Mesh

In the past, synthetic mesh, a netlike graft made of polypropylene or similar materials, was used to repair the vaginal walls and treat prolapse. Other hernias of the abdomen or groin are commonly repaired with mesh in order to provide better support for weakened tissue, and prolapse repairs are considered to be forms of hernia surgery. Unfortunately, it was discovered that mesh placed in the vagina caused complications such as erosion through the vaginal wall, bleeding, and pain. For this reason, in 2019 the U.S. Food and Drug Administration banned the sale and distribution of vaginal mesh kits, and the use of vaginal mesh was banned outright in Australia, New Zealand, and the United Kingdom.

In the United States, transvaginal synthetic mesh is used very rarely. but prolapse is still often repaired with mesh in a type of abdominal surgery called a *sacrocolpopexy*. In this surgery, which is usually done with laparoscopy or a surgical robot, a piece of mesh is attached to the cervix or upper portions of the vagina on the inside of the body, then secured to the tailbone at the base of the spine. This lifts and restores the normal positions of the vaginal walls and pelvic organs, and it is the gold standard treatment for severe prolapse and patients with a higher risk of having recurrence of prolapse. Placing the mesh inside the body poses less risk of erosion than placing through the vagina, but some surgical risk remains.

Colpocleisis

For people who are not sexually active, another option for POP repair is a *colpocleisis*, which is where the walls of the vagina are sutured together and the vaginal canal is significantly shortened and tightened; this prevents the other pelvic organs from prolapsing. This is an option only for patients who will never again engage in penetrative intercourse. It sounds extreme, but a colpocleisis is less invasive than other surgical repairs, which makes it a better option for elderly patients or people with serious medical conditions who cannot tolerate a longer or extensive repair surgery.

TAKE-HOME POINTS

- Around two hundred thousand surgeries to treat pelvic organ prolapse are performed every year in the United States.
- The most common risks for pelvic organ prolapse are pregnancy, childbirth, and menopause, but other risk factors include chronic cough, constipation, and lifting weights.
- Complete procidentia, where the entire uterus and vagina have prolapsed outside of the body, is the most extreme form of prolapse.
- Pessaries are silicone or plastic devices of different shapes (rings, disks, cubes) that are placed in the vagina to hold the pelvic organs in place.
- Surgical treatment for prolapse is usually delayed until patients are done having children, because pregnancy and childbirth can weaken the repairs and cause prolapse to return.

Urinary Incontinence

Leaking urine is a universal experience for nearly every woman at some point in their adult lives. Many patients feel relief when they learn that their experience is so common. *Urinary incontinence*, or loss of bladder control, affects up to half of all women and up to 70 percent of postmenopausal women. The same factors that cause pelvic organ prolapse—pregnancy, childbirth, menopause, chronic pelvic strain—can weaken the structures that support the bladder and urethra, so people with prolapse also commonly experience leaking of urine. Some people will only occasionally leak a few drops with the most strenuous physical exertion; others may have little to no control of their bladder.

Patients experiencing incontinence on a regular basis can feel extremely distressed: leaking can affect people's ability to work or exercise and can cause odor and vulvovaginal infections. Fortunately, there are several treatment options to help manage the leaking so people can get back to their daily activities without having to constantly search for the nearest bathroom.

TYPES OF INCONTINENCE

The different versions of urinary incontinence are *stress*, *urge*, and *overflow*. These terms describe the circumstances under which someone will leak urine, and many patients experience more than one type.

STRESS URINARY INCONTINENCE

Stress urinary incontinence is leaking that occurs with activities that put pressure on the bladder, such as coughing, laughing, and exercise. It can be caused by weakness of or damage to the support structures of the bladder and urethra. Imagine a garden hose with water flowing through. If you press down on the hose, you can block the flow of water. If you aren't able to press down firmly, the water starts to pass through.

URGE URINARY INCONTINENCE AND OVERACTIVE BLADDER

Urge urinary incontinence occurs when a person feels a sudden urge to urinate that is followed by leaking of urine. The broader term for increased urinary urge, with or without leaking, is *overactive bladder* (OAB). Overactive bladder can be caused by frequent, uncontrolled contractions of the muscle of the bladder wall, which create a sudden urge to urinate even when the bladder is not full. Bladder overactivity can also cause *nocturia*, which means an increased need to urinate overnight.

Increased bladder urgency and urge incontinence are associated with menopause, prior bladder infections, and diabetes, and it can also result from neurologic conditions such as strokes, multiple sclerosis, and Parkinson's disease. However, there is often no identifiable cause, and people with overactive bladder and urge incontinence may be seriously limited in their ability to work, travel, and socialize because they often need to search for bathrooms frequently and without warning.

MIXED INCONTINENCE

Most people with urinary incontinence leak with both stress and urge. This is called *mixed urinary incontinence.*

OVERFLOW INCONTINENCE

With *overflow incontinence,* the bladder does not empty completely, so urine can leak out when the bladder becomes too full. It can be a result of nerve damage, which prevents someone from feeling when the bladder is full, and it can occur in patients with diabetes, alcoholism, and various neurologic conditions. Overflow can also be a result of physical blockage that prevents complete bladder emptying, such as significant prolapse that distorts or kinks the urethra or medications that affect bladder sensation.

DIAGNOSIS

During an evaluation for urinary incontinence, a doctor will ask about symptoms, including how often leaking is occurring and how much urine comes out, what triggers the leakage, and if there are any associated issues, such as difficulty emptying the bladder or problems with sensation. It may be helpful to keep a diary noting frequency of urination and leakage, volume of liquids consumed per day, and any activities observed to cause leaking.

Doctors will perform an examination to assess for signs of prolapse and dryness associated with menopause or low estrogen and to check genital sensation and pelvic muscle strength. A urine sample may be obtained to rule out urinary infections.

There are also tests called *urodynamics* that a urogynecologist may perform to assess the patient's ability to fully empty the bladder and to evaluate the pressures in the bladder and urethra. Urodynamics are sometimes used to determine the type of problem present or help the doctor decide on a course of treatment. However, some types of incontinence, such as urge incontinence, can be treated without any testing beyond a basic physical exam and a urine sample.

TREATMENT

Treatment for urinary incontinence starts with lifestyle modifications and low-risk medications such as vaginal estrogen. Other medications, procedures, and surgeries may be used for patients who are not getting enough relief with less invasive treatments.

LIFESTYLE MODIFICATIONS

Making small daily changes can help prevent or minimize leaking. Basic lifestyle modifications include staying away from beverages that irritate the bladder and scheduling more frequent bathroom breaks to keep the bladder less full. This can improve urinary incontinence without the side effects of medications and the risks of surgeries.

Caffeine, Carbonation, and Alcohol Intake

Certain drinks, such as caffeinated or carbonated beverages and alcohol, can increase urine production or increase bladder urgency, so it is recommended to restrict or limit their consumption. If someone is having nocturia, they may need to stop drinking liquids after dinner. Drinking smaller amounts of water regularly throughout the day rather than large amounts less frequently may also decrease urgency and leaking.

Smoking and Constipation

Smoking and constipation can also contribute to urinary incontinence, so smoking cessation and ensuring regular bowel movements may be helpful.

Obesity

Obesity is a risk factor for developing incontinence because of increased pressure on the bladder and urethra, and weight loss for those who are obese has been shown to improve leaking from stress incontinence.

Bladder Training

Bladder training is a treatment option for urge incontinence, but it may also help with stress incontinence by keeping the bladder less full throughout the day. During bladder training, patients are counseled to urinate on a fixed schedule, starting very frequently, perhaps once an hour. They're taught distraction or relaxation techniques to control urinary urges. Once they can go entire days without leaking, the interval between timed bathroom breaks is gradually increased until the patients are satisfied with the amount of time that they can hold their bladder.

Someone who is still having urinary incontinence but who doesn't want more invasive treatment procedures may choose to wear incontinence pads to catch urine. These pads must be changed frequently, because urine and wet pads in constant contact with skin can cause vulvar irritation and yeast infections.

KEGEL EXERCISES AND PELVIC FLOOR PT

Kegel exercises to strengthen the pelvic floor muscles can help prevent incontinence. To do them, imagine that you are trying to cut off the stream of urine by squeezing the vaginal muscles. The muscles must be contracted for ten seconds and then fully relaxed, and this cycle should be repeated up to ten times in a row for three sets of repetitions each day. It may take many weeks or months to see results, but studies show that if done properly, Kegel exercises can significantly improve stress incontinence. However, Kegels are difficult to perform effectively because people may not be sure which muscles to squeeze or they might not do the exercises with enough regularity to make a significant difference. For patients who have spasms of the pelvic floor muscles, doing Kegels can also actually worsen bladder control because they further strain muscles that are already tight and dysfunctional.

Pelvic physical therapy helps guide pelvic floor and bladder training, and it's an excellent option for patients who may be struggling to perform Kegel exercises or who have other problems with pelvic floor dysfunction.

PESSARIES

In addition to treating prolapse, vaginal pessaries can also help with stress incontinence. Incontinence pessaries are a ring with a firm round knob on one side. When the pessary is placed in the vagina, the knob sits beneath the urethra and compresses it, preventing leaking of urine.

MEDICATIONS

There are two main categories of medication used to treat urinary incontinence: vaginal estrogen suppositories, which strengthen the tissues of the vagina, urethra, and bladder, and oral medications that relax the bladder. Botulinum toxin can also be injected into the bladder to decrease urgency.

Vaginal Estrogen

During perimenopause or menopause, decreasing estrogen levels can cause weakening or changes to the tissue quality of the vagina, urethra, and bladder, leading to incontinence, urgency, or frequent UTIs. This can be treated with estrogen in the form of a cream, tablet, or a ring-shaped insert placed in the vagina. Very little, if any, estrogen is absorbed into the body through the vaginal walls, so it's generally a very safe and well-tolerated medication. It's considered a first-line treatment for urinary incontinence for patients who have signs of low estrogen or are perimenopausal or menopausal.

Oral Medications

There are oral medications that can improve overactive bladder and urge incontinence by relaxing the bladder or increasing the amount of urine that the bladder can empty. A newer category of medications called beta-3 agonists, mirabegron (Myrbetriq) and vibegron (Gemtesa), are used as first-line treatments.

If beta-3 agonists aren't available or accessible due to cost, an older category of medication called anticholinergics—which include tolterodine (Detrol), oxybutynin (Ditropan), and solifenacin (Vesicare)—are just as effective, but they have a higher risk of side effects such as dry eyes, dry mouth, dizziness, constipation, rapid heart rate, vision changes, and dementia. More than half of patients will stop these medications within the first year due to side effects.

Bladder Botox

Botulinum toxin can be injected into the detrusor muscle of the bladder to relax the muscle and prevent excessive contractions. This is done under local anesthesia in the office and may need to be repeated every nine to twelve months. Botulinum toxin treatment increases the risk of urinary retention and urinary infections, so it isn't a good treatment option for patients with a history of those issues.

PROCEDURES AND SURGERIES

When less invasive methods aren't effective, there are surgical options for the treatment of incontinence. Urge incontinence can be treated with devices that use electricity to stimulate the nerves that govern bladder function, and treatments for stress incontinence include procedures that support the urethra and prevent urine from leaking through.

Neuromodulation

Stimulating the nerves in the lower spine that control the bladder can improve urinary urgency and urge incontinence. This treatment is called *neuromodulation*, and it's performed with a device that looks like a pacemaker and is implanted surgically under the skin of the upper buttock near the spine. Another procedure that can be done in the office is *percutaneous tibial nerve stimulation*. During this treatment, a thin needle connected to a battery-powered device is used to stimulate a nerve located just above the ankle that sends electrical impulses back to the spine. Over time, these electrical signals seem to improve urinary urgency and leaking. Neuromodulation procedures are also approved by the FDA for the treatment of incontinence of stool and certain types of urinary retention.

Urethral Bulking

Stress incontinence can be managed by injecting a bulking material, usually a gel, around the walls of the urethra to prevent leaking of urine. The effects are not permanent, and the bulking procedure will need to be repeated every few months or years, depending on the product used, but this may be an excellent option for people who want to have children, since the permanent surgical options discussed on the following pages are generally not performed in people who plan to become pregnant. Also, since *urethral bulking* can be done in an office, it may be recommended for people who have medical conditions that put them at risk for complications with anesthesia. In places like the UK, where synthetic sling materials are no longer used for the surgical treatment of stress incontinence, urethral bulking is a common treatment option.

Slings

The most common surgical treatments for stress incontinence are sling procedures. A sling is a narrow, lightweight mesh tape or a graft with a patient's own tissue or animal or cadaver tissue that is placed around the urethra to provide support and prevent leaking. These procedures can be performed quickly and are generally well tolerated by patients. They've been studied extensively for over twenty years and have low rates of complications. Slings are inserted while the patient is under anesthesia, and small incisions are made in the vagina and either the lower abdominal wall or the groin to pass the sling under the urethra.

Slings have a small risk of bladder injury, difficulty emptying the bladder, groin pain, pain with sex, and, if mesh is used, erosion of mesh through the vaginal wall. They can also increase urge incontinence in someone who has both stress and urge symptoms. It's recommended that people defer sling procedures until after they're done with child-bearing because the physical stresses of pregnancy and childbirth can cause incontinence to recur.

FISTULAS

A condition that can cause severe leaking of urine but that is not typically included with a discussion of other types of incontinence is a *urinary fistula*. Fistulas are connections that develop between the bladder, urethra, or ureters and the vagina or, more rarely, the co-lon, through which urine may leak uncontrollably. They're caused by trauma to the urogenital tract, such as surgical injury, cancer, cancer treatments such as radiation, and severe inflammation from diverticu-litis or inflammatory bowel disease.

Sadly, in developing countries, obstetric injuries are a common cause of fistula. The World Health Organization estimates that up to one hundred thousand cases occur per year and more than two million women live with untreated obstetric fistulas in Asia and sub-Saharan Africa. These fistulas are caused by obstructed labor—a fetus that is unable to pass through the birth canal puts pressure on the bladder, urethra, and vagina, essentially causing a crush injury of the tissue, which breaks down from trauma and lack of blood flow. Fistulas then form between the damaged organs.

Obstetric fistulas are tragic on many levels. In most cases, the baby is stillborn; if it survives, it has a high likelihood of neurological dam-age. Women with obstetric fistulas are often ostracized by their fam-ilies and communities because of the leaking of urine and stool they experience. These fistulas usually occur among women living in poverty who did not have access to emergency obstetric care, and access to treatment for fistula may be similarly limited. Women may travel for days to reach a doctor who is trained to perform the necessary surgical repairs. Even if they are able to find a doctor to conduct the surgery, fistula repair is only a small part of a larger social picture. Women may still struggle with psychological trauma or lack of acceptance within their community even after they're no longer leaking. They also face high risks of complications in future pregnancies, since the tissue may be weakened or scarred, and access to safe obstetric care is often still not available.

For these reasons, the management of obstetric fistulas requires a complete transformation of the healthcare system in communities where they often occur. Organizations such as the United Nations Population Fund, Doctors Without Borders, and the Fistula Foundation as well as individual surgeons help treat women with fistulas and train local surgeons in how to perform repairs. These organizations also work to prevent fistulas by educating birth attendants about safe childbirth practices and increasing access to emergency obstetric care, and they provide mental health services and help women reintegrate into their communities when possible. Obstetric fistulas are the result of systems of inequity that leave women and girls vulnerable to harm, and society must work toward a solution that addresses these inequities, ensures access to care, and supports women in their reproductive and social lives.

TAKE-HOME POINTS

- Up to half of women experience urinary incontinence or leaking of urine at some point in their lives, and this increases to 70 percent of women after menopause.
- Stress incontinence is leaking with coughing, laughing, or exercise. Urge incontinence is leaking associated with a sudden

cont'd

need to urinate. Most women with incontinence experience both stress and urge; this is called mixed incontinence.

- Constipation and smoking both worsen incontinence, so treatment of constipation and smoking cessation can help improve leaking.

- Botox can be injected into the bladder wall to treat urinary urgency and urge incontinence.

- The WHO estimates that a hundred thousand cases of obstetric fistula occur every year. This is when an injury from childbirth causes leaking of urine or stool.

Sexual Dysfunction

Sexuality and the definition of a satisfying sexual life may differ completely from one person to the next. Sexual activity is often constrained by socio-environmental factors. Religion and culture often dictate acceptable types of sexuality or sexual expression and can place men's pleasure over women's satisfaction. For women in many parts of the world, societal expectations position sex as an obligation to a male spouse or partner rather than as a source of joy or pleasure for oneself.

People of all genders may find it difficult to seek help for sexual health issues because they feel embarrassed or don't realize treatment options exist. But anyone who isn't satisfied deserves help in identifying and meeting personal sexual health goals, without fear or judgment. It's rare for someone to make an appointment with a doctor specifically to ask about a sexual health problem, but it's extremely common to have problems such as pain with sex, decreased libido, and trouble reaching orgasm. Up to 20 percent of women in the United States report pain with sex, and up to 40 percent experience other problems of sexual dysfunction, most commonly lack of desire. Sexual dysfunction is particularly common among perimenopausal and postmenopausal women because of hormonal changes that can affect libido, arousal, and vulvovaginal health. It's likely that the actual number of women experiencing problems with sexual health is much higher than we realize, as these are just the published statistics. Many people will not seek care, and doctors too often don't screen for sexual dysfunction during routine visits.

Unfortunately, even when people do bring up concerns with their doctor, they may receive unhelpful advice such as "You just need to relax" or "Try having a glass of wine." No amount of wine in the world will fix vulvodynia, vaginismus, endometriosis, vaginal dryness, or any of the conditions that can cause pain with sex, let alone the other physical and psychosocial causes of sexual dysfunction. Some medical professionals have limited formal training in sexual health and might not know how to properly assess and treat sexual dysfunction. While not every doctor is an expert in sexual health, every healthcare provider should be able to ask questions, conduct a basic evaluation, and coordinate referrals to appropriate specialists.

Sexual health is influenced by a complex interplay of physical, mental, emotional, and social factors; this complexity makes the diagnosis of the cause of sexual problems challenging, because so many issues may be involved. Similarly, management of sexual health requires time, patience, flexibility, and support from partners and from healthcare providers to adequately address someone's concerns and needs.

DIAGNOSIS

Individuals should reflect on their own goals for their sexual experience and decide whether they're currently meeting those goals. The main criterion for assessing the need for sexual health treatment is the level of concern that a person feels. Some people may feel upset by decreased libido or interest in sex, whereas for people who are *asexual*—meaning they naturally do not feel sexual attraction to others or have little to no interest in sexual activity—this is a normal part of their self-identity.

QUESTIONNAIRES

There are several sexual health questionnaires healthcare providers use, and the questions tend to fall into three basic categories: pain with sex, sexual desire and arousal, and orgasm. If you're experiencing sexual health issues, think about the answers to these questions. It might help to write down your answers and bring them with you when you see your doctor, as they can help guide the conversation.

Pain with Sex

- Are you experiencing pain with sex?
- If you're having pain, when does it hurt—when you or a partner touch the vulva, during vaginal penetration, orgasm, or after intercourse? Does it hurt only with certain positions or sexual activities?
- When did the pain start? Was it after childbirth or after sustaining an injury, with perimenopause or menopause, after starting a medication, or after undergoing chemotherapy or radiation?
- What kind of pain is it—sharp, burning, stabbing?
- Where does it hurt? Is it at the vulva, the opening of the vagina, the vaginal walls, deep inside the pelvis, in one specific spot? Does the pain radiate to other body parts, such as your back or your legs?
- Do you have pain at any other times, such as with periods, ovulation, bowel movements, urinating?
- Do you have vaginal dryness that causes pain with sex?
- Do you feel fear or anxiety about pain with sex?
- Do you have a history of physical, sexual, or emotional trauma?
- Do you have any other chronic health problems, including autoimmune issues?

Sexual Desire and Arousal

- Do you have interest in sex or sexual activity?
- Do you have sexual or erotic thoughts or fantasies?

- Do you initiate sexual activity? Do you feel receptive when a partner tries to initiate sexual activity?

- Do you feel interested in or aroused by visual, verbal, or written sexual cues?

- Do you feel physical arousal with sexual activity, including warmth, tingling, engorgement of the genitals, and vaginal lubrication?

- Do you feel aroused when you are *not* engaging in sexual activity, such as when your bladder is full or just randomly? *Persistent genital arousal disorder* (PGAD) is a condition characterized by frequent or constant genital engorgement or arousal, which can be very physically uncomfortable.

Orgasm

- Do you experience orgasm with sexual activity, and if so, how often?

- Has the intensity of orgasms you experience decreased?

- Has it become more difficult to achieve orgasm?

- Are you able to orgasm only with certain types of stimulation?

- Are you able to orgasm only during masturbation or only with certain partners?

PHYSICAL EXAM

In addition to the questions above, a healthcare provider may recommend a physical examination or laboratory testing or both. During the appointment, the doctor will likely address other general sexual health issues, including any need for contraception or fertility counseling, STI testing and prevention, and intimate partner safety, because these topics factor into a healthy sexual experience.

If patients are having pain with sex, the healthcare providers may inspect the vulva and vagina for pain with touch, scar tissue from childbirth, abnormalities of the hymen, vaginal dryness or narrowing, pelvic floor spasm or tenderness, and signs of endometriosis. They may check for yeast or sexually transmitted infections, order imaging studies, such as a pelvic ultrasound to look for fibroids or cysts that can cause pain, and draw blood to assess hormones and general health.

TYPES OF SEXUAL DYSFUNCTION

Problems with sexual health can be broken down into the same categories mentioned above: pain with sex, low libido or desire, difficulty with arousal, and anorgasmia (difficulty having an orgasm). These issues are often closely interconnected. For instance, pain with sex can lead to poor libido, difficulty becoming aroused, and difficulty reaching orgasm, and inadequate lubrication during arousal can lead to pain with intercourse.

PAIN WITH SEX

Patients experiencing pain with sex often assume the problem is related to the vagina, but the pain can involve almost any part of the pelvis—the vulva, vagina, pelvic floor muscles, nerves, bladder, urethra, uterus, and ovaries. Pain can be triggered by hormonal changes, injuries, nerve irritation and dysfunction, endometriosis, prior vaginal and bladder infections, and vulvar conditions.

Low estrogen levels can cause dryness and fragility of the vulva and vagina, which can lead to painful intercourse, bleeding, and tears in the tissue. These hormone-related changes can be due to menopause, testosterone use, birth control, or breastfeeding.

Physical or psychosocial trauma can cause vaginismus, which leads to a cycle of muscle tightening, pain with intercourse, and anxiety related to the experience, which can cause further muscle tension.

Neurologic disorders such as multiple sclerosis and fibromyalgia can cause pain throughout the body, including the vulva and vagina, because they affect the ways that nerves and the brain process pain signals.

Endometriosis can trigger pain with sex in several ways—it can cause inflammation and spasm of the muscles, nerve irritation, scarring of the uterus or ovaries, and pain when pushing on areas of endometriosis in the vagina or rectum.

Vulvodynia is chronic vulvar pain without a known cause. It can affect the entire vulva or only a portion, as in *vestibulodynia*, which is pain at the entrance of the vagina, or vestibule. Vulvodynia can feel like burning or stinging, even when the skin is just lightly touched.

LIBIDO AND AROUSAL

Low libido is the most common female sexual disorder. Countless factors can cause poor libido, including stress about work, home, relationships, depression, anxiety, body-image issues, hormone changes, antidepressant medications, pain, and illness.

Arousal is someone's response to sexual stimulation. This includes both mental excitement and physical changes like vaginal lubrication and engorgement of the genitals that happen when someone feels turned on. Problems with arousal can be related to the same emotional or social issues that can affect libido or to medical causes, such as thyroid disease, diabetes, multiple sclerosis, coronavirus (COVID-19) infection, cancer, cardiac problems, menopause, and certain medications.

Abnormalities of libido and of arousal used to be considered separate conditions, but because they are so closely connected in terms of both causes and treatments, they're now viewed as parts of the larger problem of sexual interest and arousal disorder.

ORGASMIC DISORDER

Orgasmic disorders are characterized by difficulty achieving orgasm, or sexual climax, despite feeling aroused. People may have delayed or less intense orgasms or no orgasms at all. Some people never experience orgasm but aren't bothered by this and are satisfied with their sex lives, whereas others can orgasm regularly but feel unhappy with the frequency or intensity. An orgasmic disorder involves both one's ability to experience orgasms and one's dissatisfaction with them.

The elements needed to achieve an orgasm differ from person to person. Some people may reach orgasm only with sufficient foreplay, clitoral stimulation, vaginal penetration, or other specific types of individual or partnered sexual activity; others can achieve orgasm just through visualization without any physical stimulation. The amount of time and the types of sexual activity needed to achieve orgasm don't factor into the diagnosis of an orgasmic disorder.

Problems with orgasm can arise from medical conditions, medications, or emotional or mental factors. In addition, for people who are sexually active with partners, inability to orgasm may be related to a partner's ability to understand and meet their sexual needs. Sometimes a partner may climax and end sex before someone is able to achieve orgasm. When doctors are discussing and treating orgasmic disorders, one of the first questions they'll ask is if that person can achieve orgasm alone during masturbation. If so, there is not a medical problem, and the issue may lie in communication or engagement with the partner.

TREATMENT

There is no single pill that can successfully treat all sexual disorders because of the complexity of the female sexual response. It's not as simple as just taking hormones or supplements that promise to balance hormones. Very often, treatment requires a multidisciplinary team, including physical therapists, urogynecologists, menopause or vulvar specialists, gynecologic surgeons, and mental health professionals. The most effective treatment strategy may involve a combination of sex therapy, partner communication, pelvic physical therapy, and, in some cases, medication and devices such as vibrators to help with libido or arousal.

SEX THERAPY

Licensed sex therapists are psychologists, psychiatrists, or social workers who have additional training in sexual health. Sex therapists help both individual patients and couples in many different ways; they provide practical guidance in terms of specific sexual skills and facilitate communication between partners. They perform cognitive behavioral therapy to discover and treat factors such as fear, unrealistic expectations, poor self-image, and other ways of thinking that can affect sexual response. Sex therapists sometimes also provide mindfulness training to increase awareness of pleasure and arousal and minimize distracting thoughts. Treatment is not limited to sessions with the sex therapist; they will often recommend exercises to try at home, either alone or with a partner. Many people think therapists treat only mental health and mood disorders, but sex therapists are skilled at helping anyone experiencing problems with sex or sexuality.

PELVIC FLOOR PHYSICAL THERAPY

For those experiencing pain with sex, pelvic floor PT is extremely helpful. Pelvic physical therapists treat conditions such as vaginismus, vulvodynia, changes of menopause, and scar tissue from childbirth or cancer treatments that can cause pain with sex. They release tight muscles and scar tissue, improve pain from irritated nerves, and can teach patients to use vaginal dilators if needed.

STIMULATORY DEVICES

Vibrators or vacuum suction devices are sometimes used for clitoral stimulation or to help with genital sensation and blood flow. Studies have evaluated the use of these devices for both men and women with neurologic conditions such as multiple sclerosis and spinal cord injury and found them to be safe and effective in treating sexual dysfunction and orgasmic disorders. Online ordering allows people to purchase toys and devices from the privacy of their homes, and several large pharmacy chains in the United States sell relatively affordable stimulatory devices with discreet packaging.

LUBRICANTS

The first-line treatment options for pain with sex caused by vaginal dryness are lubricants. Lubricants are liquids or gels used during vaginal or anal intercourse with a partner or sex toys. They can be water-, silicone-, or oil-based, and they each have pros and cons. Water- and silicone-based lubricants are commonly available at local pharmacies and online and are generally safe to use with latex condoms.

Water-based lubricants are easy to wash off and are safe to use with sex toys, but they may dry out faster than silicone and become sticky or evaporate.

Silicone-based lubricants last longer and therefore do not need to be reapplied as often and they may contain fewer irritants than water-based lubricants, but they can break down the material in some sex toys.

Oil-based lubricants such as coconut oil and olive oil should never be used with condoms, because they can break down latex. Synthetic oils such as petroleum jelly and baby oil should never be used in the vagina at all, as they can cause irritation and are difficult to wash off.

In general, when choosing a lubricant, select a water- or silicone-based product and try to avoid brands with fragrances, glycerin, and parabens because these can be very irritating to the vagina. Read the packaging carefully to see if they are safe for use with condoms and toys. Because many people prefer the smooth feel and long-lasting effect of silicone lubricants, gynecologists may recommend silicone as a first-line option as long as they're not being used with toys.

There are also topical oils or gels that have a warming effect and that claim to increase pleasurable genital sensations or arousal. The ingredients in these products can cause significant irritation or a burning sensation of the delicate vulvovaginal tissue, so they should usually be avoided.

MEDICATIONS

In general, medications are used only if other strategies, such as sex therapy and partner communication, do not resolve the problem. Hormones and other medicines are typically only used to treat desire and arousal issues, as they have not been found to be effective in managing orgasmic disorders.

Hormones

Estrogen and testosterone hormones play a role in normal female sexual response, but simply giving hormonal medications may not treat sexual disorders. Hormone treatments have generally not been found to be effective in treating sexual dysfunction in premenopausal women; the evidence is mixed for postmenopausal patients.

The Women's Health Initiative (WHI), one of the largest studies of menopausal hormone therapy (MHT), did not show that oral estrogen had any significant effect on sexual satisfaction, though smaller studies with far fewer participants have shown some potential benefit. Because menopausal symptoms such as hot flashes, poor sleep, and mood fluctuations can negatively affect sexual interest and arousal, it is still worth discussing the risks and benefits of MHT options with a healthcare provider.

Vaginal estrogen can significantly improve dryness and pain with sex in postmenopausal women or transgender men on testosterone. Very little to no estrogen is absorbed into the body when it is given this way, so vaginal estrogen is generally very safe and well tolerated by almost all patients, including trans men.

Natural testosterone levels drop in menopause, and studies have shown that testosterone supplementation can improve desire, arousal, and orgasm in postmenopausal women. The testosterone is usually administered with transdermal methods such as skin patches or topical gels. Testosterone is not currently an FDA-approved treatment of female sexual disorders, and there are some potential side effects to using it, such as acne and facial hair growth.

Antidepressant Medications

Some antidepressant medications can lower libido, but other antidepressants have actually been found to improve sexual interest and arousal. Flibanserin (Addyi), which was the first FDA-approved treatment for female sexual interest/arousal disorder, was originally developed and studied as an antidepressant. It didn't adequately treat depression, but it was discovered to have the side effect of increasing libido in female patients. The manufacturer then applied for FDA approval for treatment of hypoactive sexual desire, which was denied twice due to concerns about safety and effectiveness. In 2015, after the company submitted additional study data, flibanserin was approved by the FDA for treatment of female sexual interest / arousal disorder. It was studied and approved only for premenopausal patients, and it must be taken daily to be effective. Its use is also limited by side effects, which include low blood pressure and fainting. These problems are more common when patients drink alcohol, so people taking the medication have to wait two or more hours after drinking alcohol to take it. All these factors have limited the utilization of flibanserin, and it isn't commercially available outside of the United States and Canada.

Bupropion (Wellbutrin) is an antidepressant that is FDA approved for depression and smoking cessation, and it's been shown in small randomized studies to be effective in improving desire, arousal, and orgasm. Cost can be low because it's been used for many years for depression treatment and is available as a generic medication. However, its use for sexual dysfunction is off-label, meaning that bupropion was not specifically evaluated or approved by the FDA for this purpose. and like any medication, there are potential side effects, in this case including nausea, sedation, insomnia, and headaches.

Bremelanotide (Vyleesi)

In 2019, an injectable medication called bremelanotide (Vyleesi) received FDA approval for treatment of sexual desire disorder in premenopausal patients. It activates certain hormone receptors and is used before sexual activity. Bremelanotide has a high rate of side effects, including nausea and vomiting in up to 40 percent of patients. The need to administer an injection at least forty-five minutes before sex also limits spontaneity. For all these reasons, bremelanotide hasn't been used widely since it became commercially available.

Sildenafil (Viagra)

Perhaps the most well-known medication for sexual dysfunction, sildenafil (Viagra) is a treatment for erectile dysfunction in cis men and works by increasing blood flow. Randomized studies in women have not shown significant improvement compared with placebo. There is some early evidence it might be helpful for women experiencing sexual dysfunction from SSRI antidepressants or those with nerve-related issues such as diabetes, multiple sclerosis, and spinal cord injury. Hopefully studies will reveal other women's health applications in the future.

TAKE-HOME POINTS

- Up to 40 percent of women in the United States experience problems with sexual dysfunction, most commonly lack of desire.
- People who can achieve orgasm alone during masturbation but not with a partner do not have a medical problem. The issue may lie in communication or activity with the partner.
- Vibrators have been found to be effective for treatment of sexual dysfunction in both men and women.
- Coconut oil and olive oil should never be used as lubricants with condoms, because they can break down latex. Petroleum

jelly or baby oil should never be used in the vagina because they can cause irritation.

- Testosterone can improve desire, arousal, and orgasm in postmenopausal women. There are no FDA-approved formulations for this purpose, so its use for the treatment of sexual dysfunction in women is off-label.

Vulvovaginal Conditions

Pretty much everyone with a vulva has felt vulvar itching, burning, or irritation at some point in their lives. This can be a minor annoyance that is easily eliminated with yeast infection creams, or it can be so extreme that a person can barely sit without excruciating pain. The vulva and vagina are very sensitive and complex structures that are affected by an enormous range of different conditions that cause very similar symptoms. Vulvar pain can be due to irritation from soap, a herpes outbreak, dryness changes of menopause, vulvodynia, and even vulvar cancer. It's common for women to try to self-treat vulvovaginal symptoms with all sorts of home remedies or over-the-counter medications without lasting relief, because they don't realize that they're missing the actual problem. People who are having persistent and bothersome symptoms should see their healthcare providers for an examination, and they may need a referral to a vulvar specialist for more complex or persistent symptoms.

The major categories of vulvovaginal problems are infections, skin conditions, pain syndromes, and genitourinary changes of menopause and perimenopause. Too often, basic vulvovaginal care isn't included in health education, leading to common hygiene myths that can cause harm. It's time to start debunking these myths.

VULVOVAGINITIS

Vulvovaginitis is inflammation of the vulva or vagina, and most people with a vagina will experience some sort of vulvovaginitis in their lifetimes. Most cases are caused by either yeast, bacterial vaginosis, or STIs such as chlamydia, gonorrhea, and trichomonas. It can also result from low estrogen after menopause, chemicals, fragrances, dyes, and other irritants. Vulvovaginitis can cause bothersome symptoms, including an increased volume of discharge, odor, itching, burning, irritation, pain, discomfort with urination, and abnormal bleeding.

The medical evaluation for vulvovaginitis involves an exam of the vulvar skin and the vagina. If more of the symptoms are inside the vagina, a speculum exam may be done to check the vaginal walls, and a small cotton swab may be used to obtain a sample of vaginal discharge for testing. These tests may include assessing vaginal pH by touching the swab to a piece of pH paper, looking for yeast and bacteria under the microscope, and sending a sample to the laboratory to check for STIs.

If symptoms are more external, most of the time the examination involves an inspection of the vulvar skin. Healthcare providers will look for rashes, signs of infections such as herpes or genital warts, and other changes in the appearance of the skin. They will also check for sensation or pain of the vulva or opening of the vagina.

YEAST INFECTIONS

Three out of four women will experience at least one yeast infection in their lifetimes. Yeast infections are caused by candida species of yeast, most often a strain called *Candida albicans*. Candida can be found in up to 20 percent of reproductive-age people with a vagina, but yeast infections develop when the candida grows and causes irritation of the vulvar or vaginal tissues. Symptoms can include itching and burning, a white, curdy discharge, and sometimes a red and itchy rash of the vulvar skin. Risk factors include antibiotic use, which kills normal vaginal bacterial flora and allows yeast and other pathogens to grow; immunosuppression, such as HIV infection or steroid use; and poorly controlled diabetes with high blood sugar. Moisture, such as from damp bathing suits or urinary incontinence, also promotes growth of yeast and bacteria.

Most yeast infections are diagnosed with the basic pelvic exam described above. A sample of vaginal discharge may be viewed under the microscope. During the pelvic exam, if the doctor sees the classic white curdy discharge that looks like cottage cheese, they may offer the patient treatment for yeast without needing additional lab tests. However, if it's unclear whether a yeast infection is present or if someone is having recurrent infections, the doctor may send a sample of discharge to the lab for a culture to confirm the diagnosis and determine the type of yeast. Some rarer strains of yeast, such as *Candida glabrata*, are resistant to standard yeast treatments and may be the cause of repeat infections.

Yeast infections are treated with either oral or vaginal antifungal medications. These treatments are similar in effectiveness, but most patients prefer to use oral fluconazole (Diflucan) because fluconazole is taken as a single-dose pill, whereas vaginal creams or inserts must be used for several days. Other medications administered vaginally include boric acid, which is a weak acid that has antifungal and antibacterial properties, and flucytosine, which is a different type of antifungal medication. These vaginal treatments may be required to treat strains such as *Candida glabrata*.

Doctors may suggest weekly fluconazole treatment for up to six months if a patient is experiencing recurrent yeast infections (more than three infections per year) of common strains such as *Candida albicans*. Fluconazole is not used during pregnancy due to possible increased risk of miscarriage and birth defects, so pregnant patients are usually treated with vaginal antifungal treatments.

BACTERIAL VAGINOSIS (BV)

The most common cause of discharge in reproductive-age women is *bacterial vaginosis* (BV). It is caused by a change in the normal vaginal flora that leads to the growth of bacteria that are different from the lactobacilli that are usually found in the vagina. While both BV and yeast may cause discharge and irritation, BV tends to cause more of an odor and a thinner-looking discharge. The bacterial overgrowth increases vaginal pH and causes a gray or white discharge that may have a fishy odor. BV tends to occur more frequently with increased sexual activity and during periods, but it isn't considered a sexually transmitted infection, and partners do not need to be treated.

In most cases, BV causes only discharge, odor, and perhaps vulvovaginal irritation. In more serious cases, it can lead to preterm labor in pregnant patients and postpartum infection soon after delivery, and it can also cause pelvic infections after hysterectomy or abortion. These complications are rare, but BV infections are treated particularly carefully when they're detected before surgery or during pregnancy.

Like yeast infections, BV is usually diagnosed based on findings during office examinations and testing. *Amsel criteria* are clinical findings that suggest that BV is likely; they include the presence of thin gray-white discharge on the vaginal walls, elevated pH, bacteria seen under the microscope, and a fishy odor when a sample of discharge is mixed with potassium hydroxide. BV may also be diagnosed on vaginal swabs that are submitted for laboratory testing—these tests may be more costly than traditional microscopy-based examinations, but they can also test for yeast, gonorrhea, chlamydia, trichomonas, and other infections.

BV is treated with antibiotics, usually metronidazole (Flagyl or Metrogel) or clindamycin (Cleocin). These antibiotics can be taken as oral pills or vaginal gels or creams. It is common for BV infections to recur, and more than half of people will have symptoms again within a year of treatment. For people who have recurrent BV (three or more infections in a year), options to prevent recurrence include use of weekly metronidazole vaginal gel for up to six months and vaginal boric acid suppositories. Boric acid should be used with caution because it is poisonous if ingested by mouth and can cause skin irritation in sex partners, and it should be avoided in pregnancy.

DESQUAMATIVE INFLAMMATORY VAGINITIS (DIV)

Patients who are experiencing vaginal burning and irritation with large amounts of discharge but who don't have yeast or BV may have *desquamative inflammatory vaginitis* (DIV). This is a rare cause of vaginal discharge, inflammation, and pain. It is not caused by a known infectious organism but by a disturbance in the usual vaginal microbiome. DIV can be associated with low estrogen, or it may occur randomly. Some cases are related to medications or inflammatory conditions such as Crohn's disease.

Gynecologists diagnose DIV when they see signs of vulvovaginal inflammation, such as redness of the vaginal walls and discharge on a pelvic examination, but can find no other causes. DIV is treated with vaginal creams, either clindamycin or a steroid to calm inflammation.

STIs THAT CAN CAUSE VULVOVAGINAL SYMPTOMS

Many STIs have no symptoms, but some can cause vaginal discharge or vulvar irritation.

GONORRHEA AND CHLAMYDIA

The most common bacterial STI is chlamydia, and the CDC estimates that one in twenty sexually active teens and women has chlamydia. Because it commonly occurs with gonorrhea, these two infections are discussed together and are almost always tested for simultaneously. Most people with chlamydia and gonorrhea won't actually feel anything, but when symptoms do occur, they can be identical to symptoms of other types of vaginitis: vaginal discharge, irregular bleeding, burning or frequency of urination. Chlamydia and gonorrhea can also cause serious health risks such as pelvic inflammatory disease (significant infection of the cervix, uterus, tubes, or ovaries), infertility, and ectopic pregnancies from tubal scarring.

Because these infections are so common and cause significant health risks, the CDC recommends routine screening for gonorrhea and chlamydia. The CDC guidelines are for sexually active women to be tested at least once a year through age twenty-five and after twenty-five in those who have multiple partners or a partner who has other partners. Testing should also be considered for anyone reporting vaginitis, bladder pain, or pelvic pain symptoms without a known cause.

Gonorrhea and chlamydia are treated with antibiotics, and sex partners must also be treated because there is a high risk of becoming reinfected. All partners need to avoid sexual contact until at least a week after all parties have been treated and are no longer having any symptoms. Repeat testing is performed several months after treatment to check for reinfection.

TRICHOMONAS

A less commonly known STI that can cause vaginitis is trichomonas. Trichomonas is a parasite; observed under the microscope, it has a whip-like tail called a flagellum and can actually be seen moving in samples of vaginal discharge. They may be found incidentally on Pap smears. Trichomonas is the most common nonviral STI, with more than one hundred million cases per year worldwide. Many people with trichomonas don't have symptoms. When they occur, vaginal symptoms include a white, yellow, or green discharge, vaginal burning or irritation, and pain with sex or urination. Trich can also cause pregnancy complications such as preterm delivery.

Similar to gonorrhea and chlamydia, trichomonas is treated with antibiotics, sex partners must also be treated, all partners should abstain from sexual contact until everyone has been treated and has no further symptoms, and repeat testing is done several months after treatment to check for reinfection.

GENITAL WARTS

Genital warts are caused by strains of human papillomavirus (HPV), which is an extremely common sexually transmitted infection that almost all sexually active people will contract at some point in their lives. There are many different strains of HPV, and the strains that cause warts are usually different from those that cause cervical or vaginal cancer. Warts feel like small bumps of the genital or anal area, can be smooth or cauliflower-like, flat or raised, and though many people have no symptoms from genital warts, sometimes they can cause vulvar itching or irritation. People who are immunosuppressed due to medications or HIV infection have a higher risk of more severe wart growth.

Genital warts are diagnosed by a healthcare provider simply inspecting the genitals. If it's unclear whether a lesion is a genital wart based on appearance, the doctor may remove it for biopsy after numbing the skin.

Warts are usually treated with topical medications in the doctor's office or at home. People with warts should notify their sex partners, because even though testing for HPV in partners who are not having any symptoms is not necessary, partners should see their own healthcare providers to check for warts on examination and test for other STIs.

GENITAL HERPES

There is a great deal of fear and misinformation surrounding herpes, and people may initially be very anxious or upset when they receive a diagnosis of herpes. Genital herpes is caused by a common sexually transmitted virus called herpes simplex virus (HSV). Herpes is extremely common, affecting 12 percent or more of adults, and it is essentially the same condition as cold sores of the mouth. Cold sores are typically caused by HSV type 1 (HSV-1) and genital herpes by HSV type 2 (HSV-2). HSV-1 can also be transmitted to the genitals via oral sex, causing genital herpes.

Like cold sores, genital herpes outbreaks start as tiny blisters that then break and leave painful sores or ulcers that can take several weeks to heal. With a first, or primary, outbreak, people can also feel flu-like symptoms such as body aches, and prior to subsequent or recurrent outbreaks, there can be a tingling or burning sensation of the genitals that is usually felt before the blisters appear. The symptoms of a herpes outbreak may be mistaken for yeast infections or ingrown hairs because they can feel very similar, so people might not actually realize that they are experiencing herpes outbreaks.

Herpes is diagnosed by using a cotton swab to test fluid from the sores. Blood tests can evaluate for antibodies to HSV-1 and HSV-2, but people are not tested for antibodies if they're not having symptoms because antibodies can be present from prior exposure even if that person has never had a herpes outbreak. Blood tests may be helpful in certain situations, such as when someone has symptoms of herpes before sores appear or after the sores have healed and cannot be tested.

Herpes outbreaks are treated with antiviral medications such as acyclovir and valacyclovir (Valtrex). Antiviral medications may be used as needed when symptoms occur, or they can be taken daily to try to prevent outbreaks and lower the chances of transmitting herpes to a partner. People who are diagnosed with herpes should notify current and future partners because of the potential for infection. Barrier methods such as condoms, refraining from sexual contact during outbreaks, and daily suppressive antiviral medication can all help decrease the risk of transmission.

Medications are given prophylactically to pregnant patients in the third trimester to minimize the risk of outbreaks when the baby is born. If someone has a genital herpes outbreak at the time of birth, a cesarean delivery is indicated in order to decrease the risk of transmission to the newborn, because herpes can cause serious health problems in babies.

There is no cure for herpes, but people with herpes who are not immunosuppressed or pregnant can be reassured that herpes outbreaks are generally a manageable inconvenience and not a danger to their health. They are simply cold sores that appear on the genitals rather than the mouth. The stigma surrounding herpes is far worse than the actual condition and is based largely on false associations with promiscuity and misinformation about health risks. For people who are confused or fearful about a diagnosis of herpes, their doctors can help separate fact from fiction and discuss options for managing herpes so that it has the least possible impact on their lives.

VULVAR SKIN CONDITIONS

In many situations, symptoms of itching or irritation can be due to a problem with the vulvar skin itself, rather than an infection such as yeast or BV. These skin conditions can arise in response to an irritant like soap, or they can develop randomly.

VULVAR DERMATITIS

Vulvar dermatitis is irritation of the vulvar skin. It can be caused by chemicals, moisture, or friction. Common causes of vulvar dermatitis include fragrance and dyes in bubble baths, soap, and detergents. Some menstrual hygiene products such as pads and tampons may also be scented or contain chemicals such as chlorine bleach that can cause irritation.

If you are having persistent vulvovaginal symptoms that are unexplained, look at the labels of any products you are using on or near the vulvar skin and try changing to brands that are free of potential irritants.

VULVAR DERMATOSES

Chronic skin disorders that can affect the vulva are called dermatoses, and the three most common of these disorders are lichen simplex, lichen sclerosus, and lichen planus. These conditions can develop on the skin of other parts of the body, not only the vulva.

Lichen Simplex

When the vulva feels itchy, people scratch at the skin, which causes more irritation and actually worsens the itching sensation. This is called the scratch-itch cycle, and it is similar to what people experience with eczema. When this pattern occurs on the vulva, it is called *lichen simplex chronicus*, or just lichen simplex, and chronic scratching can make the vulvar skin look thickened and leathery.

The treatment of lichen simplex involves avoidance of triggering irritants, warm water soaks followed by a protective barrier like petroleum jelly to seal in moisture, and topical steroid creams or ointments to decrease inflammation and calm itching.

Lichen Sclerosus

Lichen sclerosus causes intense itching as well as thinning and whitening of the skin. It's more common after menopause, but it can affect anyone with a vulva. If untreated, it can cause the vulvar skin and clitoral hood to become tight, painful, or scarred, and it can increase the risk of vulvar cancer. Lichen sclerosus is treated with long-term, high-potency steroid ointment.

Lichen Planus

Lichen planus causes itchy and sometimes painful sores that can look like red or purplish bumps. Lichen planus is also treated with topical steroids.

VULVAR SQUAMOUS INTRAEPITHELIAL LESIONS (VSIL) AND VULVAR CANCER

The same strains of HPV that cause genital warts can also cause mild microscopic changes in the vulvar skin that usually resolve on their own. These are called low-grade vulvar squamous intraepithelial lesions, or VSIL. However, there are other HPV strains that cause severely abnormal cell changes, or high-grade VSIL; these must be treated to prevent progression to cancer. Both low-and high-grade VSIL can cause vulvar itching, burning, or irritated areas of the skin.

Vulvar cancer is very rare. It can be caused by HPV infection or by other types of cancer, including melanoma. People can get melanoma of the genitals even if there is no exposure to the sun. Vulvar cancer can look like a lesion or mass of the skin or a nonhealing ulcer that feels itchy or painful.

If someone is having persistent vulvar symptoms or skin changes that are not improving with attempted treatments, a biopsy of the vulvar skin may be recommended to test for vulvar dermatoses, VSIL, and vulvar cancer. This is done by numbing the vulvar skin with an injection of local anesthetic and removing a tiny sample of the skin with a scalpel or small punch instrument.

VULVODYNIA

Chronic pain of the vulva that does not have a known cause is referred to as vulvodynia. It can cause persistent pain, burning, stinging, and throbbing that is either present all the time or triggered by touch, sitting, or sex. Vulvodynia is associated with prior vulvovaginal infections, pelvic floor spasm and dysfunction, low estrogen, and pain conditions such as interstitial cystitis. It can involve the entire vulva, called generalized vulvodynia, or only a part. The most common type of vulvodynia that affects only a specific area of the vulva is called vestibulodynia, or vulvar vestibulitis. This pain occurs when the vestibule, or entrance to the vagina, is touched.

The treatment of vulvodynia is very complex, and every individual will need a personalized treatment plan based on trial and error for effectiveness. A combination of treatments is usually needed, including pelvic floor physical therapy; cognitive behavioral therapy to reduce distress caused by pain and help communication with intimate partners; medications such as topical estrogen, topical lidocaine to decrease pain with sex, anticonvulsants such as gabapentin, and antidepressants such as amitriptyline; and nerve blocks, which can potentially help with pain management. Very rarely, surgery to remove affected vulvar tissue is used to treat a focal area of pain that is not responding to any other treatments.

VULVOVAGINAL CHANGES DUE TO LOW ESTROGEN

Low estrogen can cause vulvovaginal thinning, burning, pain, discharge, narrowing of the vagina, and other problems such as pain with sex and more frequent UTIs. After menopause, this is called the *genitourinary syndrome of menopause* (GSM). People can have similar symptoms to a lesser extent with other conditions where estrogen is low, including breastfeeding, long-term birth control use, or testosterone use in transgender men.

Options for treatment of vaginal dryness include moisturizers such as hyaluronic acid and lubricants that are used with intercourse. There are also non-estrogen oral medications that exert an estrogen-like effect on vaginal tissue. Vaginal estrogen is generally the most effective treatment, and it has the additional benefits of improving the quality of vaginal and urinary tract tissue and restoring the normal pH and microbiome. Estrogen can be given vaginally in the form of a cream or a flexible ring. Very little estrogen is absorbed into the bloodstream when administered vaginally, and it does not seem to cause hormonal symptoms or increase blood clotting or breast or uterine cancer risks the way systemic estrogen does, though those with a history of blood clots or breast cancer should discuss the risks and alternatives with their own doctors.

Laser or radiofrequency (RF) devices have been marketed for the treatment of vaginal dryness and GSM. In the United States, advertisements for these treatments have claimed that they rejuvenate the vagina and help with problems like dryness, pain, incontinence, and prolapse. Unfortunately, there is limited data to support these claims, and the FDA has not approved the use of these devices for such purposes. In fact, the FDA published a warning that laser and RF devices may cause vaginal burns, pain, and scarring, and the American College of Obstetricians and Gynecologists and the American Urogynecologic Society have both issued statements that more research is needed before they can be recommended for the treatment of vulvovaginal conditions. These procedures are also quite costly and are not covered by insurance.

VULVOVAGINAL HYGIENE

Many people are surprised to hear that douches, feminine sprays, and washes can cause serious irritation and vaginal infections. It is common for women to be told that feminine hygiene products are necessary to stay clean and prevent odors. The truth is that none of these feminine cleansers and douches are needed—in fact, the scents, dyes, and chemicals within them can be serious irritants.

Most gynecologists will recommend that people simply wash the vulva with water. If people prefer to use soap, they should use soap that is free of fragrance and dyes. Douching or washing inside the vagina can disrupt this normal vaginal environment and lead to infections. The inside of the vagina should never be washed, and attempts to wash internally can cause harm to delicate vaginal tissue.

Some degree of vaginal discharge is normal. This is called physiologic discharge, and it can be white or clear, can be odorless or have a mild odor, and the appearance, amount, and consistency may change through the cycle. Discharge can also change with medications such as birth control or with stress or changes in diet.

It is a common myth that panty liners need to be used every day to absorb discharge. The fibers and fragrances in panty liners can cause irritation to vulvar skin, and they can hold moisture against the skin and potentially contribute to bacteria or yeast growth. Using liners for a few days each cycle during light-flow days is unlikely to be harmful, especially if changed regularly. But most gynecologists recommend against using liners every day because they can lead to irritation and infections.

Most gynecologists suggest people simply wear cotton underwear to wick away sweat and moisture from skin, and underwear should be changed if it becomes damp from sweat or discharge. Tight leggings or occlusive fabrics such as Spandex can also cause vulvar irritation from moisture retention or friction, so loose, breathable fabrics may be preferable for shorts, pants, or skirts.

TAKE-HOME POINTS

- Trichomonas, a microscopic parasite with a whiplike tail, is the most common nonviral STI with more than a hundred million cases per year worldwide.

- Genital herpes affects 12 percent of adults, and it is the same thing as cold sores of the mouth.

- Low estrogen from menopause, breastfeeding, birth control, or testosterone use can cause vaginal burning, pain with sex, and an increased risk of UTIs.

- Vulvar dermatitis (itching and irritation) can be caused by fragrance and dyes in bubble baths, soap, detergents, and even menstrual hygiene products like pads and tampons.

- Douches and feminine washes should be avoided because they can cause serious irritation of the vulva and vagina and may increase the risk of vaginal infections.

Premenstrual Syndrome and Premenstrual Dysphoric Disorder

Up to 75 percent of women suffer from *premenstrual syndrome* (PMS). PMS refers to emotional and physical symptoms associated with periods—including moodiness, bloating, breast tenderness, and mild uterine cramps—that are severe enough to affect quality of life. Usually when people mention PMS in casual conversation, it's considered a minor annoyance or a judgment about someone's behavior or personality. In reality, PMS is a legitimate medical condition that can affect work, activities, and relationships month after month.

Premenstrual dysphoric disorder (PMDD) is an even more debilitating form of PMS. People suffering from PMDD experience mood symptoms such as depression, anxiety, anger, and agitation that are so severe that they prevent patients from being able to function in their daily lives. It is a serious mental health diagnosis that is related to major depression and anxiety disorders, and it requires the support of a multidisciplinary team and a combination of medications and therapy to manage.

It's important to recognize that PMS and PMDD encompass a huge range of different experiences, and there is no one-size-fits-all treatment path.

PMS

Most people don't realize that there are medical criteria for diagnosing PMS. Physical, mental, and emotional symptoms must be experienced before or during periods for at least three menstrual cycles in a row. People can track their cycles and associated symptoms using a calendar or period apps to help identify patterns suggestive of PMS and PMDD.

People can have PMS without experiencing period bleeding; for example, if they've had a hysterectomy or have a progesterone IUD that prevents periods. This is because the ovaries still function and cycles of ovulation and hormone production occur whether there is uterine bleeding or not.

Most people with PMS will experience a combination of physical, emotional, and mental symptoms, and the symptoms felt may not be the same every month.

PHYSICAL SYMPTOMS

Common physical PMS symptoms include uterine cramping, lower back discomfort, tender or swollen breasts, headaches, fatigue, constipation, loose stool, abdominal bloating, food cravings, and acne.

EMOTIONAL OR MENTAL SYMPTOMS

PMS can also cause depression (sadness, crying spells, loss of interest in normal activities), anxiety, irritability, anger, trouble focusing, insomnia, and mood swings.

PMDD

PMDD is a more severe version of PMS. The physical symptoms may be the same, but the mental health effects are significantly worse. In fact, what distinguishes PMDD from PMS is that in PMDD, the mood or mental symptoms are so debilitating that they prevent people from functioning mentally or emotionally, and it can be severely disruptive to people's lives. With PMDD, someone can experience all the physical and mood problems seen in PMS but with the addition of more intense mental health issues, such as panic attacks, lack of interest in activities or relationships, a feeling of being out of control, and even suicidal thoughts.

CAUSES AND RISK FACTORS

The exact cause of PMS and PMDD is unknown. Ovarian hormones, especially progesterone, likely play a role. PMS symptoms get worse as progesterone levels rise in the luteal phase of the menstrual cycle, and they improve after progesterone levels drop. Progesterone may cause the mood symptoms, headaches, and the bloating and gastrointestinal symptoms of PMS. People with PMS don't actually have different levels of progesterone than people who don't have PMS, so it's likely that the problem is the body's response to progesterone rather than the amount of hormone in the body.

Serotonin may also be a factor. This is a neurotransmitter, or chemical signal, that is found in the brain and the gastrointestinal tract. It plays a role in mood, sleep, libido, and digestion. Levels of serotonin may be lower in people with PMS during the luteal phase than in people who do not have PMS. It is also well established that some of the most effective treatments for PMDD are antidepressants such as selective serotonin reuptake inhibitors (SSRIs), which work by raising serotonin levels in the body.

Risk factors for getting PMS or PMDD include having family members with PMS or PMDD, having a personal or family history of depression, anxiety, or other mood disorders, and having a history of trauma or abuse. PMS and PMDD are not caused by anything that a person does or does not do and may simply occur without any known risk factors.

TREATMENT

If PMS is not severe, it can be managed with lifestyle changes. More persistent or disruptive symptoms of PMS and PMDD may need to be treated with medications, cognitive behavioral therapy, and, in the most extreme cases, even surgery. The most effective treatment approach for PMS and PMDD usually involves a combination of lifestyle changes, mental health care, social support, and selected hormonal methods or antidepressants tailored to each individual person's symptoms and needs.

MEDICATIONS

PMS and PMDD may be treated with a combination of hormonal methods such as birth control and antidepressant medications. Because birth control and antidepressants can potentially have mood or physical side effects, people may need to try different options before finding a good fit. In general, studies show that birth control and antidepressants are very effective at relieving PMDD symptoms, but not every type of birth control or antidepressant suits everyone equally. There is no standard treatment algorithm, and the decision about types of medicine to try and whether to start with birth control, antidepressants, or both depends on the preferences and experiences of the patient. Some people who have previously experienced bothersome side effects with birth control or antidepressants may decide that they prefer not to use any medications at all because they get adequate relief with therapy and mental health support.

Nonsteroidal Anti-Inflammatory Drugs (NSAIDs)

Over-the-counter anti-inflammatory pain medications such as ibuprofen and naproxen can help with uterine cramping and breast tenderness.

Birth Control

Hormonal birth control that suppresses ovulation may lessen PMS and PMDD symptoms, particularly when used continuously to minimize hormone fluctuations. There is an oral contraceptive pill that is FDA approved for PMDD treatment—ethinyl estradiol and drospirenone (Yaz)—but any birth control that prevents ovulation and is well tolerated by the patient can be used.

Antidepressants

Antidepressant medications such as SSRIs can be effective for treatment of PMDD. Interestingly, antidepressants can improve some of the physical symptoms as well as the mood changes of PMS and PMDD. This effect is likely related to the impact of serotonin on bodily functions such as digestion and sleep.

Antidepressants can be either taken daily or only during the luteal phase, from around day fourteen until the period. SSRIs are usually used daily for most other mental health issues, but they seem to work in PMDD when taken cyclically. More severe symptoms may require daily dosing, but some people prefer to use the more limited luteal-phase dosing for convenience or to minimize side effects. Because the symptoms of PMDD occur only during a limited time frame, this is a unique situation where SSRIs seem to be effective when taken only on certain days of the month.

GnRH Agonists

In severe cases of PMDD when the symptoms are not improved with any other treatment, some people need more aggressive suppression of the ovaries and ovarian hormones. This may be done with a GnRH agonist like leuprolide (Lupron), an injectable medication that suppresses the ovaries and ovarian hormones. These medications are not used as long-term treatments because of health risks such as bone thinning and cardiovascular disease. They may be a good option for people who are in their late forties and close to the age of natural menopause.

SURGERIES

In the most extreme and refractory cases of PMDD, for people who don't experience relief with any other treatments, the only remaining option is surgical removal of the ovaries. Because there are long-term health risks of early surgical menopause, this is considered only for people who have debilitating symptoms without improvement from any other treatment except GnRH-agonist ovarian suppression. In these very rare cases, patients are offered hormone replacement therapy after surgery to prevent menopausal symptoms and health problems such as osteoporosis and heart disease.

HOLISTIC OPTIONS

Several natural options, including exercise, dietary changes, and cognitive behavioral therapy, improve PMS and PMDD symptoms. These methods can be tried before considering medications or in conjunction with medical treatments. Sometimes PMS and PMDD are so severe that people need to use all of these modalities together—lifestyle modifications, therapy, and medications—in order to control the symptoms fully.

Exercise

Incorporating exercise as a regular routine, not only when having symptoms, can significantly improve mood and fatigue from PMS and PMDD.

Dietary Changes

Certain dietary interventions have been shown to improve physical PMS symptoms. Avoiding or cutting back on caffeine, alcohol, and foods high in salt, fat, and sugar can minimize mood fluctuations, sleep disturbances, bloating, and headaches. There is some evidence that a diet rich in complex carbohydrates (whole grains, vegetables) and adequate calcium intake may improve PMS symptoms. Calcium, magnesium, vitamins E and B$_6$, and herbal supplements such as chasteberry and evening primrose oil have been studied for management of PMS, but they show mixed results in terms of effectiveness.

Mental Health

Cognitive behavioral therapy with a licensed mental health professional can help control depression and anxiety and decrease the intensity of distress caused by other PMS and PMDD symptoms. Relaxation and stress-relief strategies such as meditation, mindfulness, and deep breathing may also be helpful.

TAKE-HOME POINTS

- Up to 75 percent of women experience PMS, bothersome physical and emotional symptoms associated with periods.
- PMS is a legitimate medical condition that can affect work, activities, and relationships. It isn't just a minor annoyance or something to be dismissed if it's affecting someone's quality of life.
- People can have PMS or PMDD even if they're not having menstrual bleeding.
- Dietary changes, such as minimizing caffeine, alcohol, salt, fat, and sugar, and consuming a diet rich in complex carbohydrates (whole grains, vegetables) may improve PMS symptoms.
- PMS and PMDD can be treated with a combination of hormonal birth control, antidepressants, and cognitive behavioral therapy with a mental health specialist.

Perimenopause and Menopause

For people dealing with extremely painful or heavy periods, menopause may sound like nirvana. It's not uncommon for someone battling endometriosis, fibroids, PCOS, or PMDD to wish that ovulation and periods would stop forever. While menopause signifies the end of menstrual cycles and usually, but not always, the pain and suffering of conditions such as endometriosis, it unfortunately opens up an entirely new world of changes to the body and associated medical problems: hot flashes; night sweats; mood swings; dysfunction of the bladder, vagina, and pelvic floor; issues with libido and sexual function. The symptoms of menopause can be more far-reaching and debilitating than many people realize.

In the past, there was an expectation that women had to suffer through menopause as a phase of life, but in recent years, a multibillion-dollar industry has arisen to offer treatment options for symptoms. These treatments range from hormonal medications to untested and unregulated supplements. It may be difficult for people to wade through the enticing marketing for these menopausal health products, all of which promise relief of suffering and the restoration of youthfulness but have wildly varying degrees of efficacy. Let's separate fact from fiction.

MENOPAUSE BASICS

Many people may be confused about what menopause actually means. A person is considered to be in menopause after going twelve months in a row without a period. It doesn't count if a medical condition or medication stops the periods. The absence of periods in menopause reflects the natural quieting of ovarian function that occurs with age. In order to have a period, estrogen is needed to thicken the endometrial tissue in the uterus, and ovulation must occur. As someone gets closer to menopause—a time called perimenopause, or the menopausal transition—the follicle pool of the ovaries becomes depleted, and estrogen production drops. Ovulation occurs less and less often, and periods come more irregularly until they stop altogether. The menopausal transition usually begins several years before periods finally stop, and as a result, people start to experience symptoms such as hot flashes well before they are in menopause. Menopause is not defined by the presence or absence of symptoms. In fact, some people who are in menopause are fortunate enough to have no symptoms at all, and some people who are perimenopausal have severe symptoms.

Menopause is also not defined by hormone levels. Generally, estrogen, progesterone, and testosterone will be low in menopause, but hormone levels may change from day to day and moment to moment. This is why hormone testing isn't usually necessary or helpful to confirm menopause. The average age of menopause in the United States is fifty-one to fifty-two, so when people in their late forties or early fifties start to skip periods, the cause is usually assumed to be the menopausal transition. However, people who are forty years old or younger who are missing periods may need hormone testing to distinguish premature menopause (also called premature ovarian insufficiency) from conditions such as PCOS and thyroid disease.

Surgical menopause is menopause induced by the removal of the ovaries. Removing both ovaries has serious health risks even for women well into their fifties, including higher rates of cardiovascular disease, osteoporosis, and overall risk of death. For these reasons, it's rare for doctors to induce surgical menopause by removing the ovaries in premenopausal patients unless patients have a serious health risk, such as a high likelihood of ovarian cancer with genetic mutations in *BRCA1* or *BRCA2*.

SYMPTOMS

The range of symptoms experienced in perimenopause and menopause is enormous and can affect almost every aspect of someone's physical, mental, and emotional health.

VASOMOTOR SYMPTOMS

When most people think of menopause, the first words that come to mind are probably *hot flashes.* Hot flashes are a sensation of heat that can be felt day or night and may occur as frequently as once an hour. They are often associated with sweating, chills, flushing of the skin, and palpitations, and these experiences are known collectively as vasomotor symptoms. Vasomotor symptoms can be mild, or they can feel extremely oppressive and anxiety-provoking to the point that someone cannot even go to work.

MOOD

Mood fluctuations are also common. People can feel irritable or tearful and experience significant depression or anxiety. Having a prior history of depression or a mood disorder increases the risk of having worsened depression in menopause. Factors such as poor sleep, bothersome symptoms, changes in the body, problems with sexual function, and loss of fertility can also understandably contribute to feelings of depression or anxiety.

SLEEP AND FOCUS

Sleep patterns change during menopause and it may be more difficult to fall or stay asleep. This is sometimes due to hot flashes, night sweats, or having an increased need to get up in the night to urinate, but sleep disturbances can occur even if other symptoms are not present. Some people experience difficulty focusing or remembering details, which is sometimes referred to as brain fog. These problems with focus or memory might also be a result of depression or poor sleep, which are themselves symptoms of menopause.

SEXUAL DYSFUNCTION

Decreasing estrogen and testosterone levels in menopause can cause decreased libido and arousal and an inability to achieve orgasm. Sexual problems may also be related to genitourinary syndrome of menopause, including problems with insufficient vaginal lubrication, vulvar blood flow and engorgement, and pain with sex due to narrowing of the vagina or fragility of the vaginal tissue.

GENITOURINARY SYNDROME OF MENOPAUSE (GSM)

GSM can also involve weakening of the pelvic floor and pelvic organ prolapse, as well as changes in the tissue of the urethra and vagina leading to urinary frequency, urgency, UTIs, vaginal dryness, burning, and discharge.

SKIN CHANGES

Collagen content of the skin can also decrease with dropping estrogen levels, leading to changes in appearance such as wrinkling or sagging of the facial or body skin.

WEIGHT GAIN

Weight gain, slowing metabolism, and loss of muscle mass are all related to aging in general as well as to menopause. Menopausal symptoms such as poor sleep and mood symptoms may also affect someone's eating habits and ability to exercise, further contributing to weight gain.

HEALTH RISKS

Menopause and low estrogen are associated with increased risks of serious health conditions such as cardiovascular disease and stroke. Decreasing estrogen levels can cause a rise in LDL (low-density lipoprotein) cholesterol, which is the bad cholesterol that can build up in the blood vessels of the heart and the vessels leading to the brain. This makes it particularly important for people who are postmenopausal to consult their primary care doctors regularly for blood pressure, cholesterol, and other health screenings and to discuss exercise and nutrition.

Low estrogen can lead to bone loss and osteoporosis, a condition where the bones are weakened and have a higher risk for fractures. Loss of bone mass actually starts before the menopause transition, and continues after menopause occurs. People can lower their chances of osteoporosis by ensuring adequate calcium and vitamin D, avoiding smoking and alcohol, which can further weaken bones, exercising to strengthen the bones and improve balance to prevent falls, and getting routine screening for osteoporosis with bone-density scans. People who are diagnosed with osteoporosis are treated with medications to improve bone density and decrease risk of fractures.

TREATMENTS

Many of the physical, emotional, and mental symptoms of menopause are interconnected, so treatments for these symptoms may overlap. Hormonal medications may improve many of these problems, but simply taking hormones or any single medication may not fully alleviate all symptoms, and a multidisciplinary approach to treatment is often needed.

MENOPAUSAL HORMONE THERAPY (MHT)

Estrogen containing *menopausal hormone therapy* (MHT), formerly known as hormone replacement therapy, is the most effective treatment for vasomotor symptoms and GSM. There are options for MHT that contain only progesterone or testosterone, but the versions that include estrogen have been more extensively studied and are more commonly used. MHT can be taken as an oral pill or a patch worn on the skin, less commonly as a topical gel or spray. These are called systemic methods, because hormones travel throughout the body via the bloodstream after being absorbed through the skin or the gut. This is in contrast to vaginal estrogen treatments, which are administered as a cream, tablet, or ring inserted into the vagina. Very little to no hormone actually gets absorbed into the body through the vagina, so vaginal estrogen is considered a local treatment for GSM symptoms.

Systemic Estrogen Therapy

Hormone pills or disposable patches worn on the skin are mostly prescribed for vasomotor symptoms, but they can also improve other symptoms such as mood fluctuations and sleep disturbance. For people who have a uterus, systemic hormones never consist of estrogen alone because estrogen used by itself can increase the risk of uterine cancer. Oral or transdermal estrogen is always combined with a progesterone for people who have not had a hysterectomy in order to counteract the effect of estrogen on the uterus and prevent cancer. The progesterone can be included in the same pill or patch as estrogen or given as a separate prescription. Because vaginal estrogen has very little systemic absorption, it can be given without progesterone unless someone has a particularly high risk of developing uterine cancer.

There are several different pill and patch formulations and doses.

In general, healthcare providers will start with a low dose and then increase as needed, because using the lowest dose needed to control symptoms helps minimize the risk of side effects. In terms of which type of formulation to choose, many gynecologists will recommend transdermal patches rather than pills for several reasons: convenience of dosing (patches are applied once or twice a week rather than taken once daily like pills), more stable blood hormone levels, and less of an impact on cholesterol and lower risks of blood clots and strokes compared with oral pills.

Cost

Because MHT can be expensive in the United States, insurance companies often limit the brands and types of hormone treatments that they will cover for patients. It is not uncommon for people to find that the MHT prescription given to them by their doctors is not covered by their insurance plans. To minimize inconvenience, people can call their insurance companies and request a list of covered hormone formulations before seeing their doctors to discuss menopausal symptoms or before picking up a prescription from the pharmacy. The doctor can consult the list and choose from covered options or change the prescription if necessary. Sometimes even with insurance coverage, the cost may still be too high to afford. For these situations, there are coupon card programs through drug manufacturers and companies such as GoodRx that may bring down the out-of-pocket cost. If medication price is preventing patients from using MHT, their healthcare providers can try to help find one of these solutions. Unfortunately, cost can be a barrier to access to care for many, and it's a source of frustration for both patients and healthcare providers.

Risks

Historically, MHT was prescribed routinely to perimenopausal and menopausal women for prevention of osteoporosis, heart disease, vasomotor symptoms, and GSM. Then, in 2002, a landmark study called the Women's Health Initiative (WHI) showed that systemic MHT was associated with higher risks of coronary artery disease, blood clots, stroke, and breast cancer, though the breast cancer risk was higher only with combined estrogen and progestin formulations, not estrogen alone.

After the WHI results were published, rates of MHT prescriptions plummeted, and healthcare providers became wary of giving hormones. When the data was scrutinized more closely, researchers noted that the study population in the WHI was mostly older postmenopausal women with an average age of sixty-three. Subsequent studies have since shown that the cardiovascular and cancer risks of MHT in younger women are significantly lower than those reported in the initial WHI findings, which makes sense, as the rates of these diseases naturally increase as people age. Vasomotor symptoms tend to be the worst in the few years around the menopause transition, primarily affecting people in their forties and fifties.

Most of those who need MHT will be able to use it. There are no strict cutoffs for duration of use or age as long as symptoms are being controlled and the person does not develop new health conditions such as cancer or blood clots. In order to minimize the health risks as someone ages, doctors may discuss trying to wean off hormones if symptoms are no longer present. MHT is no longer given to prevent health problems such as osteoporosis and heart disease—it is prescribed only for treatment of symptoms that are affecting quality of life.

Vaginal Estrogen

Estrogen can be given vaginally in the form of a cream, small pill, or plastic ring, and the choice of method may depend on insurance coverage and individual preference.

Vaginal estrogen poses minimal risks of blood clots and uterine and breast cancer compared with systemic hormone methods. Even some breast cancer patients may safely use vaginal estrogen. Many breast cancer patients have significant GSM symptoms because some breast cancer treatments work by dropping estrogen levels, and chemotherapy can also cause early menopause. In the past, all hormones were avoided in breast cancer patients to prevent stimulating cancer recurrence. In recent years, studies have shown that vaginal estrogen doesn't increase the risk of cancer recurrence except in certain circumstances; therefore, oncologists have started allowing some people with a history of breast cancer to use vaginal estrogen if they have severe GSM symptoms.

Progesterone

Progesterone is typically not prescribed by itself for the treatment of menopausal symptoms because estrogen is more effective. However, for patients with risk factors for blood clots or other contraindications to estrogen, progesterone pills or the Depo-Provera birth control injection have also been shown to have some benefit in treating vasomotor symptoms.

Testosterone

Testosterone is converted into estrogen by fat cells in the body, so it could be used to treat menopausal symptoms. However, there are currently no testosterone methods that have been approved by the FDA for the treatment of menopause. It's sometimes used off-label to treat low libido in postmenopausal women.

Bioidentical and Compounded Hormones

The term *bioidentical* refers to hormones structurally similar to those produced by the ovaries. There are FDA-approved bioidentical hormones, such as 17-beta-estradiol (Estrace) and micronized progesterone (Prometrium). However, the term *bioidentical* in women's health marketing usually refers to hormone formulations that are specially compounded by a pharmacy, sometimes based on lab testing, rather than those produced by a pharmaceutical company. They are often promoted as supposedly being more natural than traditional MHT preparations.

The reality is that all commercial MHT estrogen is actually derived from natural sources, either plants or the urine of pregnant mares (Premarin). Compounded estrogen is derived from essentially the same plant-based precursors as those in commercial formulations. There is no evidence that compounded hormones are more effective or safer than commercial MHT. In fact, the American College of Obstetricians and Gynecologists and the North American Menopause Society both recommend against using compounded hormones, because unlike FDA-approved formulations, there is no standardization or regulation of compounded hormone methods and therefore no data about safety or effectiveness.

Some bioidentical hormones are given as pellets that are embedded under the skin. These medications are not FDA approved and are not covered by insurance. Pellets cannot be removed, which is problematic if someone experiences side effects. Some of these pellets contain testosterone, which can cause masculinizing symptoms that may feel bothersome to some cis women. There's also a risk of uterine polyps, precancer, or cancer if the pellets do not contain sufficient progesterone to protect the uterus from estrogenic effects.

Many providers who prescribe compounded hormones obtain repeated hormone-level tests, often through saliva testing, and usually at additional cost to the patient. NAMS and ACOG do not support these practices; hormone testing is not necessary to guide treatment, since hormone levels fluctuate daily. The most important part of treatment is how patients feel and how well their symptoms are controlled, not their lab results.

NONHORMONAL MEDICATIONS

Estrogen-containing medications are the most effective treatments for menopausal symptoms. However, many people cannot take hormones because they have medical risks such as breast cancer, and others simply prefer not to take hormones. Fortunately, there are several nonhormonal options for the treatment of vasomotor symptoms.

Antidepressants

The most effective alternatives to estrogen are antidepressant medications such as selective serotonin reuptake inhibitors (SSRIs) and serotonin-norepinephrine reuptake inhibitors (SNRIs). Of these, only a low-dose version of the SSRI paroxetine (Brisdelle) has been approved by the FDA for the treatment of hot flashes, but other SSRIs, such as citalopram and escitalopram, and SNRIs, such as venlafaxine, have also been shown to be effective.

Anti-Seizure Medications

Gabapentin (Neurontin) and pregabalin (Lyrica) are anti-epileptic medications that are also used to treat nerve pain, and these medications have some efficacy in preventing vasomotor symptoms. Because they can cause sedation, gabapentin and pregabalin are usually taken in the evening for those who are having more severe symptoms at night and may be having difficulty sleeping.

Neurokinin 3 (NK3) Receptor Antagonist

In 2023, the FDA approved a medication called fezolinetant (Veozah) for the treatment of moderate to severe menopausal vasomotor symptoms. This is the first of a new class of drugs that work by blocking neurokinin, a neurotransmitter that triggers hot flashes and sweating. When neurokinin receptors in the part of the brain that control temperature sensation are blocked, vasomotor symptoms improve.

Taken daily, fezolinetant was shown to significantly decrease the frequency and intensity of hot flashes. It may affect the liver, so liver enzymes must be monitored while patients are taking the medicine, and it cannot be used by people with liver cirrhosis or kidney failure. It can also cause abdominal or back pain, diarrhea, or difficulty sleeping. Since it's a new medication, insurance coverage and cost may limit access.

HOLISTIC OPTIONS

Complementary and alternative therapies are commonly used for menopausal symptoms when people are searching for an alternative to medications or simply want to use a more natural approach. These can take the form of supplements, acupuncture, meditation and mindfulness, and exercise. The literature has not shown that any of these are significantly more effective than placebos for the treatment of menopause symptoms, but they may help with reclaiming a sense of overall health and well-being.

In general, if people feel better when engaging in holistic health practices, they don't need research studies to justify continuing to enjoy them. Keeping active and minimizing stress can naturally improve mood, sleep, and overall health for everyone, not just those in perimenopause or menopause.

Nutritional Supplements

There are many dietary supplements with vitamins and herbal compounds that are marketed toward menopausal women, but like compounded hormones, supplements are not standardized, rigorously studied, or regulated, and there is little to no evidence to support their safety or effectiveness.

Phytoestrogens are compounds in plants that act similarly to estrogen. They are present in dietary sources such as soy products, flaxseed, legumes, and some fruits and vegetables. Soy phytoestrogens may also be taken as nutritional supplements. There are also herbal remedies such as black cohosh that are used for menopausal vasomotor symptoms. The data on soy and black cohosh is mixed; a few small studies show some benefit in terms of symptom relief, but most studies do not show any significant improvement.

Acupuncture

One of the most commonly used alternative treatments for hot flashes is acupuncture. This is a traditional Chinese practice in which very fine needles are placed in the skin to redirect the flow of energy, or *qi*, through the body. Acupuncture can be very effective for the treatment of some medical conditions, such as musculoskeletal pain and headaches. Randomized studies have not shown significant differences between acupuncture and placebo treatments for the relief of hot flashes, but it's difficult to standardize research on acupuncture given differences in techniques. Since there are minimal risks, if patients experience relief of symptoms with acupuncture, it's worth continuing.

Exercise

According to several studies, exercise does not significantly improve hot-flash intensity or frequency except when it is associated with weight loss in overweight or obese patients. Exercise is still a very important part of maintaining health in menopause because it helps with sleep and prevents cardiovascular disease and bone thinning.

Mental Health

Cognitive behavioral therapy may improve sleep disturbance and decrease the extent to which hot flashes are bothersome. In general, therapy can be beneficial in managing mood swings, depression, anxiety, and sexual dysfunction that some people experience during perimenopause and menopause. Ensuring mental and emotional well-being are as important as treating the physical symptoms of menopause, and a mental health professional can be an important part of the menopause care team.

TAKE-HOME POINTS

- Patients who go through twelve consecutive months with no spontaneous periods have entered menopause. Menopause is not defined by hormone levels or symptoms.
- People can be in the menopausal transition—with hot flashes, sweats, mood swings, and genitourinary symptoms—for years before their periods actually stop.
- Estrogen-containing hormone therapy is the most effective treatment for menopausal symptoms.
- The estrogen in commercially available menopausal hormone treatments is derived from natural sources, such as plants and the urine of pregnant horses. Compounded

cont'd

hormones are not any more natural or effective than those available from a traditional pharmacy.

- Hormone levels don't need to be checked in patients receiving menopausal hormone therapy. Treatment and adjustment of doses are based on how they feel, not on what their lab results show.

Infertility

Infertility is incredibly common. The WHO estimates that 48 million couples and up to 186 million people globally live with infertility. Despite these staggering numbers, people struggling to get pregnant often feel alone, because the process of trying to conceive is such a private and personal experience. In many cultures, it is considered taboo to discuss sex or conception, and people can feel uncomfortable talking about fertility problems even with close family members or friends. Having difficulty becoming or staying pregnant can involve a heartbreaking combination of medical challenges and emotional, financial, and interpersonal stressors. It may feel confusing and frustrating, and it's compounded by the fact that in up to a third of cases, testing doesn't reveal a clear answer as to the root cause. This is called *unexplained infertility*. People dealing with reproductive challenges may feel anger, grief, or self-doubt. If society normalizes discussing these issues, people facing infertility will be able to better understand their options and feel empowered to talk with their doctors, and they'll realize that they're far from alone in their struggles.

BASICS OF INFERTILITY

People who are unable to become pregnant after one year of trying regularly are said to be infertile. Couples don't need to wait a full twelve months before seeking testing; issues such as missing or irregular periods warrant earlier evaluation. Fertility testing should be considered after six months of trying regularly if the partner with a uterus is thirty-five or older because there is a higher likelihood of difficulty conceiving as someone ages.

People may have trouble getting pregnant even if they have had children before. This is called *secondary infertility* and it can be due to age, changes in health, or a partner with fertility issues.

Same-sex couples may seek out assisted reproductive treatments such as insemination and in vitro fertilization to build their families, and they can experience infertility if they have difficulty conceiving using these methods.

CAUSES OF INFERTILITY

In order for conception and pregnancy to occur, a sperm must fertilize an egg, the sperm and egg must be genetically normal, and the resulting fertilized egg must divide into a multicelled embryo, travel through the fallopian tube, and reach the uterus. The embryo implants in the endometrium of the uterine cavity and develops a placenta that will support the pregnancy in terms of hormone production and nutrient exchange.

Problems at any step of the conception or implantation process can lead to infertility. Factors related to the female organs include issues with egg quality or number, problems with ovulation, fallopian tube blockage, and abnormalities of the uterine cavity or cervix. Male factors include problems with erections, ejaculation, sperm production, and sperm transport. In almost all circumstances, the causes of infertility are biological conditions outside of people's control, not something that they did wrong.

OVARIAN FACTORS

Ovarian factors include issues with the number or quality of eggs, or with ovulation. As people age, the number of eggs and egg quality diminishes. Pregnancy rates drop with age, and miscarriage rates increase, making it more difficult to conceive and stay pregnant. The likelihood of pregnancy per cycle starts to decline slowly in patients in their early thirties, and the rate of decline accelerates rapidly when they are in their late thirties. At this point, only about 10 percent of a person's original egg supply remains.

Sometimes the pool of available eggs, the *ovarian reserve*, is lower than expected; this is called *diminished ovarian reserve*. Sometimes the ovaries stop functioning normally, leading to early menopause. This is also known as *primary ovarian insufficiency* or *premature ovarian failure*. Someone with this condition will stop having periods before age forty and may no longer ovulate. Diminished ovarian reserve and premature ovarian failure can happen without any clear reason, but there are some factors that damage the ovaries or eggs and affect ovarian function. These include cancer treatments such as chemotherapy and radiation, smoking, autoimmune diseases, and genetic conditions such as Turner's syndrome where a woman is born with only one copy of the X chromosome.

Problems with ovulation and the release of eggs can be due to a diminishing egg pool or hormonal problems. One of the most common causes of infrequent or missing ovulation is PCOS. Endocrine conditions such as thyroid, pituitary, and adrenal diseases, chronic liver or kidney disease, autoimmune conditions, and certain medications may also affect ovulation. Physical and mental stresses can alter the signals from the hypothalamus to the pituitary that are necessary for follicle development and ovulation. This change in hypothalamic function is why people who exercise intensely, lose a great deal of weight, or experience a significant illness or physical or emotional stress may temporarily lose their periods and stop ovulating.

TUBAL FACTORS

Blockage of the fallopian tubes prevents an embryo from reaching the uterine cavity. Tubal factors include any condition that scars or obstructs the tubes; common causes are prior pelvic infections with gonorrhea or chlamydia; endometriosis; abdominal surgeries; and inflammatory bowel disease. Tubal scarring is also a significant risk factor for ectopic pregnancies, since an embryo that is unable to enter the uterus may implant and begin to grow within the tube. Most people with blocked tubes will not have any symptoms, and it is usually diagnosed only when they undergo infertility testing.

When the end of the tube closest to the ovary is blocked, the tube can fill with fluid and become large and swollen, forming a hydrosalpinx. The fluid inside a hydrosalpinx is inflammatory and can prevent the implantation of an embryo or increase the risk of miscarriage by flowing backward and creating an inhospitable environment in the uterine cavity. Surgical removal of a damaged tube that has turned into a hydrosalpinx is one of the only situations where removing a tube actually improves someone's fertility. A single remaining tube can draw in an egg from the opposite ovary, and pregnancy rates in IVF are better after removal of a hydrosalpinx.

UTERINE FACTORS

Structures that affect the size and shape of the uterine cavity can prevent implantation of an embryo or increase risk of miscarriage. These include fibroids that grow within the cavity or distort it, endometrial polyps, and scar tissue in the cavity from prior surgeries or infections.

Scarring of the cervix from prior infections or surgical procedures can also cause infertility by blocking the passage of sperm into the uterus. Especially thick mucus in the cervix can also prevent passage of sperm.

MALE FACTORS

There is a wide range of estimates for the number of cases in which infertility is due to a male factor. A WHO study reported that in developed countries, 8 percent of cases were due to male factors alone, and 35 percent were due to a combination of male and female factors. Other studies report that about a third of cases are due to male factors alone, and half are due to both male and female factors. This is important to recognize, because in some cultures, problems with conception are attributed to the female alone, and women face stigma related to infertility that male partners don't.

Male infertility can be due to problems with sperm production, ejaculation, or erections, and these in turn can result from aging, obesity, or hormonal, genetic, infectious, and environmental causes. Elevated temperature in the testicles can also affect sperm production and quality. This temperature effect can be seen in a condition called varicoceles, which are dilated veins in the testicle. If varicoceles are large, the blood in the veins raises the temperature and causes problems with the number and shape of sperm that are produced. Nicotine, cannabis, alcohol, and drugs, including anabolic steroids and testosterone used in bodybuilding, can also affect sperm production.

As this book focuses primarily on gynecologic health, this is just a small sampling of possible causes of male-factor infertility. A reproductive urologist can do a full evaluation that addresses the entire range of potential issues.

UNEXPLAINED INFERTILITY

Almost a third of infertility cases have no apparent explanation, with all tests coming back normal. Receiving a diagnosis of unexplained infertility can feel confusing; it may be a relief to find that everything is normal, but it can be frustrating to hear that there is no clear problem that can be fixed.

FERTILITY TESTING

It may take several months of trying to conceive before someone becomes pregnant. Even under the best of circumstances, the likelihood of getting pregnant is 25 percent or less during each cycle. This is why fertility testing is not usually done until someone has been trying to conceive with regular intercourse for twelve consecutive months, or six months if the partner with the uterus is thirty-five or older. Because egg number and quality decline rapidly beginning in one's late thirties, getting timely testing and a referral to a board-certified specialist as soon as possible offers patients the best chances of conceiving.

Fertility testing involves evaluation for ovarian, tubal, uterine, and male factors. These tests assess ovulation and ovarian reserve, whether the tubes are open and the uterine cavity is normal, and whether there are enough sperm of normal shape and function.

TESTS OF THE OVARIES

To test the partner with female reproductive organs, a doctor takes a medical and menstrual history and orders lab tests and imaging studies. The medical history can provide important information about fertility. For instance, patients who are having regular periods approximately every four weeks are most likely ovulating, and patients who skip multiple periods are most likely not ovulating during those months.

Blood tests are obtained to check hormone levels and ovarian function. Because female hormones can fluctuate throughout the menstrual cycle, fertility labs are usually obtained around day three of the cycle if possible (with day one being the first day of regular flow) in order to standardize result interpretation. Levels of estrogen, follicle-stimulating hormone, and anti-Müllerian hormone (AMH) are used to assess how the ovaries are functioning. AMH decreases with age, and a very low level may predict a poor response to in vitro fertilization. Additional tests are sometimes used to evaluate the ovarian reserve, including an antral follicle count, which is an ultrasound assessment of the number of eggs.

None of these tests can evaluate egg quality. Abnormalities in sperm can be seen under the microscope, but there is no equivalent test to assess the quality and structure of eggs.

TESTS OF THE UTERUS AND TUBES

The shape and contour of the uterine cavity and fallopian tubes can be checked with an X-ray called a hysterosalpingogram, or HSG. This test is usually done by a fertility doctor or a radiologist. A dye is injected through the cervix and then an X-ray is taken that shows whether the cavity of the uterus is a normal shape and whether the tubes are open. An HSG identifies abnormalities of the cavity, such as scarring and fibroids, and it can also show blocked or dilated fallopian tubes. An REI doctor can also evaluate the uterine cavity and tubes by performing a special ultrasound in which saline and air are injected into the uterus.

If an abnormality such as polyps, fibroids, or scar tissue is found in the uterus, the patient is treated with *hysteroscopy*, a minor surgical procedure where a thin camera is inserted through the vagina and into the uterus. Small instruments, such as scissors, graspers, electrical loops, or tiny spinning blades, may be used through a hysteroscope to remove the abnormalities.

Some fertility specialists suggest testing the endometrial tissue inside the uterus to rule out microscopic problems such as abnormal cells or mild infections. This testing is done with an *endometrial biopsy*, where a thin straw is inserted through the cervix and into the uterine cavity to pick up loose endometrial tissue.

When there is suspicion for endometriosis or pelvic scar tissue that could be affecting the tubes, laparoscopic surgery may be suggested to remove endometriosis or adhesions.

TESTS OF THE SPERM

Male fertility testing is done primarily through a semen analysis. A semen sample is obtained through masturbation, and the number, shape, and movement of the sperm are evaluated under the microscope. If there are no sperm in the semen or if the patient has a problem with ejaculation, sperm may be removed from the testes with a minor surgical procedure done under anesthesia. This is called testicular sperm extraction (TESE) and it can be used for both testing and to collect sperm for fertility treatments such as IVF.

FERTILITY TREATMENTS

Once testing has been completed, doctors use the results to help patients evaluate their fertility treatment options. These can include medications to stimulate ovulation; *insemination*, which is a procedure to place sperm directly into the uterus; and in vitro fertilization. Each strategy has different risks and likelihoods of success. The fertility doctor will discuss these differences and help patients understand which options give them the best chances of getting pregnant and having a baby.

OVULATION INDUCTION

Stimulating the ovaries to induce ovulation may increase pregnancy rates. This can be done with oral medications, such as clomiphene or letrozole, especially for patients with PCOS. If these aren't effective, injectable hormones such as FSH and LH may be recommended. These medications are combined with either timed natural intercourse or insemination (intrauterine insemination, or IUI). A medication is given to trigger egg release, then the couple may have sex or the fertility doctor will perform an IUI as described on the following page. Ovulation induction is usually more affordable and less invasive than IVF, so many couples will choose this as an initial treatment option.

Ovulation induction medications can cause the release of more than one egg, so they can lead to multiple-gestation pregnancies—such as twins, triplets, and quadruplets—which are more high risk than pregnancies with a single baby. For this reason, follicle development is usually monitored carefully with ultrasounds during ovulation induction. If several follicles seem to be maturing and may release at the same time, the treatment cycle may be canceled. Insemination would not be performed, and couples would be counseled to avoid intercourse in order to prevent multiple eggs from being fertilized.

There's also risk of *ovarian hyperstimulation syndrome* (OHSS), a serious condition that can cause enlarged ovaries and leakage of fluid into the abdomen from the ovaries. Mild OHSS can cause abdominal bloating, weight gain, pain, and nausea, but severe OHSS can cause difficulty breathing, dangerous blood clots in the veins, electrolyte abnormalities, and kidney failure, and it requires emergent medical treatment. OHSS is seen more commonly with injectable fertility hormones but can also occur with oral medications.

INTRAUTERINE INSEMINATION (IUI)

Insemination may be helpful if a couple is unable to have intercourse because of a problem such as vaginismus or erectile dysfunction, if a same-sex female couple is trying to conceive using donor sperm, or if there is a cervical or male factor where placing a concentrated number of sperm directly into the uterus increases the chances of pregnancy. IUI can also improve pregnancy rates when given with ovulation induction medications.

For IUI, a semen sample from a male partner or a sperm donor is washed and prepared, and the sperm are introduced into the uterus with a small catheter inserted through the cervix. IUI is usually performed in an office or procedure room using a speculum; it's similar to what is done during a Pap smear. It isn't usually painful and doesn't typically require pain medication, though antianxiety medication or sedation may be offered if patients have difficulty with vaginal procedures.

IN VITRO FERTILIZATION (IVF)

In vitro fertilization is a procedure in which eggs are retrieved from the ovaries, combined with sperm in a lab to create embryos, and the embryos are transferred into the uterus. The term *in vitro* means "in glass" in Latin and comes from the idea of creating embryos in glass test tubes or petri dishes. IVF is the most effective form of assisted reproductive technology (ART) because it results in the highest pregnancy rates. It can be done with a couple's own egg and sperm or a donor egg or sperm. IVF can also be performed with a gestational carrier, which is a person who will carry the pregnancy on behalf of another person or couple.

Less invasive options such as IUI are usually performed first, but in some scenarios, couples may proceed directly to IVF. These include situations where the tubes are completely blocked or the sperm is extremely abnormal. Some couples who haven't experienced infertility may choose to undergo IVF in order to screen embryos for genetic conditions such as sickle cell disease if one or both partners are carriers for affected genes and their children are at risk of inheriting the disease.

An IVF cycle generally involves stimulating the ovaries with medications to produce multiple follicles. Hormone testing and ultrasounds are used to monitor follicle development. When the follicles appear to be ready, the eggs are retrieved with a minor procedure that is performed under sedation: an ultrasound is used to guide insertion of a needle through the vagina to remove eggs from the follicles.

The eggs are then fertilized with sperm in a lab. Male partners will provide a semen sample on the day of the egg retrieval, or previously frozen or donor sperm can be used. Fertilization can be done by inserting a single sperm into each egg with an extremely fine needle, a procedure called *intracytoplasmic sperm injection* (ICSI).

The embryos are then grown in a lab for several days and carefully monitored by embryologists as they develop. Embryologists assign each embryo a grade based on appearance and number of cells with the goal of identifying the highest-quality embryos. The decision of which embryos and how many to transfer during a cycle is very complex and based on many factors, among them the patient or egg donor's age, the quality of the embryos, and prior reproductive history.

In most cases, only a single embryo is transferred during each IVF cycle to minimize the potential of having multiple-gestation pregnancies. People undergoing IVF may wonder why more embryos aren't transferred to ensure the highest possible chances of pregnancy. This is because twin and higher multiple pregnancies have significantly more medical risks for both the parent and fetuses, including pregnancy loss and extremely premature birth. Even if only a single embryo is transferred, it can split and become twins, and two embryos can become quadruplets. For this reason, every country has specific guidelines on how many embryos should be transferred, with a single embryo recommended for most cycles.

During IVF cycles, embryos can be tested for genetic abnormalities. *Preimplantation genetic testing* (PGT) involves growing embryos in the lab for five to six days, removing a few cells from each, then freezing the embryos while genetic testing is performed. PGT can screen for serious medical conditions such as Huntington's disease, sickle cell anemia, cystic fibrosis, and cancer-risk mutations such as *BRCA*. PGT may also be used in cases of recurrent miscarriages or failed IVF cycles because genetic abnormalities can lead to miscarriage. Selecting genetically normal embryos to transfer increases the chances of successful pregnancy.

IVF can be a costly and emotionally as well as physically challenging process. There may be side effects from the hormone medications, and there is a small chance of serious complications such as OHSS and ectopic pregnancy. Finances or access to infertility specialists may limit IVF services in many parts of the world. Couples may face ethical decisions about what to do with unused embryos, how many embryos to transfer per cycle, and how many cycles they are able and willing to pursue in order to conceive. Despite these challenges, IVF is a miraculous technology that can be the best hope for some patients to achieve their goal of pregnancy. There have been eight million babies born through IVF, and in places such as Scandinavia and Israel, where IVF is covered through the healthcare system, up to 10 percent of pregnancies are a result of IVF.

HOLISTIC OPTIONS

Some studies suggest that certain vitamins, supplements, and complementary treatments such as acupuncture may help fertility. The data tends to be mixed, and the size and quality of the studies may be limited.

Vitamin D

Follicle development in the ovaries can be affected by vitamin D. Observational studies suggested that IVF outcomes are improved if vitamin D levels are normal, and vitamin D deficiency may be associated with other reproductive conditions, such as endometriosis, fibroids, and PCOS. A large randomized study of vitamin D supplementation in women who were vitamin D deficient did not show any difference in pregnancy rates with IVF. Because there are other potential health benefits to restoring vitamin D levels, supplementation may still be suggested for those who are deficient.

Antioxidants

Coenzyme Q10 (CoQ10) is an antioxidant that protects cells from damage. Antioxidants have been investigated for possible benefit in terms of egg and sperm quality. CoQ10 occurs naturally in the body and is also found in foods such as fish and organ meats. It may also be taken as a dietary supplement. Studies have shown that CoQ10 supplementation during fertility treatment cycles may improve some features of ovarian response but doesn't seem to improve birth rates.

DHEA

Dehydroepiandrosterone (DHEA) is a testosterone hormone produced by the adrenal glands that plays a role in follicle development. Some studies show potential benefits for women with diminished ovarian reserve or poor ovarian response undergoing IVF cycles. People with PCOS or other conditions where testosterone levels are high should not take DHEA.

Acupuncture

Acupuncture is thought to potentially improve hormone balance and blood flow to the uterus, and it may help with management of anxiety and stress during infertility treatment. There is some evidence that acupuncture slightly improves pregnancy rates when used alongside fertility treatment such as IVF.

Mental Health

Mental health care and personal wellness are a vital part of fertility and infertility care. Having trouble getting or staying pregnant can be incredibly difficult emotionally, and people going through infertility treatments face severe financial, physical, and relationship stressors. Working with a therapist or psychiatrist can help with management of stress, depression, anxiety, and partner communication. Support from friends, family, and partners is also incredibly important. If you're going through difficulty with fertility, please treat yourself with grace and patience and lean on your medical team and loved ones for help. You are not alone.

TAKE-HOME POINTS

- Up to 186 million people globally are living with infertility.
- Infertility is defined as not being able to become pregnant despite trying regularly for one year. Fertility testing may be recommended sooner if a woman is over thirty-five years old or having irregular periods.
- About a third of cases of infertility are due to a medical issue involving the male partner.

cont'd

- In most IVF cycles, only a single embryo is transferred in order to minimize the chance of a multiple pregnancy, which has higher medical risks than pregnancies with a single baby.

- IVF offers the highest pregnancy rates of any fertility treatment, and more than eight million babies have been born through IVF worldwide.

Miscarriage

Similar to infertility, miscarriage is extremely common. Up to 25 percent of recognized pregnancies end in a miscarriage. The actual rate of miscarriage is likely far higher, because many losses occur before people even know that they are pregnant. It is estimated that up to 70 percent of fertilized eggs will result in a miscarriage. Most people don't realize that pregnancy losses are so common, in part because in many cultures, miscarriages are kept private and considered taboo to discuss. Many couples wait until the second trimester to announce that they're expecting, because they would feel uncomfortable telling friends, coworkers, and even relatives if they lost the pregnancy. Unfortunately, this culture of secrecy can create the false impression that miscarriages are rare. People going through miscarriages can feel alone or wonder if there is something wrong with them. Many people will scrutinize everything that they ate, drank, and did, worrying that they caused the loss. Very rarely is it something that the pregnant person did.

This chapter will cover what happens in a miscarriage, management, risk factors, and testing for women who have experienced recurrent miscarriages. These topics can be very difficult to read about for people who have experienced pregnancy losses. I've had two miscarriages myself and deeply understand how emotionally and physically painful they can be, no matter how early in pregnancy they occur. However, I hope that this information can help readers see past the myths and misinformation that surround the topic of miscarriage and support those who are trying to conceive.

BASICS OF MISCARRIAGE

The word *miscarriage* refers to a spontaneous loss before the twentieth week of pregnancy. A loss after twenty weeks is called a *stillbirth*. The risk of miscarriage decreases as a pregnancy progresses. Most miscarriages occur within the first twelve weeks of pregnancy, and once a pregnancy reaches the second trimester, miscarriage risk drops to 1 to 5 percent.

People may discover that they are having a miscarriage because they're experiencing symptoms such as vaginal bleeding, cramping pain, or passage of tissue, but sometimes there are no symptoms at all, and the miscarriage is discovered during a routine ultrasound.

The medical term for miscarriage is *spontaneous abortion*. It can be confusing or painful for people to see this term in a medical chart, because the general public usually uses the word *abortion* to refer to an elective termination of pregnancy. In medical terminology, *abortion* simply means the ending of a pregnancy.

There are different types of miscarriage. These are distinguished by how far along the pregnancy was before it stopped growing and what symptoms, if any, the person is experiencing. Conditions such as ectopic pregnancies, which must be terminated for the safety of the mother, also represent a type of pregnancy loss.

BIOCHEMICAL PREGNANCY

A *biochemical pregnancy* is a very early miscarriage in which the pregnancy stopped developing before anything was visible on an ultrasound. A pregnancy test may be positive only briefly. Sometimes early biochemical pregnancy losses are mistaken for regular or slightly delayed periods.

MISSED MISCARRIAGE

A *missed miscarriage* is when the pregnancy stops growing without any symptoms of bleeding or pain. Missed miscarriages are often found when a patient goes for a routine ultrasound or prenatal visit. An embryo may be seen on ultrasound, but no heartbeat is visible. An ultrasound might also show a pregnancy sac but with no embryo inside; this scenario is called a *blighted ovum*, and it occurs when the pregnancy stops growing before an embryo develops.

THREATENED MISCARRIAGE

A *threatened miscarriage* is when the patient has symptoms such as bleeding or cramping but an ultrasound shows a normally developing pregnancy. In these situations, it is unclear whether a miscarriage will occur, but it is possible that it may. Fortunately, many pregnancies in these scenarios will continue to develop normally.

SEPTIC MISCARRIAGE

Septic miscarriages occur if the pregnancy tissue and uterus become infected. The pregnant person may feel pain and show signs of infection such as fever and abnormal vaginal discharge. This type of miscarriage can be very dangerous, and the pregnancy must be removed and antibiotics given as soon as possible. In other types of miscarriage, the pregnant person can take several days or even weeks to consider options or wait for the pregnancy tissue to pass on its own, but this is one of the few situations where a miscarriage must be treated immediately, because if it isn't, the patient can become extremely ill.

RECURRENT MISCARRIAGE

Recurrent miscarriage is when someone experiences two or more miscarriages. In most cases, the loss of one or two early pregnancies is the result of random chance and not a sign of a medical problem.

ECTOPIC PREGNANCY

Ectopic pregnancies are pregnancies that implant outside of the uterine cavity. They're not considered miscarriages, but they are still a type of loss because the pregnancy cannot be allowed to continue. The most common place for ectopic pregnancies is the fallopian tubes, but they can also occur in the cervix, the muscle of the uterus, a cesarean section scar, the ovary, and the abdominal cavity.

These pregnancies cannot grow into normal full-term fetuses. They're life-threatening because they can burst and cause internal hemorrhaging, so they must be treated urgently to prevent rupture. Options for treatment include methotrexate—a type of chemotherapy medication that is given as a shot in the muscle—and surgery, which may be required to remove the pregnancy.

People who have an ectopic often don't realize there's anything wrong until they develop pain or abnormal bleeding. In addition to suddenly facing a potentially life-threatening situation, they may also be grieving the end of what had seemed to be a normal pregnancy.

MOLAR PREGNANCY

Molar pregnancies are similar to ectopics in that they unfortunately can't develop into full-term babies. These are rare conditions, occurring in less than 1 percent of pregnancies. They form when there is an abnormality of fertilization—either a sperm fertilizing an empty egg or two sperm fertilizing one egg. A large amount of placental tissue develops, and the uterus can feel like it is growing very quickly. Pregnancy hormone levels can be very high, and the pregnant person might experience severe nausea and vomiting, pelvic pain, and abnormal bleeding. Molar pregnancies can also lead to serious medical conditions such as high blood pressure and thyroid abnormalities. One form of molar pregnancy can even become cancerous, so people with molar pregnancies must not conceive again for up to a year so that pregnancy hormone levels can be carefully monitored.

Because of these health risks, molar pregnancies must be treated with a dilation and curettage (D and C), a procedure in which pregnancy tissue is surgically removed.

DIAGNOSIS

A miscarriage may be discovered when a patient experiences vaginal bleeding or pain and goes to a doctor's office or the emergency department for evaluation. In other cases, there may be no symptoms at all, and people may find out that they've had a miscarriage at a routine prenatal visit or ultrasound appointment.

Miscarriages are usually confirmed with a combination of pelvic ultrasound imaging, blood work to measure pregnancy hormone levels, and a pelvic exam to check for bleeding and passage of tissue. Early in pregnancy, ultrasounds are performed vaginally because it is difficult to look inside the uterus through the abdominal wall. As pregnancies grow and the uterus becomes larger, it is possible to see the fetus through the abdomen. Depending on how far along someone is, the doctor may try to do the ultrasound through the abdomen first and then vaginally if they cannot see well enough.

Sometimes it isn't clear if a miscarriage is occurring or if someone is simply so early in pregnancy that an embryo has not yet developed. In these cases, ultrasounds and pregnancy hormone levels will be repeated in a few days or weeks to check for growth. If the levels have dropped or plateaued, the ultrasound shows no growth of the embryo or development of a heartbeat, or if the patient passes the pregnancy tissue, these unfortunately confirm a miscarriage.

TREATMENT

Patients who are experiencing a miscarriage will be presented with several options for management. They can choose to watch and wait to see if the miscarriage will pass naturally on its own, use medications to help pass pregnancy tissue, or undergo a D and C procedure to re-move the pregnancy.

All options for management of miscarriage can be associated with incomplete removal of pregnancy tissue, which may require additional doses of medication or D and C treatments. Therefore, follow-up eval-uations with pregnancy hormone tests, ultrasounds, or both may be suggested. Healthcare providers will usually schedule appointments during and after the miscarriage to ensure that the patient is healing well both emotionally and physically. There isn't a standardized regimen for follow-up after a miscarriage; doctors will make recommendations based on how far along the patients were and what symptoms they are having. Different practices and hospital systems may have their own protocols, but they should all ensure that the miscarriage has com-pletely resolved and that the patient is not having any signs of infection or heavy bleeding.

EXPECTANT MANAGEMENT

People who want to minimize medical or surgical intervention may choose to wait to see if the pregnancy tissue will pass on its own. This is called *expectant management*, or watchful waiting. Up to 80 percent of first-trimester miscarriages will resolve naturally, though it may take several weeks. The only major risk of waiting is the possibility of uter-ine infection developing. Treatment is recommended if the pregnancy has not yet passed after four weeks or if any signs of infection develop.

MEDICATIONS

Medications can be used to treat a miscarriage if a patient wants to avoid surgery but doesn't want to wait for the miscarriage to start naturally. The medicines prescribed are misoprostol and mifepristone, the same drugs used for elective abortions. *Misoprostol* softens the cervix and induces uterine contractions; *mifepristone* causes the pregnancy to detach from the uterus. A combination of mifepristone and misoprostol is more effective than misoprostol alone in treating miscarriages, but in many parts of the world, mifepristone may not be accessible due to restrictions on its use for medical abortions.

Passage of a miscarriage either with medications or with expectant management can cause heavy bleeding and painful cramping. People often require pain medication, and if bleeding is extremely heavy, they may need to go to the emergency department for urgent treatment. Second-trimester miscarriages can pose particularly high risks for bleeding and pain, and it may be emotionally difficult to pass the fetus. Therefore, people in the second trimester are often counseled to undergo medical management of miscarriage in a healthcare facility rather than at home.

SURGERIES

A *dilation and curettage* (D and C) is a minor surgical procedure used to remove pregnancy tissue; it is done for both miscarriages and elective terminations of pregnancy. In these procedures, a speculum is inserted in the vagina, the cervix is gently opened, and either a narrow suction tube or instruments are used to remove the pregnancy tissue. D and Cs for early miscarriages can be done with local anesthetic in an office, but if patients prefer to receive more significant anesthesia or if the pregnancy is further along and there is more risk of bleeding or pain, they may undergo the procedure in an operating room.

People may choose a D and C if they're anxious about experiencing the bleeding or pain that can be associated with a miscarriage. The procedure also makes it possible to collect pregnancy tissue for genetic testing. D and Cs have minor risks of infection, scarring, and injury to the cervix or uterus, though they're generally considered low-risk procedures.

If a pregnancy has progressed to the second trimester or beyond, the procedure may be called a *dilation and evacuation* (D and E), though sometimes healthcare providers use the terms D and C and D and E interchangeably. Second-trimester D and Es have higher surgical risks of bleeding and incomplete removal of placenta tissue because the pregnancies are more advanced.

RISK FACTORS

More than half of miscarriages are due to an abnormality in the embryo's chromosomes. Most of those chromosomal issues develop due to random chance as the embryo's cells divide and multiply, and they aren't usually a sign of an inherited problem from either parent that would recur in a future pregnancy.

Health factors can increase the risk for miscarriage. Some risk factors, such as smoking, are modifiable risks, meaning that a person can make lifestyle changes or undergo treatment to lower the risk of miscarriage. Other risk factors, such as age and genetic issues, cannot be modified, but miscarriage risk can decrease with the use of assisted reproductive technologies such as donor eggs and preimplantation genetic testing.

AGE

Because egg quality diminishes over time as eggs age, miscarriage rates increase with age. On average, the risk of miscarriage is 10 percent for women ages twenty-five to twenty-nine and over 50 percent for women in their mid-forties.

CHRONIC MEDICAL CONDITIONS

Endocrine conditions, such as insufficiently controlled diabetes, thyroid disease, and PCOS, and chronic medical problems, like lupus and kidney and heart disease, can increase risk of miscarriage.

Antiphospholipid syndrome (APS) is a type of clotting disorder that increases the risk of blood clot formation in the placenta and can cause pregnancy loss.

INFECTIONS

Certain viruses and bacteria can infect the placenta or fetus and cause pregnancy loss. COVID-19 infection in pregnancy can lead to miscarriage and stillbirth, possibly because of inflammation or blood clot formation in the placenta. Another group of infections that can pass through the placenta, infect the fetus, and cause miscarriage, stillbirth, or birth defects are known as the *TORCH infections*; TORCH is an acronym for toxoplasmosis, other (syphilis, varicella, parvovirus B19, listeria), rubella, cytomegalovirus, and herpes simplex virus.

SUBSTANCE USE

Smoking, alcohol consumption, and drugs such as cocaine may all increase the risk of miscarriage.

UTERINE ABNORMALITIES

Any structural abnormalities that compress or block the uterine cavity can increase the risk of pregnancy loss. These include fibroids, polyps, and *uterine septa* (a uterine septum is a fibrous wall of tissue running down the middle of the uterine cavity).

Fibroids, polyps, and septa can be removed using hysteroscopy to restore a more normal cavity and lower the risk of miscarriage.

GENETIC ABNORMALITIES

In a *balanced translocation*, a piece of chromosome breaks off and attaches to another chromosome. People who have a balanced translocation have a normal number of chromosomes, so they usually experience no health issues themselves. However, when their sperm or egg cells develop, those cells end up with the chromosomes that have either an extra piece or a missing piece. Any resulting embryos will have an abnormal number of chromosomes, and this can lead to miscarriage.

MYTHS ABOUT MISCARRIAGE RISK

It's equally important to discuss what are *not* risk factors for miscarriage. There are myths in almost every culture about activities and actions that should be avoided to prevent miscarriage. These can include exercise, sex, lifting objects, working, and stress. Most of these are completely false. Most miscarriages are due to either a chromosomal abnormality that developed spontaneously or health issues that are out of someone's control. Dealing with pregnancy loss is already extremely difficult; people should not be made to feel that they somehow caused their miscarriages because they were stressed or working too much.

Some people may have heard that low progesterone levels can cause miscarriage. In most cases, low progesterone is a sign of a pregnancy that is not viable and will most likely end in miscarriage; it's not the cause of the miscarriage. Giving supplemental progesterone has not been shown to significantly lower the risk of miscarriage except in very specific cases of people with a history of recurrent miscarriages who are experiencing bleeding in a current pregnancy.

TESTING FOR RECURRENT MISCARRIAGE

People who have experienced two or more miscarriages may wish to undergo testing to evaluate for underlying conditions that could be causing the miscarriages. More than 50 percent of patients experiencing recurrent pregnancy loss have no abnormalities found on testing, which means that the losses were unexplained. The good news is that most people will actually go on to have normal pregnancies in the future. In one study, 77 percent of people with a history of recurrent miscarriage went on to give birth, and the success rate was 71 percent even for those who had a risk factor found on testing.

An evaluation for recurrent miscarriage may include a routine health assessment, a basic physical examination, and screening for issues such as diabetes; thyroid, kidney, and heart disease; and antiphospholipid syndrome. Both partners may get a blood test of the chromosomes called a karyotype to check for balanced translocations.

The shape of the uterus will be assessed with a pelvic ultrasound. Additional tests, such as a hysteroscopy and a hysterosalpingogram, may be suggested to evaluate the uterine cavity for abnormalities such as fibroids or polyps.

RECOVERY AFTER A PREGNANCY LOSS

It can obviously be extremely upsetting and difficult to experience any sort of pregnancy loss. People may feel grief, anger, confusion, and fear in addition to the physical pain that may accompany a miscarriage. Self-care for mental and emotional well-being is as critical as physical healing. Individuals and couples experiencing a miscarriage may benefit from counseling by a mental health professional to help with grieving and processing the complex emotions they experience.

Many people ask how long they need to wait before trying to get pregnant again. Doctors often recommend pelvic rest with avoidance of sex for a few weeks to minimize the risk of infection and ensure that the miscarriage is complete. In many cases, for people who have recovered physically after a loss, there may not be a medical need to wait longer than this. However, people may choose to wait longer so they can prepare emotionally and mentally before trying to conceive again.

It's common to still feel very anxious or guarded in subsequent pregnancies, even if everything is going well. For this reason, it is important that people continue to be gentle with themselves and lean on loved ones and healthcare providers for all of the mental and emotional support they need.

TAKE-HOME POINTS

- Up to 25 percent of recognized pregnancies end in miscarriage, but the actual rate of miscarriage is likely far higher because many pregnancies end before people even know that they are pregnant. Up to 70 percent of fertilized eggs may result in a miscarriage.

- Most cases of miscarriage are due to random chance and are not a sign of other medical problems.

- It's possible to have a miscarriage and not experience any symptoms. This is called a missed miscarriage.

- Up to 80 percent of first-trimester miscarriages pass naturally without treatment, but it may take several weeks.

- The majority of people who experience multiple miscarriages will go on to have normal pregnancies and deliveries.

Gender Diversity

There's an enormous amount of misinformation about gender and sex—starting with what these terms actually mean. The simplest way to understand the difference is that *gender* has to do with identity and the social meaning of being female, male, or other, whereas *sex* refers to biology, including genes and chromosomes, reproductive organs, genitals, and hormones. *Gender* and *sex* are not interchangeable terms, and neither is limited to a simple male-versus-female binary.

In fact, millions of people worldwide are *gender diverse*, meaning that they are transgender and do not identify as the gender that they were assigned at birth or that they are nonbinary or gender fluid and do not identify solely as male or female. Data from the CDC analyzed by researchers at the University of California, Los Angeles, estimated that there are 1.6 million transgender people ages thirteen and up in the United States. These numbers likely underestimate the true transgender population, as many people may not publicly identify themselves as transgender or may be in the process of understanding their gender identity.

For those who exist outside of the gender binary, issues of gender and sex may affect almost every aspect of their physical, emotional, and social lives. They can even be a matter of life and death. In a

2018 study, the American Academy of Pediatrics reported that more than half of transgender male teens had attempted suicide, and the risk was 30 percent and 42 percent in transgender female and non-binary teenagers, respectively. Bullying, rejection by family or peers, and other social factors can also contribute to these staggeringly high rates. Fortunately, healthcare that allows people to safely explore and affirm their gender identity has been shown in many research studies to significantly improve depression and anxiety and reduce the risk of self-harm. For these reasons, gender-affirming care can be truly lifesaving and allows gender-diverse people to lead full, healthy, and joyful lives.

It's necessary to discuss gender diversity in a book on gynecologic issues because gender-affirming care is an important and legitimate part of reproductive healthcare. Despite this, transgender and non-binary people face serious hurdles on their path to seeking medical treatment; they may experience discrimination or even legal threats simply for trying to live authentically as themselves. I want this chapter to serve as a resource for those who may be exploring their own gender identity and are seeking medical care to affirm that identity. I also cover these concepts for readers who want to better understand gender diversity but are struggling to distinguish truth from misinformation in the media or their communities.

GENDER EXPLAINED

Gender is a multifaceted term that includes a person's sense of identity and their relationship to the social world around them. The WHO defines *gender* as the "characteristics of women, men, girls and boys that are socially constructed. This includes norms, behaviors and roles associated with being a woman, man, girl or boy." What it means to be a man or woman, masculine or feminine, differs from culture to culture and changes over time.

If the broader concept of gender is shaped by the society around us, *gender identity* involves a person's experience of gender. One's gender identity may or may not match someone's sex assigned at birth or fit neatly into gender categories.

TERMINOLOGY

If someone's gender identity matches the sex they were assigned at birth, they are cisgender. Being transgender means that someone's gender identity does not match the sex they were assigned at birth. *Cis* and *trans* are used as adjectives; a cis man is someone who identifies as a man and was assigned male at birth. A trans man is someone who identifies as a man but was assigned female at birth. Someone who identifies with aspects of both male and female identities or with neither may consider themselves nonbinary, genderqueer, or agender. People who are nonbinary are also technically transgender, since they do not identify fully with the sex assigned at birth. Gender identity may change and vary over time in someone who is gender fluid. Language is also ever evolving, so these categories (and the terms that an individual may choose to use for themselves) may also shift and change over time.

Gender is not the same as sexuality or sexual orientation. It's an aspect of a person's sense of self, whereas sexuality refers to who someone is attracted to. People of all genders can be homosexual (attracted to those of the same gender), heterosexual (attracted to the opposite gender), bisexual (attracted to men and women), pansexual (attracted to people of all genders), or asexual (experience little to no sexual attraction to people of any gender).

TRANSGENDER HEALTH

In the past, it was estimated that 0.3 to 2 percent of the population was transgender or nonbinary; however, the most recent data from the Pew Research Center showed that 5 percent of adults under thirty identified with a gender that differed from the sex assigned at birth. This increasing percentage probably doesn't represent a change in the actual number of people who are transgender. Rather, it's likely that younger generations are more accustomed to gender diversity represented in the media and among peers and have access to the language and concepts that allow them to characterize their own identity. Older generations and those who live in more conservative environments may feel significant pressure to confirm to conventional gender roles. In many parts of the world, coming out can lead to persecution or bodily harm. All these factors make it difficult to accurately assess the number of people who are transgender, but it's likely that the available data significantly underestimates the true population worldwide.

Transgender people often face enormous social and health challenges. They can feel severe distress because of the discordance between their identity and the sexual characteristics of their physical body. This feeling is known as gender dysphoria, and it can be triggered by physical appearance or experiences such as menstruation, sex, and medical exams. Not everyone who is transgender experiences severe dysphoria, but when it occurs, it can be debilitating and is a serious risk for self-harm.

A point of hope is that gender-affirming medical care, which allows a transgender person to more closely align their physical body with their gender identity, can help relieve the depression and anxiety associated with dysphoria. The inverse of gender dysphoria is gender euphoria, which means the sense of joy, comfort, and peace that someone feels when their body and gender expression match their identity; this is the ultimate goal of care. Gender-affirming care involves a combination of psychosocial support, hormonal medications to suppress pubertal changes or alter secondary sex characteristics such as facial or body hair growth, and sometimes surgical treatments to remove the reproductive organs or alter the appearance of the face, genitals, or body.

Unfortunately, gender care is one of the most politicized types of medical treatment. Despite the fact that every major medical society has published statements supporting the medical necessity and safety of gender-affirming care for adults as well as minors, in America, more than half the states have enacted laws or proposed bills that ban gender-affirming care for minors. Such laws may impose criminal penalties on healthcare providers or parents who assist a minor in obtaining any gender-affirming treatments. Similar to laws banning abortion, laws that criminalize gender-affirming care directly contradict evidence-based standards of medical care. Studies have shown that access to gender-affirming care drastically decreases rates of depression, suicidal thoughts, and self-harm, with up to 70 percent reduction in suicidality in transgender youths. It is truly lifesaving care.

GENDER-AFFIRMING CARE FOR MINORS

Much of the opposition to gender-affirming care is grounded in misinformation about what it actually entails, particularly when it involves children and adolescents. There are myths that doctors are commonly performing irreversible genital surgeries on minors who are too young to actually know their own minds and that there is a high risk of regret and detransitioning. Both of these are false and do not reflect the reality of gender-affirming care.

Gender-affirming treatment in minors is mostly nonsurgical and involves supporting the child emotionally and physically so they can explore and solidify their gender identity. There is no one-size-fits-all approach to management; some children may simply want to know that they are safe and supported and may not need other treatments at all. Others will require treatment to stop pubertal changes, such as breast growth, that may trigger dysphoria. No medications or surgeries are ever offered to prepubertal children; care in this age group is purely supportive. Only a small percentage of teenagers will need surgery because of severe dysphoria that cannot be managed with medications alone, and most doctors will recommend deferring genital surgeries, such as phalloplasty, until after age eighteen.

The rate of detransitioning—stopping treatment and returning to the sex assigned at birth—is also extremely low: 98 percent of transgender adolescents will continue treatment into adulthood. Most gender-affirming care for minors centers on psychosocial support and reversible medical options when possible because children and teens may have different feelings about their identity or goals for medical treatment as they get older. Even if someone ultimately decides to de-transition, gender-affirming care is still important because it provides that person with freedom from dysphoria and the resources to better understand themselves and their identity.

Supporting Children and Families

Parents of a transgender child may feel overwhelmed or worry about how to best help their child through a process that is extremely med-ically and emotionally complex. The healthcare team will guide par-ents and families through each choice and help them think through options, including any potential long-term health considerations such as fertility. Consent for gender-affirming treatment of children must always be obtained from a legal guardian, so parents will be closely involved in the counseling and decision-making process. Children on pubertal suppressants and hormone therapy are monitored very closely by healthcare professionals in terms of their physical and emotional health. They are seen regularly for checkups to assess their growth, and they will receive individual and family counseling with mental health professionals. Treatment decisions are reevaluated as the child grows and matures. For instance, they may decide to start or stop hormone therapy, or doses may be adjusted over time.

The treatment team, which is usually based at a major medical cen-ter or children's hospital, typically includes pediatricians, social work-ers, and psychologists or psychiatrists with expertise in gender identity. Sometimes endocrinologists, gynecologists, urologists, and plastic surgeons are involved. Gender-diverse children and their parents need to navigate school systems as well as relationships with peers and other family members. Social workers and mental health specialists can help families communicate with teachers and school officials to cre-ate a safe and supportive environment for the child. This can include using chosen names and pronouns, ensuring privacy and not revealing the child's gender status without their permission, and providing protection against harassment and bullying. Ensuring the health and well-being of a transgender child extends far beyond the hospital and involves the support of parents, teachers, and other members of the child's community.

Medications: Pubertal Suppressants and Hormones

Gender-diverse children do not usually start to feel dysphoria until they go through puberty. This is when their bodies start to change, and they develop sexual characteristics, like breast growth and the onset of periods, that can be extremely distressing. For this reason, pubertal suppressants are one of the main types of medication used to treat transgender children. The medications—GnRH agonists—are also used to treat precocious puberty, endometriosis, and fibroids. They work by preventing the development of sexual characteristics. This allows relief from gender dysphoria so that the child can have time to explore and clarify their gender identity. If they decide to stop the medication, normal pubertal development usually resumes within a few months. GnRH agonists are not started until a child shows physical changes of puberty. Medications are not given to prepubertal children because there is no need: they do not yet have the sexual characteristics, such as breast or facial-hair growth, that can cause dysphoria.

Hormone treatments with estrogen or testosterone may be used to achieve desired physical sexual characteristics in teens. For transgender boys, this can include facial-hair growth, deepening of the voice, and suppression of periods. Because estrogen and testosterone treatment can affect long-term fertility in transgender adolescents, families will be referred to specialists to discuss options for fertility preservation before a minor starts hormones.

Surgery

Permanent surgical treatments are performed in minors only when there is very severe gender dysphoria, especially when risk of self-harm is high without surgery. Top surgery is by far the most common surgery in minors. This is removal of breast tissue with reconstruction of a more masculine-appearing chest contour. Top surgery is also the most commonly requested gender-affirming surgery in transgender men. This is because chest dysphoria related to the presence and appearance of breast tissue can be debilitating, since breast tissue is more difficult to hide than other sexual characteristics. Transgender boys and men may bind their breasts, but this can be painful or even physically harmful to the skin or chest wall and may not provide adequate relief of dysphoria. Early initiation of pubertal blockers can prevent chest dysphoria, but many transgender youth do not start gender-affirming treatment until after the breasts have developed. For these teens, top surgery can provide enormous relief of distress.

Genital surgeries and surgeries to remove internal organs, such as hysterectomies and oophorectomies, are very rarely performed on minors. Medications can suppress periods, and because the uterus and ovaries are not visible, their presence is not nearly as triggering for gender dysphoria as the breasts can be. This is the reason that hysterectomies and genital surgeries are usually delayed until the child has reached adulthood.

GENDER-AFFIRMING CARE FOR ADULTS

A wide range of hormonal and surgical gender-affirming options exist for transgender adults, and every individual will have different goals for their own care. When choosing which treatments best fit their needs, transgender people should consider what their goals are—what degree of masculinization or feminization is desired, how they would feel about undergoing surgery, and whether they are interested in future fertility. Some people may decide that they do not need any medical or surgical treatment at all, whereas others will choose hormone therapy as well as facial, top, and bottom surgery. Some transgender patients assigned female at birth may wish to maintain fertility and carry pregnancies, whereas others will request tubal sterilization or removal of the uterus or ovaries. These are extremely personal choices and there is no right or wrong answer, only what is right for each individual person.

Medications: Hormone Therapy

For transgender men, hormone treatment consists of testosterone therapy that is usually given as an injection, though it can be given as a topical gel for those unable to tolerate needles or those who are seeking a slower rate of masculinization. Testosterone will produce male secondary sexual characteristics such as facial and body hair, increased muscle mass, voice deepening, enlargement of the clitoris, and testosterone injections will stop menstrual periods. Levels of testosterone are usually monitored during treatment, and doses are adjusted to keep levels in a normal masculine range. People on testosterone therapy should be carefully monitored by experienced healthcare providers, as there may be some risks of increased cholesterol and red blood cells.

Surgery

Some transgender men may wish to have a hysterectomy to avoid future periods or risk of pregnancy or because of persistent irregular bleeding or cramping, which can trigger dysphoria. The decision about removal of the ovaries may be more complex; there is little long-term data about health in transgender men after bilateral oophorectomy. Testosterone provides hormone support and seems to protect the body from health risks, like osteoporosis, that are seen in cis women who go through surgical menopause. However, it is unclear if, over time, transgender men will have as high a risk of cardiovascular disease and osteoporosis as cis women do when the ovaries are removed at a young age. Removing the ovaries without preserving the eggs also eliminates the possibility of having biological children, so some transgender youth and men choose to undergo egg retrieval and freezing before having the ovaries removed, allowing a cis female partner or gestational carrier to carry future pregnancies.

Genital surgery options for transgender men include vaginectomy (removal of all or part of the vagina), scrotoplasty (creation of a scrotum, with or without testicular implants), metoidioplasty (increasing the length of the clitoris to create a small phallus), or phalloplasty (creation of a penis using skin flaps from the arm, leg, or side). Bottom surgery may also involve lengthening the urethra so someone can urinate while standing and insertion of an erectile device so that the patient can achieve erections. Each individual who chooses to have bottom surgery will have different goals: to achieve a more masculine appearance or to be able to urinate or have sex as a male. Sometimes people do not want to fit a traditional male-versus-female binary; for instance, they may undergo a phalloplasty but also keep the vagina.

Genital surgeries may carry risks of complications such as infection, breakdown of wounds, urethral narrowing from scar tissue, and problems with nerve sensation. For this reason, people choosing to undergo genital-reconstruction surgery should seek out high-volume, experienced gender-affirming surgeons if possible and carefully consider the risks and benefits of different options. Undergoing surgery with a surgeon with expertise in these complex cases gives people the best chance of safely achieving the appearance and bodily function that fit their personal goals.

ROUTINE HEALTHCARE

Beyond hormones and surgeries, transgender patients also need basic healthcare, including contraception and Pap screening for cervical cancer for those with a uterus, testing for STIs, breast cancer screening for those who still have breast tissue, and other routine wellness exams. Even trans male patients who are on testosterone and no longer have periods can still ovulate, so it's important for them to discuss birth control options with their providers if they want to avoid pregnancy.

It may be very challenging for transgender people to find doctors who they're comfortable seeing and who are experienced and competent in caring for gender-diverse patients. Transgender men may feel uncomfortable in an OB-GYN clinic where there may be very feminine office decor or many pregnant patients in the waiting room. Physicians and office staff should provide a more inclusive and welcoming environment by routinely asking patients about their pronouns and gender identity as part of the intake process, using a patient's name of choice, avoiding gendered decor, honoring a patient's autonomy if they do not feel comfortable undergoing pelvic exams, and, most important, centering the patient in all counseling, testing, and treatment decisions. Healthcare workers should educate themselves on best practices for providing care for gender-diverse patients using the educational resources of the World Professional Association for Transgender Health (WPATH).

HOW TO ACCESS CARE

If you're transgender or nonbinary and have had negative experiences with the medical system or if you're struggling to find providers with experience in gender-affirming care, there are a few strategies to try. The WPATH website (wpath.org) has a searchable directory of specialists who are committed to providing care for transgender patients. The directory includes primary care providers, mental health professionals, gynecologists, urologists, and plastic surgeons and can be searched by geographic location. Many people will also find doctors through the recommendations of friends or connections in social media groups or community organizations.

If you are starting the journey of exploring your gender identity and aren't even sure where to begin, the first step is to schedule an appointment with a primary care provider (PCP) who has expertise in gender care. For minors, this is a general pediatrician. You can search for a doctor on the WPATH website, or you can see if there is a center for gender care near you; these are usually based at academic medical centers and children's hospitals. PCPs can explain the process, help you navigate the system, and arrange referrals to therapists, endocrinologists, and surgical specialists as needed. Many PCPS will also prescribe hormone therapy in addition to providing routine medical care such as health screenings and contraception.

If there are no providers with experience in gender-affirming care near you, services such as mental health counseling and prescriptions for hormone therapy can be accessed via telemedicine. Having a local PCP for other routine medical care and physical exams is also important. Even if your PCP does not have experience caring for gender-diverse patients, you can forge a constructive and positive relationship if you are able to communicate freely with your provider.

Limited access to care for transgender and nonbinary people is a significant issue, particularly outside of major metropolitan areas. Many providers who currently treat transgender patients sought out educational resources on their own because they felt a commitment to serving this community. However, medical schools and residency programs are starting to include formal training in caring for gender-diverse patients in their curricula, and many commercial and public insurance plans now cover gender-affirming care. Hopefully, over time, it will not be so challenging for transgender and nonbinary people to access the medical treatments they need to live authentic, emotionally and physically healthy lives.

TAKE-HOME POINTS

- There are at least 1.6 million transgender teens and adults in the United States.
- Access to gender-affirming care drastically decreases rates of depression, suicidal thoughts, and self-harm, with up to 70 percent reduction in suicidality in transgender youths.
- Approximately 98 percent of transgender adolescents will

continue treatment into adulthood. Rates of detransitioning are extremely low.

- Most gender-affirming care in minors is not surgical but supportive and allows the child to explore their gender identity safely as they grow.

- The WPATH website has a searchable directory of health-care providers who specialize in helping gender-diverse patients.

Intersex

Intersex describes a person whose reproductive anatomy doesn't fit a typical male-versus-female binary. Some intersex conditions, also known as differences of sex development, or DSDs, may present at birth as genitalia that does not clearly appear to be either a penis and scrotum or a clitoris and vulva. Starting in the 1950s, doctors began counseling parents of intersex infants to surgically change the genitals to appear more male or female, purportedly to help the child fit established gender norms. Families often hid the surgeries and diagnoses from the children and raised them in selected gender roles. Unfortunately, in many cases, the gender selected at birth did not match that which the children actually identified with as they grew older, leading to severe confusion and trauma. The surgeries, which include removal or surgical reduction of an enlarged clitoris and removal of the testicles or ovaries, can cause decreased genital sensation, scarring, infertility, altered sexual function, and psychological distress.

Most intersex advocates now condemn the practice of performing genital surgeries on infants and children as potentially physically and psychologically harmful. This has led major children's hospitals in the United States, such as Boston Children's Hospital and Lurie Children's Hospital in Chicago, to stop performing medically unnecessary surgeries on intersex children. In speaking out about their experiences, intersex people and the parents of intersex children are advocating for their right to bodily autonomy and helping the medical community to view differences of sex development as valid variations of sex rather than abnormalities that must be altered.

INTERSEX BASICS

Biological sex is far from simple, and there's a wide and complex spectrum of situations where the biology doesn't fit a neat binary. Sex is made up of several different components: genetics, hormones, reproductive organs, and genitals. There may be discordance between whether these components are male or female or there may be elements of both. For example, there is a condition called Swyer syndrome in which people have XY—male—chromosomes and a uterus, vagina, and female external genitalia.

Sex can be compared to the color spectrum, which is made up of wavelengths of light. There are wavelengths that can be seen as red or orange, but in reality, there are many wavelengths in between, and the distinction between what is considered red and orange is at some point arbitrary. Genes, reproductive organs, genitals, and hormones may have a similar wide range of variations. For instance, the measurements that define clitoromegaly, which means a clitoris that is larger than usual, and a micropenis, a penis that is smaller than usual, are essentially arbitrary cutoffs based on statistical distributions of size within a population. The same is true for levels of testosterone and estrogen. Many people think that only males have testosterone and only females have estrogen, but the reality is that everyone has both testosterone and estrogen; there are just different ranges of hormone levels found in most males and females. In other words, what is considered to be male and female in terms of physical features is simply what is most commonly seen, and at some point, the cutoffs are social constructs and not biological absolutes.

For this reason, it is difficult to estimate the number of people who are intersex. Being intersex is an umbrella term for an extremely wide range of people and conditions. There are dozens of hormonal and genetic conditions that can lead to differences of sex development, and there is some disagreement in the medical and intersex communities about what conditions are actually considered to be DSDs. But in general, being intersex is far more common than most people realize. Up to 1.7 percent of the population may be intersex or have an intersex variation. Approximately one in 1,000 to 4,500 infants are identified as intersex at birth, but other DSDs may not be discovered until later in life. Suffice it to say that even by conservative estimates, there are millions of intersex people in the world.

TERMINOLOGY

The intersex community is definitely not a monolith. Just like in the general population, every individual is different, and their identity, perspective, and experience is unique. Even the choice of what term is preferred—*intersex* versus *DSD*—differs from person to person. Many prefer the term *intersex*, as *DSD* also stands for "disorders of sex development," and the word *disorder* implies that there is something abnormal about the body that requires treatment or correction.

The more antiquated terms of *hermaphrodite* and *pseudohermaphrodite* have almost universally been rejected by healthcare professionals and advocates as being inaccurate. There is a myth that intersex people have both male and female genitals, though this is not physically possible, and the term *hermaphrodite* perpetuates this myth. However, it is possible to have both XX and XY chromosomes, and some people with this genetic makeup prefer to call themselves *chimeras*, because genetic chimerism means possessing different sets of DNA.

In general, the word *intersex* is used to describe people, and *DSD*, or differences of sex development, is used to refer to medical conditions, but readers should be aware that people may prefer different terms or conventions and the language is ever evolving. Also, some people who have DSDs or intersex variations in sexual characteristics don't choose to self-identify as intersex.

Being intersex does not imply a certain gender identity. Some people who are intersex identify with the sex that was assigned to them at birth; others consider themselves transgender, nonbinary, or agender; still others identify primarily as intersex. As we discussed in the previous chapter, none of this is the same as sexuality, which has to do with who the person feels attracted to.

DIAGNOSIS

Most intersex conditions are discovered in childhood, either at birth or when an adolescent doesn't go through typical pubertal changes. Some intersex people are diagnosed later, as adults, when they first attempt to be sexually active or try to conceive. The medical evaluation of an intersex patient usually requires a multidisciplinary healthcare team, including pediatricians or primary care doctors, endocrinologists, geneticists, urologists or gynecologists, and mental health professionals. Genetic and hormone testing, a physical examination, and imaging studies to assess internal anatomy may be needed to understand someone's unique biology.

TREATMENT

There are only a few circumstances where emergency medical care of intersex infants is truly necessary. For example, if a newborn baby is unable to urinate because of abnormalities of the genitals or urethra, that may require immediate surgical treatment. Beyond specific cases like these, most DSDs don't need treatment. Simply having genitalia that don't fit the typical appearance of a vulva or penis and scrotum doesn't necessitate surgical correction. Surgeries that are not medically necessary shouldn't be chosen for children until they are old enough to understand the risks and alternatives and decide whether or not they want the procedure.

Some intersex people may eventually want or need medical or surgical treatment because their anatomy is affecting their ability to be sexually active or because they want to conceive or carry a pregnancy. Assisted reproductive treatments can make it possible for intersex people to have children, sometimes through the use of donor eggs, sperm, embryos, or a gestational carrier. If one's hormones and physical appearance do not correspond with that person's gender identity, options for gender affirmation should be discussed.

Certain DSDs may be associated with an increased risk of cancer of the gonads, and in the past, surgical removal of the testes or ovaries in childhood was recommended to decrease the risk of cancer. However, recent data suggests that the risk of early cancer in some of these conditions may have been overestimated, and families may decide to delay surgery until the child has undergone puberty or is old enough to consent for themselves. Some families may decide not to remove the gonads at all, preferring instead to monitor carefully for signs of cancer.

Intersex people and their families should receive social support and counseling to help them navigate the medical system and understand their own identities, goals, and options. Ultimately, intersex children and adults deserve the basic right to bodily autonomy—to have healthcare professionals discuss the risks and benefits of all of their medical options without paternalism or judgment. If patients are not comfortable with the recommendations they are given, they should seek a second opinion with specialists who are experienced in intersex care. Presently, this may require traveling to an academic medical center or a major children's hospital or seeking telemedicine consultations. It is fortunate that remote options exist, but increasing access to quality care for all intersex people will require the broader medical community to commit to learning, listening, and increasing formal training on intersex health.

TAKE-HOME POINTS

- Intersex people have bodies that do not fit a typical male-versus-female binary.

- Up to 1.7 percent of the population may be intersex.

- Some people may not learn that they are intersex until they are adults and attempt to be sexually active or try to conceive.

- Most intersex people don't need treatment. Medically unnecessary surgeries on infants and children should be avoided so that the individuals can make their own health-care decisions as adults.

Cancer

Many medical situations share the "it's not hysteria" pattern: women suffering from pelvic pain and other disturbing symptoms try desperately to get help, but must fight for testing before finally receiving a diagnosis. In some cases, symptoms such as pelvic pain, nausea, vomiting, and abnormal bleeding may actually be signs of a serious medical problem such as cancer—and unfortunately, the stakes for a delayed diagnosis become life and death.

The best possible scenario with cancer is preventing it from developing in the first place. If prevention is not feasible, detecting it and starting treatment as early as possible gives someone the best chance of beating the cancer. Raising awareness can go a long way in prevention and early detection, and it can empower women and people assigned female at birth to ask questions and advocate for their health.

SYMPTOMS

Certain symptoms should always be taken seriously and warrant some sort of diagnostic testing. These include a large unexpected weight gain or weight loss without any changes in diet or exercise, vaginal bleeding after menopause, rectal bleeding, new breast masses, and lymph nodes in the underarm or groin area that don't resolve within a week or two.

While most people experiencing these symptoms don't have cancer, they can still be signs of a serious medical condition and should prompt a thorough evaluation. If your healthcare providers don't offer any sort of exam or testing, you can advocate for yourself by asking them what they think the symptoms are from and why they're not recommending any further workup. Your provider may suggest trying another course of treatment first, but if your symptoms continue, you're not getting answers, or you feel uncomfortable with the plan for management, you should seek a second opinion as soon as possible.

Some common symptoms may not necessarily be concerning if they happen only occasionally and resolve on their own, but if they persist, keep recurring, or worsen, see your primary care doctor or gynecologist for evaluation. These include sporadic abdominal, pelvic, or back pain, nausea, bloating, and constipation or other significant changes in bowel habits.

DIAGNOSIS

The process for evaluating any concerning symptom starts with your doctor taking a medical history, including what symptoms have been felt and for how long, what other medical problems you have, if you're up to date on routine health tests such as cancer screenings, and if there is a family history of cancer. If several relatives on one or both sides of the family have had cancers, especially if they were diagnosed at a young age, this might suggest an increased genetic risk of cancer in the family.

The healthcare provider, usually a primary care doctor or gynecologist, should perform at least a basic physical examination, which may include a breast or pelvic exam depending on the area of concern. If imaging is needed, that will usually start with an ultrasound for the pelvic organs or a breast ultrasound or mammogram for breast concerns. Additional testing may be suggested based on the symptoms or exam findings.

Cancers are diagnosed with a biopsy or surgical procedure to obtain a sample of the tissue that is then analyzed by a pathologist. Throughout this process, the healthcare provider performing the evaluation should always clearly explain what testing is being recommended and why, and what a patient may experience during tests or procedures such as biopsies.

If patients are diagnosed with cancer or if the doctor has a very strong concern for cancer, they will be referred to an oncologist. Decisions about treatment are made by a team of medical experts including oncologists, surgeons, pathologists, and radiologists. In the field of gynecology, gynecologic oncologists perform surgeries for treatment of uterine, ovarian, tubal, cervical, vaginal, and vulvar cancers, and they may also help manage medical treatments such as chemotherapy.

GYNECOLOGIC AND BREAST CANCERS

Some of the cancers that primarily affect women actually represent major success stories in the world of public health. Cervical cancer and breast cancer both have good screening options; testing for these cancers is done regularly; precancers and cancers can often be detected early; and there are effective treatment options that can prevent cancer from developing or give patients a good chance of beating the disease. There is even a vaccine to prevent cervical cancer.

These successes exist because of a combination of factors, including a large amount of research, funding, and education campaigns for both healthcare providers and the public. Though other gynecologic malignancies do not yet have such effective methods for screening and prevention, cervical and breast cancer serve as an example of what is possible with research, advocacy, and awareness.

CERVICAL CANCER

Cervical cancer is one the few cancers that could potentially be completely eradicated. This is because there are interventions to prevent the source of the cancer and simple methods to detect and remove precancerous cells before they turn into cancer. More than 99 percent of cases of cervical cancer are caused by a sexually transmitted infection, human papillomavirus (HPV). Vaccines to protect HPV infection are given to adolescents before they become sexually active, and these vaccines significantly decrease the risk of developing cervical precancer and cancer. There is also a widely available screening test, the Pap smear.

Cervical cancer is generally very slow growing; it usually takes many years for cervical cells infected with HPV to develop precancerous changes—called cervical dysplasia—and a few years more for dysplasia to become cancer. This slow rate of change makes it possible for dysplasia to be detected and treated before it progresses to cancer.

Risk Factors

The risk factors for developing cervical cancer are mostly related to someone's likelihood of getting HPV and the body's ability to clear an HPV infection. People with more sexual partners over their lifetimes have a higher risk, since it is possible to contract HPV from each partner even if barrier methods such as condoms are used. Anything that weakens the immune system also increases the risk of cervical cancer; this includes smoking, immunosuppressant medications such as steroids, and human immunodeficiency virus (HIV) infection. A weakened immune system may not be able to clear HPV, and the longer that an HPV infection is active, the more chance it has to cause changes in the cervical cells.

Cervical cancer is far more common in countries where much of the population does not have access to Pap screening and HPV vaccines. The disparity in cervical cancer cases and deaths reflect serious economic and social inequities; almost 90 percent of cervical cancer deaths occur in low- and middle-income countries. In 2020, the WHO adopted a global strategy for cervical cancer elimination that focuses on increasing access to vaccinations, Pap tests, and treatment of dysplasia and cancer. However, the success of this strategy will require large-scale, systemic changes, including training health-care providers and educating the population about HPV and cervical cancer prevention.

Exposure in utero to a synthetic hormone called *diethylstilbestrol*, or DES, is a relatively rare risk factor for cervical cancer. DES was given to mothers from 1940 to 1970 in order to decrease the risk of miscarriage. In the 1950s, it was discovered that DES did not significantly improve miscarriage rates, so usage decreased, but it was still used in some countries until the 1970s. Children who were exposed to DES while in the womb have increased risks of both vaginal and cervical cancers, and therefore need more frequent testing for cervical cancer than the general population.

HPV Vaccine

Almost everyone who is sexually active, at least 80 percent, will contract a strain of HPV at some point in their lives. This is true even for people who have a single lifetime partner, because that partner may have been previously exposed to HPV. While many of these strains don't cause symptoms, some of them are considered high-risk, meaning they can increase the risk of malignancies such as cervical cancer.

Commercial vaccines that protect against HPV were introduced in the United States in 2006. Since then, countries that have widespread HPV vaccination have seen significantly decreased rates of cervical dysplasia and cervical cancer. Vaccines also decrease the risk of other HPV-related cancers, such as vulvar, vaginal, anal, penile, and oral cancers.

HPV vaccines protect against the two most dangerous strains of HPV, 16 and 18, which cause approximately 70 percent of cervical cancers; they also protect against several other strains that can cause cancer and genital warts. The most recent version of the vaccine available in the United States, Gardasil 9, protects against nine different strains. Because there are hundreds of types of HPV, vaccination doesn't completely eliminate the risk of dysplasia or cancer, but it is highly effective, preventing 98 to 99 percent of cervical precancers and cancers.

The vaccines are usually given as a series of two or three doses, typically in adolescence before children are sexually active. The vaccines are recommended for children of all genders, not just those who can get cervical cancer. They protect vaccinated children from other HPV-related cancers, and decreasing the amount of HPV in a population lowers overall rates of transmission, protecting everyone. The vaccine can also be given to adults, and in the United States, the Gardasil 9 vaccine is now FDA approved for use in both women and men through age forty-five. Even people who have already had HPV may still benefit from vaccination, because they may be protected from contracting other strains if they have more than one sexual partner or if they will have new partners in the future.

There is a great deal of misinformation about HPV that may make people nervous about getting the vaccine. Some parents feel that HPV vaccines aren't necessary for their children or that they somehow promote promiscuity. There are also myths that the vaccine may cause autism, infertility, and other health risks. None of these are true. The vaccine is extremely safe: hundreds of millions of doses have been administered, and the main side effects are temporary irritation at the injection site and mild symptoms such as headache and dizziness—no major or long-term side effects have been seen. HPV vaccination also does not influence future sexual behavior. It is safe and well tolerated and can provide significant cancer protection for people of all genders.

Symptoms

The most common symptom of cervical cancer is irregular vaginal bleeding, including bleeding after sex, between periods, and after menopause. There might also be persistent vaginal discharge that is watery or foul-smelling and can be mistaken for vaginal infections. Because these symptoms can be the result of so many different conditions, people having persistent bleeding or discharge should get testing to determine the cause—especially if they are postmenopausal.

Diagnosis

Cervical dysplasia and cervical cancer may be seen on a routine Pap smear, or patients might present to their healthcare provider with symptoms of abnormal bleeding or discharge, and a cervical mass may be found on pelvic exam. In these cases, the doctor will recommend a biopsy to test the cervical tissue and establish the diagnosis of precancer or cancer.

Pap Smears and HPV Screening

Pap smears can usually detect abnormal cervical changes well before they turn into cancer. In the United States, Pap testing is recommended starting at age twenty-one, regardless of sexual activity. In the past, Paps were performed as soon as someone became sexually active or turned eighteen. However, the risk of cervical dysplasia or cancer before age twenty-one is extremely small, and these early screenings can lead to unnecessary biopsies and treatments without significantly decreasing the number of people who develop cancer. For this reason, Paps are no longer done as often as they used to be, and people who have not had any abnormal Paps can get testing done every three to five years. Pap smears are still recommended starting at age twenty-one even if someone has not been sexually active because there are some rare cervical cancers which are not caused by HPV. Because people who have never been sexually active may not feel comfortable with the pelvic exam that is necessary to obtain a Pap smear, they can discuss the risks and benefits of screening with their healthcare provider, and it is their right to decline the test if they wish.

Testing for high-risk HPV strains can also be added for cervical cancer screening starting at age thirty. HPV is very common among sexually active people in their teens and twenties, but as they get older, their immune system often clears the infection. If someone has persistent high-risk HPV that has not resolved, they may have a higher chance of developing cervical dysplasia and cancer. HPV screening is performed using the same Pap smear specimen and helps to triage a person's risk for cancer. Someone with a positive high-risk HPV test will be monitored more closely as long as the test is positive, but the good news is that most people with HPV will clear the infection before it can cause dysplasia or cancer.

People who do not have high-risk HPV have a very low likelihood of developing cervical cancer. In fact, some organizations, such as the American Cancer Society (ACS), recommend HPV screening alone—without Pap smears to evaluate the appearance of cells—for people ages twenty-five to sixty-five.

General Pap screening guidelines for average-risk people differ from guidelines for people with higher risk of cervical cancer. People with high-risk HPV, prior abnormal Pap smears or cervical dysplasia, or immunosuppression may require more frequent monitoring.

Cervical Biopsies

A *colposcopy* is performed when a Pap smear shows abnormal cells or detects a particularly high-risk strain of HPV such as 16 or 18. During this test, a microscope is used to inspect the cervix and vagina, and small biopsies of the cervix are taken. If an actual mass is seen on the cervix, this can be biopsied directly.

If a colposcopy reveals dysplasia, other procedures may be performed to provide more detailed testing and also to treat the dysplasia. Mild dysplasia does not need treatment, but a more high-grade dysplasia with more abnormal-looking cells will be removed to prevent development of cancer. Dysplasia can be treated with a laser to vaporize the abnormal cells, cryotherapy to freeze them, or, more commonly, with a *loop electrosurgical excision procedure*, or LEEP. In this procedure, the cervix is numbed with local anesthetic and a thin electrified wire loop is used to remove a small piece of the cervix. If there is concern for actual cancer, a *cone biopsy* is usually performed; during this procedure, a doctor uses a scalpel to cut out a larger piece of cervical tissue while the patient is under anesthesia in the operating room. Cancer can be found on biopsy during colposcopy, LEEP, or cone biopsy.

UTERINE CANCER

While cervical cancer is the most common gynecologic cancer in resource-limited countries, in other countries such as the United States, uterine cancer is the most common. There are two parts of the uterus that can become cancerous: the endometrial tissue in the cavity, and the muscle and connective tissue of the uterine walls. Usually when healthcare providers say *uterine cancer* they mean endometrial cancer, because this is by far the most common type.

Risk Factors

The risk of endometrial cancer goes up with age, and most cases occur in people above fifty. An imbalance in estrogen and progesterone can also increase the risks. Estrogen stimulates the growth of endometrial tissue, particularly if there is also a lack of progesterone, which usually controls endometrial cell growth. This combination of factors can allow endometrial cells to mutate and grow aggressively, which can lead to abnormal thickening of the tissue called *hyperplasia*, a precancerous condition. If the cells continue to grow, endometrial cancer can develop.

For these reasons, PCOS is a risk factor for endometrial hyperplasia and cancer because it can cause missed periods and low progesterone. Obesity also increases the risk, because adipose cells produce estrogen, and some people with PCOS may be overweight. The endometrial tissue builds up even further if there are not regular periods to flush out the tissue. This is the reason that people with PCOS who do not have periods regularly are treated with progesterone—to protect them from developing endometrial cancer.

The dangers of unopposed estrogen, meaning estrogen without the protective effect of progesterone, is the reason that birth control and hormone replacement therapy are never given as estrogen-only medications for people who have a uterus; it is always combined with a progesterone. If someone doesn't have a uterus, estrogen can be taken alone for menopausal hormone therapy or gender affirmation.

There is a medication called tamoxifen that is not a hormone but can stimulate endometrial tissue like estrogen does. It is used for breast cancer treatment because it blocks the effects of estrogen in the breast, but it can unfortunately act like estrogen in other parts of the body such as the uterus. For this reason, tamoxifen use increases a woman's risk of developing endometrial cancer.

A higher number of lifetime menstrual cycles, from an earlier age at first period to a later age of menopause, also increases the risk of endometrial cancer because the more times that the endometrium is stimulated and grows, the more possibility there is for abnormal cells to develop.

There are also genetic conditions that increase the likelihood of uterine cancer; the most well known of these is Lynch syndrome, which causes a high risk of gastrointestinal cancers such as colon and stomach cancer and also raises the risk of endometrial cancer. The *BRCA1* mutation, which is more famously associated with breast and ovarian cancers, may also pose a slightly increased risk of endometrial cancer. People with this mutation may be offered hysterectomy at the same time as surgery for removal of the tubes and ovaries.

There are certain rare types of endometrial cancer that are not related to estrogen exposure. These cancers may occur in people who have none of the typical risk factors that we discussed above and are generally more aggressive types. Other forms of uterine cancer include leiomyosarcomas, cancers of the uterine muscle and connective tissue which appear similar to fibroids. These are also much less common and more aggressive than endometrial cancers.

Symptoms

The most common symptom of uterine cancers is abnormal vaginal bleeding, especially bleeding after menopause; 90 percent of postmenopausal women with endometrial cancer experienced vaginal bleeding before they were diagnosed. For this reason, anyone with postmenopausal bleeding must be tested to ensure that cancer is not the source. Most cases of postmenopausal bleeding are not from cancer; the cause is usually a benign condition like polyps, fibroids, or genitourinary syndrome of menopause. However, testing is still offered quickly because around 10 percent of women with postmenopausal bleeding do have cancer, and the prognosis is best when the cancer is caught early.

Diagnosis

Endometrial cancers are diagnosed by testing a sample of tissue from inside the uterine cavity. This can be done in a medical office with an endometrial biopsy, which is a thin straw that is inserted through the vagina into the uterus and used to pick up loose endometrial cells. A hysteroscopy may also be recommended in order to look into the uterine cavity, and this is usually paired with a dilation and curettage to obtain tissue for testing.

OVARIAN CANCER

Ovarian cancer is perhaps the most feared gynecologic cancer, because unlike cervical cancer, there are no effective methods for screening or prevention, and unlike uterine cancers, symptoms may not appear until the cancer has progressed to an advanced stage. Fortunately, there are ways to decrease the risks of getting ovarian cancer, and these can be as straightforward as using hormonal birth control or getting a tubal sterilization.

There are several different types of ovarian cancer, and some are less aggressive than others. Each part of the ovary—the follicles and eggs, the hormone-producing cells, and the rest of the ovarian tissue—can form its own type of cancer. These cancer types include germ-cell tumors, which arise from the eggs; sex cord–stromal tumors, which involve hormone-producing cells; and epithelial tumors, which come from the surface of the ovary. The most common types of ovarian cancer are epithelial; when people think of ovarian cancer as an aggressive, late-stage disease, they are usually thinking of this type of cancer.

Fallopian tube cancers are virtually identical to epithelial ovarian cancers and are treated the same way. Many epithelial ovarian cancers actually start from the ends of the tubes but grow to involve the ovaries by the time they are detected. For this reason, removing the fallopian tubes for sterilization or during a hysterectomy significantly decreases someone's risk of developing ovarian cancer.

Risk Factors

Risk factors for ovarian cancer include age, although germ-cell tumors are usually seen in younger patients. Like endometrial cancer, the more lifetime menstrual cycles or number of times that ovulation occurs, the higher someone's risk of developing ovarian cancer. Because of this, early age of first period, later age of menopause, and not having had any pregnancies are risk factors for ovarian cancer. Birth control that prevents ovulation also decreases the risk.

Genetic cancer syndromes, such as *BRCA1* or *BRCA2* mutations, also carry a high risk of ovarian cancer. People with these mutations will be counseled to have their ovaries and tubes surgically removed when they're done having children, or by age thirty-five to forty, to decrease their likelihood of developing cancer.

Symptoms

Signs of ovarian cancer can be common symptoms such as pelvic pain, bloating, a feeling of abdominal fullness, nausea and vomiting, and changes in bowel habits such as constipation. Patients and their healthcare providers may initially think that they have irritable bowel syndrome or indigestion because the symptoms are virtually identical. Because these symptoms may be attributed to other common and benign conditions, ovarian cancer is unfortunately often not diagnosed until it is fairly advanced.

Diagnosis

Ovarian cancers may be seen on ultrasounds, which are performed if someone is experiencing pain or abdominal bloating. A pelvic ultrasound or MRI may reveal features concerning for possible ovarian cancer, but surgery is needed to test the tissue and get a diagnosis.

Ovarian cancers cannot generally be biopsied because of the risk of spillage of cancer cells into the abdomen if a needle is inserted into the mass, so they are diagnosed surgically when a cyst or the entire ovary is removed.

VULVAR CANCER

With fewer than twenty thousand cases per year in the United States, vulvar cancer is very rare compared to other gynecologic cancers. The symptoms of vulvar cancer can mimic those of common conditions like yeast infections, and because these cancers are so rarely suspected, they may not be diagnosed until someone has had symptoms for quite some time.

Risk Factors

Vulvar cancers can be similar to other skin cancers, and there can even be melanoma of the vulva. Many vulvar cancers are HPV-related, like cervical cancer. For this reason, smoking and conditions and medications that weaken the immune system also increase the risk of vulvo-vaginal cancers, and HPV vaccines decrease the risk. The chance of having vulvar cancer also increases with age, particularly after menopause. Lichen sclerosus causes chronic inflammation of the vulvar skin and can also increase risk of vulvar cancer.

Symptoms

The symptoms of vulvar precancer or cancer can be very similar to those of yeast infections and genital warts: chronic irritation of the vulvar skin, a wartlike bump, thickening of the skin, or a sore that doesn't heal.

Diagnosis

Anyone experiencing vulvar itching, irritation, or skin lesions that are not improving despite treatment should see the gynecologist for a physical exam. A vulvar biopsy may be recommended to test the tissue.

VAGINAL CANCER

Only about a thousand women are diagnosed with cancer of the vagina each year in the United States, so it is extremely rare. Most cancers found in the vagina are actually from other nearby organs, most commonly the cervix or uterus. Vaginal cancers that originate from the vagina itself are similar in many ways to cervical and vulvar cancer caused by HPV. Just as there can be precancerous cells of the cervix and vulva, there is also a precancerous condition of the vagina called *vaginal intraepithelial neoplasia*, or VAIN, that can be detected and treated before it progresses to cancer.

Risk Factors

Vaginal and cervical cancers share the same risk factors, most notably HPV infection and in utero exposure to DES. Women who were exposed to DES are some of the only people that need Pap smears of the vaginal walls, because their lifetime risk is particularly high. Otherwise, vaginal cancer is so rare that it does not need to be screened for in the general population.

Symptoms

Many cases of VAIN or early vaginal cancer will not have any symptoms, though possible symptoms include irregular vaginal bleeding, bleeding with sex, or watery vaginal discharge. When vaginal cancer progresses, it may be felt by the person or by a partner or doctor as a lump in the vagina. Advanced vaginal cancer can cause pelvic pain or even urinary frequency or constipation if it spreads and affects the bladder or rectum.

Diagnosis

VAIN and vaginal cancer are diagnosed with colposcopy and biopsy, just like cervical dysplasia and cancer. In fact, many cases of VAIN are found incidentally at the time of a colposcopy for an abnormal

242 IT'S NOT HYSTERIA

cervical Pap smear, because the walls of the vagina are also inspected at that time.

BREAST CANCER

Breast cancer is the second most common cancer diagnosed in women, after skin cancer. As many as one in eight women will be diagnosed with breast cancer in their lifetime, and many families will have at least one relative who had breast cancer. Fortunately, there is a good screening test—mammograms, or X-rays of the breasts—that can detect breast cancer very early. Advocacy groups and breast cancer survivors have helped raise awareness about the importance of mammograms as well as early evaluation of breast lumps found on self-exam.

Types of Breast Cancer

Breast cancer can affect different parts of the breast. *Lobular cancer* involves the milk glands, while *ductal cancer* involves the tubes, or ducts, that carry milk to the nipple. There are other types of cancer that affect the rest of the breast tissue, including the skin or nipple. *Ductal carcinoma in situ* (DCIS) and *lobular carcinoma in situ* (LCIS) are early or stage 0 cancers, which means that cells have become cancerous but they haven't spread outside of the duct or milk glands. Once the cancer cells start growing into the surrounding tissue, they are called *invasive ductal* and *lobular cancer*, respectively.

Risk Factors

Risk factors for breast cancer include age, a family history of breast or ovarian cancer, longer lifetime exposure to ovarian hormones (such as an earlier age of first period or later age of menopause), having dense breasts, and having a history of radiation of the chest. Obesity is a risk factor for breast cancer in postmenopausal women, but for unclear reasons, this effect is not seen in premenopausal women.

Lifestyle modifications, such as exercising regularly, not smoking, and reducing alcohol intake, can lessen the likelihood of getting breast cancer. Breastfeeding can also decrease the risk of breast cancer for those who are able and want to breastfeed.

People may worry about whether birth control causes cancer. While hormonal birth control methods may pose a slight increased risk of breast cancer, this risk is low and seems to go away after the birth control is stopped. In fact, people who use hormonal birth control have lower overall lifetime risks of cancer than those who don't, because the hormones also decrease the risks of uterine and ovarian cancers.

Postmenopausal hormone replacement therapy treatments that contain both estrogen and progesterone may slightly increase the risk of breast cancer, though studies suggest that short-term use of less than four to five years may not significantly affect risk, and breast cancer rates may go up only with prolonged use. Interestingly, estrogen-only hormone treatment, which is used for people who do not have a uterus, does not seem to affect breast cancer risk.

Mutations in genes such as *BRCA1* and *2* are associated with an up to 85 percent lifetime risk of developing breast cancer. Certain elements of a patient's family history may suggest a genetic cancer risk: several family members who had breast or associated cancers such as ovarian cancer; a family member with multiple different types of cancers; Ashkenazi Jewish heritage; cisgender male family members with breast cancer. If there is concern for a possible cancer gene mutation, genetic counseling should be considered to discuss testing. People who are positive for mutations in *BRCA1* or *2* will be offered options such as more frequent cancer screening, the addition of breast MRIs to mammograms for screening, and cancer prevention surgeries such as prophylactic mastectomy.

Symptoms

More than a third of all breast cancers may be found by patients themselves rather than by routine breast imaging. This is because cancers may develop during the year or two between mammograms or before someone is old enough get routine mammograms. Patients may feel a lump in the breast while showering or changing, or a lump may be felt by a partner. Other signs of breast cancer include persistent red or inflamed-appearing rashes of the skin or nipple, swollen lymph nodes that do not go away, and a nipple suddenly retracting inward.

Diagnosis

Even if a third of breast cancers are found by patients themselves, the other two-thirds of patients do not have symptoms and the cancers are found by doctors or on a mammogram. Routine screening mammograms are very important for the detection of small cancers before they cause symptoms or grow into a mass that can be felt.

For people with average breast cancer risk, routine screening mammograms should begin between ages forty and fifty. They are performed every one to two years until age fifty, once yearly from ages fifty to eighty, with individual counseling about when to stop screening after age eighty. Different organizations have unique guidelines for frequency and age to begin mammograms; this is because guidelines must balance potential improvement in breast cancer survival and outcomes with an increase in possible false-positive results, unneeded biopsies, anxiety, and X-ray exposure. People with increased risks of breast cancer based on family or personal history will definitely need an individualized plan for screening.

It used to be recommended that women perform breast self-exams at home every month, feeling the breast tissue and underarm area to check for masses. However, it was discovered that these frequent self-exams did not change the outcomes of breast cancers detected and might lead to unnecessary imaging or biopsies. ACOG now recommends that women practice breast self-awareness, which means that people should get to know what their breasts normally look and feel like, and notify their healthcare provider immediately if they notice any changes in the appearance of the skin or nipple or if they feel any new masses of the breast or underarm area.

Clinical breast exams done by a healthcare provider at routine checkups do not seem to improve detection for average-risk patients, but they may still be offered, especially for those with risk factors for breast cancer. The WHO notes that clinical exams may be an import-ant way to check for breast cancer in low-resource settings where pa-tients may not have access to routine mammography.

What every expert organization does agree on is that mammog-raphy is vastly superior to thermography, which is a method that de-tects breast temperature. Alternative health practitioners may promote thermography, but this has never been shown to be effective at detect-ing breast cancer. The FDA issued a safety communication in 2011 stating that thermography is not a replacement for mammograms, and that thermography on its own is not an effective screening tool. Those who prefer thermography usually do so for two reasons: concern about X-ray exposure and discomfort with the compression of the breasts during mammograms. However, the dose of X-rays with routine mam-mograms is very small and extremely safe at the recommended screen-ing intervals.

It's true that breast compression with mammograms can be un-comfortable or even painful, but the images require only a few seconds to obtain, and most people feel pressure, not pain. Newer mammo-gram technologies are making the exam less uncomfortable. Schedule nonurgent mammograms during the week or two after your period in order to avoid times when the breasts are more sensitive or tender.

If breast imaging shows a mass or other concerning-appearing findings, a breast biopsy will be recommended. Biopsies may be per-formed using guidance from an ultrasound, mammogram, or MRI, and they are done by a breast radiologist or a breast surgeon.

Because of early detection with mammograms and effective treat-ment options, the outcomes for breast cancer are generally very good, with an overall five-year survival rate of 90 percent, and 99 percent five-year survival if the cancer has not spread beyond the breast. Breast cancer is an excellent example of a disease where groundbreak-ing changes can occur if there is access to research funding, insurance coverage for screening and treatment, public education and awareness, and a commitment by the medical community to find more effective treatment options.

TAKE-HOME POINTS

- Almost all cervical cancers can be prevented with HPV vaccination and regular Pap screening.

- Uterine cancer is the most common gynecologic cancer in the United States.

- 10 percent of women with vaginal bleeding after menopause will have uterine cancer. In the other 90 percent, bleeding is from a benign cause like polyps, fibroids, or changes of menopause.

- Hormonal birth control and removal of the fallopian tubes can significantly decrease someone's risk of getting ovarian cancer.

- More than a third of breast cancers are found by the woman herself, but routine screening with mammogram is important for detecting breast cancer before it can be seen or felt.

PART III

What Are the Treatments?

Birth Control

Few classes of medication are as simultaneously championed and vilified as birth control. Since the introduction of contraceptive pills in the 1960s, birth control has given people with a uterus autonomy over their reproductive lives, allowing them to prevent or space pregnancies to focus on education, work, and other personal goals.

Hormonal birth control is also used to treat a wide range of gynecologic problems, providing relief from sometimes debilitating period or premenstrual symptoms. Critics may feel that healthcare professionals rely too heavily on birth control for the treatment of conditions such as endometriosis, fibroids, and PCOS, sometimes to the exclusion of other options, and there may be an element of truth to this. However, there's also rampant misinformation about the potential harms of hormonal birth control methods, including myths that they cause health problems such as infertility. Entire industries have risen out of this misinformation; there are expensive hormone detox supplements and treatments that supposedly reverse the harms inflicted by birth control—even though there is no evidence that significant long-term harms exist or that detox treatments have any benefit.

Like any medical treatment, birth control methods are simply tools; they have benefits and risks, and they're not universally good or bad. They may help some people and cause side effects or complications for others. There is no one method that is perfect for everyone, only the best possible fit for each individual person. When considering hormonal and nonhormonal birth control options, patients and doctors should review the risks, benefits, and effectiveness of each method.

When discussing the effectiveness of different birth control methods, *typical use* refers to percentage of users that successfully avoid getting pregnant during a year of using the method. Sometimes, a method can be very effective when it is used perfectly every time, but if it is difficult to use or remember, pregnancies can occur. For example, people may forget to take a daily pill, so the typical-use effectiveness of the pill is lower than the effectiveness could be with perfect use.

If you're currently deciding on a birth control method, please consider the risks of not choosing any birth control method at all—specifically, the potential psychological and physical risks of having to undergo a pregnancy and childbirth or an abortion if an unplanned pregnancy occurs. It's worth noting that potential side effects of hormonal birth control, including mood symptoms, weight gain, breast tenderness, nausea, and blood clots, are side effects of pregnancy too, because pregnancy also causes increases in estrogen and progesterone hormones.

HORMONAL BIRTH CONTROL

Hormonal birth control methods, with the exception of progesterone-containing intrauterine devices, or IUDs, prevent pregnancy by suppressing the release of eggs from the ovaries. They block signals from the brain that normally stimulate follicle growth and ovulation, and if eggs are not released, fertilization and pregnancy can't occur. Progesterone also thickens cervical mucus, which can prevent the passage of sperm into the uterus. All hormonal birth control methods contain progesterone, but the combined birth control pills, contraceptive patch, and vaginal ring also contain estrogen.

It's possible for all hormonal contraceptive methods to cause mood symptoms such as depression and anxiety, especially if someone has these mood disorders at baseline. They can also cause irregular bleeding or spotting, though hormonal birth control methods usually lighten or take away period bleeding or cramping. This is why they are used to treat symptoms of endometriosis and fibroids.

Estrogen-containing birth control has a small risk of causing blood clots in the veins—*deep venous thrombosis* (DVT) of the legs, *pulmonary emboli* (PE) of the lungs, and strokes in the brain. Fortunately, for people with average blood clot risk, the likelihood of developing a clot or stroke is far less than 1 percent, meaning only a few cases per thousand people using the method. The risks are higher after age thirty-five or if someone has other risk factors for blood clots, such as smoking, high blood pressure, and migraines with auras (visual, sensory, or stroke-like symptoms). Patients who have any of these risk factors may need to avoid estrogen-containing birth control.

People who have actually had a blood clot or stroke or who have a clotting disorder that carries a very high risk of developing clots may need to avoid hormonal birth control method altogether, because progesterone can also slightly increase the risk of clot formation. When weighing the risks, remember that pregnancy itself poses a significant risk for blood clots and stroke; clotting risk is actually increased fivefold in pregnancy and for several weeks after having a baby, so becoming pregnant may pose greater health risks than using a progesterone method.

The estrogen-containing methods such as the pill, patch, and ring are usually taken as three weeks of hormones, followed by one week of placebo pills or a hormone-free break, which allows a period to occur. In a typical menstrual cycle, a drop in progesterone levels triggers period bleeding. If progesterone stays at the same level, no periods will occur, and it's common for patients' periods to disappear while they're using progesterone-only birth control or methods with low doses of estrogen.

When people use hormonal birth control, there's actually no medical reason that they must have periods; progesterone suppresses the growth of endometrial tissue in the uterine cavity, so periods aren't needed to flush out old tissue. This is great news for people who have painful or heavy periods or severe period-related symptoms such as menstrual migraines, PMS, and PMDD. There are only two potential downsides to skipping the periods using birth control. One is that some people prefer to have periods to reassure themselves that they are not pregnant, and another is that if there are no periods, there can be unpredictable breakthrough bleeding.

Progesterone-only birth control may be suggested instead of estrogen-containing methods for people who have recently had a baby. This is because there is an increased blood clot risk for several weeks postpartum, but also because estrogen might suppress lactation if someone wishes to breastfeed.

Many transgender men prefer progesterone-only methods. Estrogen can suppress testosterone levels, which might blunt the desired effects of testosterone medications. Estrogen can also cause feminizing side effects such as breast swelling and tenderness, which can worsen dysphoria. Transgender men can still become pregnant even if testosterone has suppressed their periods, so trans men should not depend on testosterone alone as a birth control method.

THE PILL

Most birth control pills contain both estrogen and progesterone. One pill is taken daily. Packs usually contain three weeks of hormone pills followed by one week of placebo pills, which will induce a period. For people who wish to skip their periods, some pill packs have either no placebo pills or placebo pills only every three months, but the same effect can be achieved with any contraceptive pill by simply skipping the placebos and taking hormone pills continuously without breaks.

There are hundreds of types of birth control pills, and they differ by the amount of estrogen and the amount and type of progesterone they contain. There is overall no difference between different pill formulations in terms of contraceptive effectiveness, but they may have different side effect profiles. For instance, there are types of progesterone that are stronger than others, and these can cause more mood symptoms. Pills with lower levels of estrogen, the so-called low-dose pills, are better at preventing side effects like nausea, but they are also more likely to cause breakthrough bleeding.

Each pill formulation has possible benefits and drawbacks. When seeing a healthcare provider before starting a pill, patients should discuss their priorities and concerns about possible side effects; this can help the doctor choose which pill to prescribe. The good news is that for many pill users, any hormonal side effects experienced tend to resolve within a few months with continued use.

Combined estrogen and progesterone birth control pills also have a secondary benefit: they can improve acne. Dermatologists often recommend birth control purely for acne treatment, even if the patient doesn't need to prevent pregnancy. Estrogen stimulates the production of proteins that bind testosterone in the bloodstream, and the resulting decrease in testosterone levels can improve acne. The higher the estrogen, the better the effect.

There are also progesterone-only pills. These are traditionally made of a progesterone called norethindrone and referred to as the minipill. They are not as effective at preventing pregnancy as estrogen-containing pills, and the minipill must be taken at the same time every day within a three-hour window, otherwise pregnancy can occur. Because of this, the minipill is used mostly by people who are breastfeeding and prefer to take a pill instead of using another more effective method, such as an IUD. In 2023, the FDA approved a progesterone-only birth control pill containing norgestrel (Opill) for sale over the counter. Being able to obtain birth control without a prescription helps to remove barriers to access, but users should be aware that Opill must also be taken within a three-hour window each day. There is a progesterone-only pill containing drospirenone (Slynd) that does not need to be taken within that narrow time frame. However, cost may be an issue with Slynd because there are no generic versions, and insurance may not necessarily cover it.

Compared with other contraceptive methods, the benefits of birth control pills include simplicity of use, affordability, and accessibility. Pills also wear off within a day if someone is experiencing side effects or wishes to try to conceive immediately after stopping. The downsides are that any birth control pill must be taken every single day, and ovulation and pregnancy can occur if a dose is missed. Because of the potential for forgetting pills, the typical-use effectiveness is 93 percent with combined pills and 91 percent with progesterone-only pills. Cell phone reminders may be helpful, but for people who work irregular hours, travel across time zones frequently, or otherwise feel they may have difficulty remembering daily medications, birth control pills may not be the best method.

VAGINAL RINGS

Contraceptive vaginal rings are thin, flexible rings that release estrogen and progesterone that are absorbed through the vaginal walls. Rings are inserted at home by gently squeezing the ring and inserting it into the top of the vagina with the fingers. The ring is left in the vagina for three weeks, and then removed by the user and left out for one week to experience a period. Rings do not need to be removed for sex, can be used with tampons, and are not felt by the patient or their sexual partners if inserted correctly. Most contraceptive rings are thrown away and replaced every month, but there is a newer brand of ring that can be reused for up to one year.

Vaginal rings have very low doses of estrogen, and since they are not taken by mouth, they may be good methods for people who had nausea with pills or other estrogen-related side effects. Because there is still some estrogen, they have the same contraindications as any estrogen-containing methods. They have about the same effectiveness as pills: 93 percent with typical use. Since they are inserted only once a month, they may be more convenient than pills but can potentially be hard to remember to change. Rings would not be a good method for someone with significant vaginismus or who feels uncomfortable with vaginal insertion of products such as tampons or menstrual cups.

PATCH

The contraceptive patch is another combined estrogen and progesterone method. The patches are placed on the skin once a week for three weeks, and the fourth week is patch-free to allow for periods. They may be preferable for people who don't want to remember a pill every day but don't feel comfortable with vaginal rings or other longer-acting procedures for contraception. The patch has 93 percent typical-use effectiveness, which is the same as the pill and the ring.

Patches may have a slightly higher blood clot risk than most birth control pills and may also have a higher pregnancy failure rate at higher body weights. The main contraceptive patch in the United States has a prescribing warning that it should not be used in people with body mass index (BMI) higher than thirty because of the potential increased blood clot risk. Sometimes the patch may become loose or fall off, and some users may find the adhesive irritating.

BIRTH CONTROL SHOT (DEPO-PROVERA)

Depot medroxyprogesterone acetate (Depo-Provera, also known as Depo) is a progesterone that is injected into the muscle once every three months. It's administered in a clinic or doctor's office. Because it's a progesterone-only method, many users will have few to no periods or irregular periods. People may choose this method because of convenience.

It's one of the few birth control medications that can cause weight gain, and therefore it may not be a good option for someone who is concerned about gaining weight. Other birth control methods such as pills have not been clinically shown to significantly increase weight, though people's individual experiences may differ.

There's a risk of temporary thinning of the bones while Depo is being used. When this effect was discovered, some doctors started imposing limits on the number of years that they allowed patients to use this method. More recent studies have shown that the loss of bone density is only temporary, reverses once the medication is discontinued, and does not increase the risk of bone fracture, so people can use Depo for as long as they wish unless they are at high risk for osteoporosis or fractures. Generally, people on Depo should ensure they're getting enough calcium, vitamin D, and exercise, and avoid smoking in order to keep the bones strong.

Depo is the birth control method that can take the longest to wear off. Though it must be given every three months to ensure effectiveness for pregnancy prevention, periods and ovulation may sometimes not return for several months after stopping. This can be confusing and bothersome for people who want to try to conceive, so it may not be ideal for those who want to contracept for only a short time. People on Depo who are planning for pregnancy in the near future may want to switch to a rapidly reversible method like a pill for a few months before they plan to start trying.

The effectiveness of the Depo shot is higher than the methods mentioned earlier, 96 percent with typical use. This is because users do not have to remember to take a method on their own, beyond making appointments for the shot. To make it easier for patients, most doctors' offices will schedule the next appointment when a patient is there for Depo injection.

PROGESTERONE IMPLANT (NEXPLANON)

The progesterone implant (Nexplanon) is a small, thin rod that is inserted just under the skin of the upper arm and releases a hormone called etonogestrel. It is approved for use for up to three years. This is a type of long-acting reversible contraceptive (LARC) device, like an IUD. The implant is usually inserted and removed in a doctor's office or clinic, or it can be placed right after having a baby. The insertion procedure is very quick—the skin is numbed with local anesthetic, and the device is inserted under the skin using a needle. They're an excellent option for people who want a long-acting method but want to avoid pelvic procedures. Unlike the Depo shot, it does not seem to cause weight gain. And though the effectiveness may be somewhat decreased at higher body weights, the implant is among the most effective birth control methods for obese patients.

The most common side effect of the implant is irregular vaginal bleeding. Users may not have regular periods but may experience unpredictable breakthrough bleeding. Fortunately, there are ways to control the bleeding if it becomes bothersome, including taking anti-inflammatory medications such as ibuprofen.

Because LARC devices like Nexplanon do not require users to remember to take birth control on their own, they have the highest effectiveness rates: more than 99 percent.

INTRAUTERINE DEVICES (IUDs)

Intrauterine devices are long-acting reversible contraceptives of different shapes and materials that are placed in the cavity of the uterus. They usually have an attached string that is used to remove the device, but in some countries, like China, IUDs do not have strings and are left in place as permanent birth control methods.

IUDs that are used in the United States are T-shaped and made of either copper or plastic embedded with progesterone that is released into the uterus. It's generally thought that IUDs work by causing a mild inflammatory reaction that affects both the motility of sperm and the health of the egg. Like other progesterone birth control methods, progesterone-releasing IUDs thicken the cervical mucus to block passage of sperm.

There is a myth that IUDs prevent the implantation of embryos and cause abortions by disrupting an established pregnancy. IUDs do not dislodge pregnancies that have already implanted in the uterus, and they do not seem to prevent implantation if fertilization of an egg has occurred. There were studies performed in the 1970s and 1980s in which researchers analyzed the fallopian tubes of women with and without IUDs who were undergoing tubal sterilization. The tubes of people with IUDs did not contain either sperm or fertilized eggs, whereas people without IUDs who were not using other contraception were found to have both. These findings may reassure people who have ethical concerns about using IUDs because they've heard that they can cause abortions.

The progesterone-containing IUDs come in two different sizes with different amounts of hormone. The smaller IUDs were designed to be inserted more comfortably in younger patients or those with a smaller uterus or a narrow cervical opening. These smaller IUDs, Skyla and Kyleena, are approved for three and five years of use, respectively. They have lower levels of hormone than the larger IUDs, and periods are unlikely to be fully suppressed with use, meaning that most people who use them will experience periods. The larger IUDs, Liletta and Mirena, are only a few millimeters longer and wider in size but contain more hormone and therefore have more of a suppressive effect on period bleeding. Up to half of people who use the larger progesterone IUDs won't have periods while the IUD is in place. For this reason, Liletta and Mirena may be preferable for people who want to treat heavy and painful periods. These brands are both approved for up to eight years of use.

The copper IUD (Paragard) is hormone-free and may be left in place for up to ten years. It is a good long-term method for patients who want to avoid hormones. The downside of the copper IUD is that it can increase the heaviness of menstrual bleeding and may worsen menstrual cramping, so it may not a good choice for those who are already having painful or heavy periods.

Before IUD insertion, testing must be done to rule out cervical or uterine infections such as gonorrhea and chlamydia. If an IUD is placed while there is an active infection, there's a risk of pelvic inflammatory disease (PID), which is a dangerous infection of the uterus, tubes, and ovaries. Testing for these infections can be performed with a vaginal swab obtained at the time that the IUD is inserted. Patients with symptoms of infection such as fever, abnormal vaginal discharge, and unexplained pelvic pain should avoid having the IUD placed until any infection is fully treated and symptoms have resolved.

IUDs are placed in a clinic or doctor's office. (Please see chapter 24 for more detail on gynecologic office procedures.) Strings attached to the end of the IUD are left outside of the cervix. When it's time to remove the IUD, the strings are pulled. These strings can be felt at the top of the vagina, and patients should expect their doctor to teach them to periodically check the strings to ensure that the IUD remains in place. The strings of the IUD can be pushed into the cervical canal with sex, especially if they are trimmed too short, and this can make removal more challenging.

There are risks of IUDs. The device may not be placed correctly or may be expelled if the uterus cramps or bleeds heavily. IUDs can cause irregular spotting or bleeding, which typically resolves within a few days or weeks but can persist for longer in some women. Patients may feel cramping or pain for a few hours to days after placement, though usually this can be controlled with over-the-counter medications such as ibuprofen. If the cervix is tightly closed or if the anatomy of the uterus is unusual (distorted by fibroids or tipped sharply forward or backward), an IUD may not be able to be placed. The device can embed in the muscle of the uterus or, in rare cases, perforate the wall of the uterus and enter the abdomen. For these reasons, if it is difficult to insert the device, the healthcare provider will usually stop the procedure or use an ultrasound to guide placement.

In general, most people can have IUDs inserted in the office with proper counseling and a plan for pain prevention. Because IUD insertions can potentially be painful, those who have significant pain or anxiety with speculum exams may prefer a different contraceptive method or may consider IUD placement under sedation.

Like the implant, IUDs are among the most effective birth control methods and are also more than 99 percent effective when placed correctly. Progesterone IUDs have very slightly better effectiveness compared with the copper IUD; it is extremely rare for pregnancy to occur with a progesterone IUD, even if it is not perfectly positioned, whereas a copper IUD can fail to prevent pregnancy if it is sitting too low within the uterus or cervix.

EMERGENCY CONTRACEPTION

While most methods of birth control are started before having sex, emergency contraceptives are used to prevent pregnancy after unprotected sex occurs. When most people hear the term *emergency birth control*, they think of pills like Plan B, but copper IUDs placed after unprotected sex are actually the most effective method for preventing pregnancy in these situations.

There are several commercially available emergency birth control pills, also known as morning-after pills. These include pills containing a progesterone called levonorgestrel (brand names include Plan B and Julie) and a medication that acts on progesterone receptors called ulipristal (Ella). The most common brands are taken as a single pill, though some emergency birth control formulations require two doses. Levonorgestrel methods like Plan B are available over the counter in pharmacies without a prescription, but ulipristal is prescription only, so it may be more difficult to access urgently. Multiple doses of regular combined estrogen and progesterone birth control pills can also be used as emergency birth control after unprotected sex. This is called the Yuzpe method, and whereas other emergency birth control such as levonorgestrel can be bought over the counter, the Yuzpe method requires a doctor to explain how many pills must be taken depending on the dosage and type of pill that someone is using.

Emergency birth control is often mistaken for the abortion pill. They are actually very different, because emergency birth control pills don't disrupt an implanted pregnancy; they work by preventing ovulation, just like any other birth control pill.

Ulipristal is more effective than the other emergency contraceptive pills, preventing up to 98 percent of pregnancies even up to five days after unprotected sex; compared to levonorgestrel pills, which are 85 to 97 percent effective up to three days after unprotected sex. The Yuzpe method is the least effective option. Because ulipristal has the highest likelihood of preventing pregnancy, people may want to ask their doctor for a prescription to have on hand in case they ever need it.

In comparison to all of these methods, the copper IUD is the most effective form of emergency contraception, with a greater than 99 percent effectiveness rate when inserted up to five days after unprotected sex. The copper IUD is also effective regardless of body weight, whereas the pills lose some effectiveness in people who are overweight or obese: levonorgestrel pills may be ineffective above a BMI of 30, and ulipristal may be ineffective above a weight of 195 pounds or BMI of 35. If someone with a higher BMI cannot or does not want to have a copper IUD inserted, ulipristal is the next best choice.

Ultimately, the effectiveness of emergency birth control depends on ability to use it as soon as possible after unprotected sex. Many people will be able to get emergency birth control pills more quickly than they're able to schedule an urgent appointment for IUD insertion, so they should proceed with the method they can access first.

BARRIER CONTRACEPTIVES

Barrier methods work to prevent pregnancy by physically blocking sperm from reaching the egg during sex. They may be used by people who want to avoid hormones or other birth control methods or who prefer the simplicity of using a method only when having penis-in-vagina sex. Condoms also have the additional benefit of protecting users from STIs.

CONDOMS

The most commonly used barrier method is the male *condom*, which is placed over the penis when it is erect and before any genital contact occurs. Condoms are made of latex (rubber), polyurethane (plastic), or natural materials such as lambskin (which is not literally skin but tissue from lamb large intestines). The latex and polyurethane condoms are much more effective at protecting against STIs because natural materials can have microscopic holes that may allow bacteria or viruses to pass through. When used perfectly, all male condoms can prevent up to 98 percent of pregnancies, but because many couples don't use condoms perfectly, the typical effectiveness rate is 85 percent.

For perfect use, condoms should be stored properly, avoiding extremes of temperature that can weaken the material. Condoms shouldn't be kept in pockets, wallets, or cars. Packages should be opened carefully to avoid tearing. Only water- or silicone-based lubricants should be used, because oil-based lubricants, such as coconut oil, can weaken the condom material.

When putting on a condom, the reservoir tip should be held to allow space for semen, and the condom is then unrolled over the penis with the rolled side facing out. Right after ejaculation, the penis should be withdrawn from the vagina while grasping the condom around the base to prevent it from slipping off. The condom should be thrown away and a new condom used if having sex again. Condoms should never be reused or doubled up because the friction can cause tearing. Couples should read the instructions on condom packages if they are unsure how to properly use or remove condoms.

Female condoms are larger than male condoms, are made of nitrile (plastic), and have flexible rings at both ends—one to hold the condom inside the top of the vagina and one to keep the condom open at the vaginal entrance. They're called female condoms because they have traditionally been placed in the vagina but they can also be used to prevent STIs with anal sex. Female condoms are inserted before intercourse and removed and thrown away after ejaculation. Male and female condoms shouldn't be used together because the friction can tear the material. Female condoms are used less commonly than male condoms because they aren't as widely available and are more expensive. Typical effectiveness is also lower than male condoms, 79 percent, possibly because people may be less familiar with female condoms and may not know how to use them correctly.

SPONGE

The *contraceptive sponge* is a soft foam device that contains spermicide. It is moistened with water to activate the spermicide and inserted at the top of the vagina. It can be inserted up to twenty-four hours before sex and should be left in place for at least six hours after sex, but shouldn't remain in the vagina for more than thirty hours because of a small risk of toxic shock syndrome (TSS), a rare but dangerous infection caused by bacteria. The sponge can be used for multiple acts of sex within twenty-four hours and doesn't need to be replaced each time. Afterward, the user pulls on a loop attached to the sponge to remove it.

The sponge isn't as widely available as male condoms, doesn't protect against STIs, and has a higher failure rate for women who have had a vaginal birth of a baby. Typical-use effectiveness is 86 percent for people who have never given birth but 78 percent for women who have given birth, likely because the cervix can be more open after childbirth. The spermicide in the sponge can also cause vaginal irritation or burning.

SPERMICIDE AND CONTRACEPTIVE GEL

Spermicide and *contraceptive gel* are methods that are placed in the vagina before sex to immobilize or block sperm. Spermicide contains chemicals that affect the sperm's ability to swim and can also physically block the sperm from entering the cervix. It comes in the form of creams, foams, and vaginal inserts, which all have different instructions for when they must be inserted and how often they must be reapplied. By itself, spermicide is one of the least effective birth control methods, with typical-use effectiveness of only about 70 percent, but it can also be used with condoms to provide additional pregnancy protection.

There is a new prescription-only vaginal contraceptive gel that contains lactic acid, citric acid, and potassium bitartrate (Phexxi). It works by lowering the vaginal pH, which immobilizes sperm. It's inserted into the vagina with an applicator before sex, lasts for one hour, and must be reapplied with every act of intercourse. The gel can be used with condoms but shouldn't be used with the vaginal contraceptive ring. The vaginal gel has a typical-use effectiveness of 86 percent. Neither a spermicide nor the vaginal gel will protect against STIs, so doctors recommend using these methods in combination with condoms.

DIAPHRAGM AND CERVICAL CAP

The remaining barrier methods, the *diaphragm* and *cervical cap*, are no longer commonly used in the United States because they aren't as effective and convenient as other methods. The diaphragm, a flexible disk inserted into the vagina, was one of the most commonly used birth control methods in the United States until the birth control pill was introduced in the 1960s. The diaphragm and cervical cap work by holding spermicide over the cervix and blocking passage of sperm. The diaphragm is wider and covers the upper vagina and cervix, and the cervical cap is a small disk that fits snugly directly over the cervix. Both must be fitted by a healthcare professional to ensure the proper sizing. They must be filled with spermicide and inserted before sex. After each act of intercourse, the diaphragm or cervical cap must be removed, refilled with spermicide, and reinserted. They must then be left in place for at least another six hours but no longer than twenty-four hours. Users should inspect the cap or diaphragm regularly to look for any cracks or holes.

The cervical cap is less effective than the diaphragm, likely because it can be harder to place exactly over the cervix. Similar to the sponge, both have a high failure rate for people who have given birth because the opening of the cervix may be harder to block; the typical effectiveness of the cervical cap is 71 percent for people who have given birth, and 86 percent for those who have not. The typical effectiveness of the diaphragm is 87 percent. Neither the diaphragm nor the cervical cap can prevent STIs. Because condoms are far simpler to use, don't require fitting or maintenance, and prevent STIs, many people who want to use a barrier method will choose condoms rather than diaphragms or caps, but the diaphragm can be considered as an alternative for someone who wants to avoid hormones, is at low risk for STIs, and doesn't want to use an IUD or condoms.

THE WITHDRAWAL METHOD

The pullout or withdrawal method involves pulling the penis out of the vagina before ejaculation occurs. This method has a high pregnancy-prevention failure rate because fluid may escape the penis before ejaculation, and this pre-ejaculate fluid can contain sperm. Also, if pulling out does not occur before ejaculation starts, semen can get onto the vulva or the opening of the vagina and cause pregnancy. Because there is so much room for error, the typical-use effectiveness is 80 percent, meaning that one in five couples who depend on withdrawal as their only contraception will become pregnant within a year.

NATURAL FAMILY PLANNING /
FERTILITY-AWARENESS METHODS

Natural family planning is an umbrella term for methods that rely on knowledge of one's own natural cycle to identify ovulation and the fertile window when pregnancy can occur. This technique can be used to prevent pregnancy or to optimize the chances of conception for couples who are trying to conceive. Some people prefer natural methods for contraception because they don't want to use hormones, IUDs, or barrier methods or because they have experienced side effects with other types of birth control.

There are multiple different methods of natural family planning. The most basic is the *standard days method*, which involves abstaining from intercourse or using other contraceptive methods from days eight through nineteen. This method can be used only if a woman's cycles are always between twenty-six and thirty-two days long.

For the *rhythm method*, or *calendar method*, cycles are tracked on a calendar or app for several months, and the fertile window is calculated based on the longest and shortest measured cycles. To estimate the first fertile day, subtract eighteen from the shortest measured cycle length. For a person whose shortest cycle length is twenty-eight days, the first fertile day is the tenth day of the cycle. The last fertile day is estimated by taking the longest measured cycle length and subtracting eleven. If the same person has a longest cycle length of thirty-five days, the last fertile day would be the twenty-fourth. This person would need to abstain or use barrier methods from day ten to twenty-four of each cycle.

Natural family-planning methods have a higher risk of pregnancy than other contraceptive options in typical use. Many people don't have perfectly regular or predictable cycles; ovulation may occur at unexpected times; and it may be difficult to abstain or use other methods such as condoms during the entire fertile window every month. The standard and calendar methods have a typical-use effectiveness rate of about 75 percent, which is almost the same as using no method at all. Effectiveness improves when the rhythm method is combined with other natural family-planning techniques such as fertility-awareness methods.

These *fertility-awareness methods* involve tracking other signs of ovulation, including body temperature and cervical mucus, to more accurately identify when someone may be ovulating. Basal body temperature, taken in the morning before getting out of bed, will increase after ovulation occurs. The increase may be only a fraction of a degree, so a special basal-body-temperature thermometer must be used. Cervical mucus is a fluid produced by the cervix that can be found in the vagina. The consistency of this mucus changes with ovulation. Cervical mucus can be checked by inserting clean fingers into the vagina or checking the mucus that appears on underwear. Leading up to ovulation, the cervical mucus can feel sticky or tacky. Immediately before or after ovulation, the mucus looks and feels like raw egg white: clear, slippery, and stretchy when pulled between the fingers.

It's important to note that many of the signs of ovulation, such as rise in basal body temperature and egg-white cervical mucus, don't appear until after ovulation has already happened—meaning that if someone has been having unprotected sex, by the time these changes are noticeable, it's too late to prevent pregnancy. Fertility awareness should never be used as the only birth control method until someone has been tracking their cycles for several months to identify ovulation patterns. The effectiveness of fertility-awareness methods is 77 to 98 percent, and using basal body temperature, cervical mucus, and the calendar method together is necessary to achieve the higher rates of effectiveness. Checking cervical mucus and temperature daily and abstaining or using backup methods consistently over many years demands a significant amount of dedication. The effectiveness of this method also depends on the regularity of someone's cycles and is not a good method for anyone with irregular periods or who isn't be able to commit to the necessary tracking.

DECIDING ON A CONTRACEPTIVE METHOD

When choosing a birth control method that will best fit your needs, there are many factors to consider. It may feel overwhelming to hear such a long list of options, but once you weigh the pros and cons and consider your own preferences, you'll likely narrow the choices down quickly.

Questions you should consider include:

- How is the method taken or used? Are the instructions convenient for your lifestyle?
- Will you be able to remember to take or use the method on schedule? The pill may not be a great option for someone with a very irregular schedule who has difficulty remembering daily medications.
- Does the method allow for spontaneity with having sex or require significant planning, as in the case of barrier methods or spermicide? The LARC devices, such as IUDs and the Nexplanon

implant, are among the most effective contraceptives and do not require users to remember anything except when the device will expire.

While some people prefer natural family planning or barrier methods to minimize potential side effects, these methods have the highest risk of pregnancy unless very strict monitoring practices are used. This may not be a problem for someone who is open to getting pregnant but could be a serious concern for a person who doesn't want children. Since every birth control method can potentially fail, people who don't want to conceive should use a backup method such as condoms or consider sterilization if they're ready for a permanent option.

Cost or ability to access a method may limit the types of options available. In the United States, all commercial and state insurance plans are required by law to cover contraceptive methods, including the LARC devices and sterilization, but they may not necessarily cover every brand of birth control, and some birth control methods may be more expensive. For patients who don't have insurance or a gynecologist or primary care doctor to prescribe birth control, Planned Parenthood clinics can offer affordable access to all types of contraception, including via telemedicine if there is not a clinic nearby.

TAKE-HOME POINTS

- All hormonal birth control methods can be used to skip periods.
- Some birth control pills can help improve acne because they decrease levels of testosterone.
- IUDs don't cause abortions, meaning they don't disrupt pregnancies that are already implanted.
- The copper IUD is the most effective form of emergency birth control.
- Withdrawal or the pullout method has a very high failure

rate, because sperm can be present in fluid that escapes the penis before ejaculation occurs.

- Natural family-planning methods such as the calendar method have a high risk of pregnancy unless someone also tracks signs of ovulation such as basal body temperature and cervical mucus.

Hysterectomy

More than four hundred thousand people undergo hysterectomies every year in the United States, making it one of the most common surgeries performed. The word *hysterectomy* often elicits a strong negative reaction from people who have heard that it can cause menopausal symptoms such as hot flashes or loss of sex drive, or that it requires a long and difficult surgical recovery. There's a great deal of confusion about what exactly hysterectomies are, how and why they're done, and what risks they actually present, especially in terms of long-term health and well-being.

Many of the myths surrounding hysterectomies are based in historical truths but no longer reflect most people's experiences today. Women are often pleasantly surprised that there are not as many long-term health effects as they thought. While there are certainly risks like any other surgery, it's not uncommon for patients who were initially scared of hysterectomies to decide that it's the right choice for them once they learn the facts.

HYSTERECTOMY AND OOPHORECTOMY BASICS

A hysterectomy is a surgery to remove the uterus. It's important to know that the term *hysterectomy* refers to removal of the uterus only, not the ovaries. Surgical removal of the ovaries is called an oopho-rectomy. In the past, gynecologists were more likely to recommend removing the ovaries at the time of hysterectomy in order to avoid ovarian cancer, and more than 50 percent of women undergoing hysterectomies also had their ovaries removed, even as recently as 2008. That meant that women as young as their thirties were sometimes plunged into surgical menopause, leading to symptoms such as hot flashes, mood fluctuations, prolapse and incontinence, and decreased libido. Many people associate hysterectomies with these menopausal symptoms because young patients used to go through menopause when the ovaries were taken out at the time of hysterectomy. However, the uterus itself doesn't produce hormones, so removing the uterus alone doesn't cause menopause.

In 2008, ACOG recommended that the ovaries should be preserved in premenopausal women as long as the hysterectomy was not for the treatment or prevention of cancer. Therefore, the default is now to keep the ovaries in place if a hysterectomy is done unless someone has a significant risk of breast or ovarian cancer. Postmenopausal women may still choose to have the ovaries removed to decrease their risk of ovarian cancer, but they should discuss the possible health risks with their doctor.

REASONS FOR HYSTERECTOMY

Conditions that are treated with hysterectomy include uterine fibroids, adenomyosis, endometriosis involving the surface of the uterus, uterine precancer or cancer, genetic conditions that increase the risk of uterine cancer, and gender dysphoria. Hysterectomies are considered the definitive treatment for medical problems involving the uterus, which means that removal of the uterus is thought to completely eliminate these conditions. The exceptions are endometriosis and cancer, both of which can recur after hysterectomy.

There is a myth that hysterectomies are an option for anyone who simply wants to stop having periods or who doesn't want to have any future pregnancies. In reality, a hysterectomy should be used only as a treatment for serious medical conditions if less aggressive treatments have not worked. On a practical level, insurance won't cover a hysterectomy unless there is a medical indication such as fibroids or painful and heavy periods, and it definitely will not cover hysterectomy as a method for sterilization. More important in terms of someone's health and well-being, a hysterectomy is often the most invasive option for treatment. It's a major surgery involving removal of an organ, so patients should choose to have a hysterectomy only when medications or more minor procedures have failed to control bothersome symptoms. This is to minimize the risk of experiencing a complication, which is possible with any type of surgery.

SURGICAL TERMINOLOGY

Hysterectomy terminology can be confusing because the language of medical professionals sometimes differs from the language of the general public. For instance, many people think *partial hysterectomy* means a surgical removal of the uterus with the ovaries left behind. This term actually doesn't exist in medical terminology. Doctors don't call surgeries "partial hysterectomies," since it's unclear whether the ovaries, cervix, or tubes are being preserved. These differences in expressions can create confusion and miscommunication, but if patients and their doctors share a common language, they can understand each other better and work together to find the best treatment path. Here are some basic definitions:

- *Total hysterectomy*: The entire uterus is removed, including the cervix. Again, this does not mean that the ovaries are removed, just the uterus and cervix.
- *Supracervical hysterectomy*: The uterus is removed, but the cervix is left in place.
- *Salpingectomy*: The fallopian tube or tubes are removed; bilateral salpingectomy means removal of both tubes.

- *Oophorectomy / salpingo-oophorectomy*: The ovary or ovaries are removed. Since the fallopian tubes are almost always removed when the ovaries are, doctors usually use the term *salpingo-oophorectomy* for removal of the tube plus ovary.

TYPES OF HYSTERECTOMY

Before the 1990s, most hysterectomies were performed with a large abdominal incision, called a laparotomy or open hysterectomy. Open surgeries generally require a long recovery, with a delay in returning to work or exercise of up to two months. There are now minimally invasive options for hysterectomy: laparoscopic (or robotic) and vaginal.

Laparoscopic and vaginal hysterectomies allow patients to recover faster, with less pain and risk of surgical complications, so gynecologists aim to perform hysterectomies with these minimally invasively methods if possible. However, individual surgeons have different levels of training, expertise, and comfort levels performing vaginal or laparoscopic hysterectomies, and removing large fibroid uteri may require open surgery. Patients considering a hysterectomy may want to seek out opinions from surgeons with different types of expertise to explore all available options.

VAGINAL HYSTERECTOMY

Vaginal hysterectomy is done entirely through the vagina, with no abdominal incisions. This method is great for patients with uterine prolapse and is often done as part of urogynecologic surgery when the patient is undergoing other vaginal repairs for pelvic organ prolapse or incontinence.

There are technical limitations on how large a uterus can be removed through the vagina. Fibroids, in particular, can cause the uterus to become very large, sometimes even filling the pelvis or extending into the upper abdomen. A vaginal hysterectomy cannot safely remove such a large uterus because the vagina has only enough space for a small surgical incision. Furthermore, vaginal surgery doesn't allow the surgeon to evaluate or manage other conditions inside the abdomen, such as endometriosis.

Not every gynecologist offers vaginal hysterectomies; as laparoscopic surgery has become more common in recent decades, expertise in vaginal surgery has become rarer. But when they are offered, vaginal hysterectomies are excellent options because there are no abdominal incisions and recovery is usually very smooth.

LAPAROSCOPIC HYSTERECTOMY

A laparoscopic approach for hysterectomy is great for treating conditions such as scar tissue and endometriosis, which may be difficult or impossible to see with vaginal or abdominal incisions. As with vaginal hysterectomy, there are some size constraints in terms of how large a uterus can be removed laparoscopically. Fibroid uteri may need to be cut into smaller pieces to fit through an incision in the vagina or one of the abdominal incisions. This cutting process can take several hours, and is avoided in cases of suspected cancer because of the risk of spreading cancerous cells. Even if the uterus doesn't need to be cut for removal, laparoscopy often takes more time to perform than open surgery because the instruments are small; therefore the patient has to be healthy enough to tolerate the physical stresses of a longer time under anesthesia.

Laparoscopic surgery can also be performed using a surgical robot. Some surgeons may prefer robotics because it makes certain skills, such as laparoscopic suturing, easier to perform, but ultimately the robot is simply a tool controlled by the surgeon, not a different or superior type of surgery.

ABDOMINAL OR OPEN HYSTERECTOMY

An abdominal or open hysterectomy is performed through a single large incision in the lower abdomen. It's used for removal of very large fibroid uteri, or if there is concern for uterine cancer and the uterus cannot be cut into smaller pieces for removal. Abdominal hysterectomy may also be recommended for people who have medical conditions that might make a longer surgery more dangerous. Given the larger incision, open hysterectomy requires a longer recovery than laparoscopic or vaginal hysterectomy and carries more risk of complications such as infections or hernias.

HYSTERECTOMY AND THE CERVIX

Patients often ask if the cervix should be left in place when a hysterectomy is done because they've heard that it is necessary for sexual or bladder health or to prevent vaginal prolapse. Many studies have shown that there is no medical benefit to leaving the cervix behind. There's no difference in sexual satisfaction, bladder function, or risk of prolapse. Therefore, the default is to remove the cervix with hysterectomy, as this has the benefit of eliminating the risk of cervical cancer. In the United States, if the cervix is removed with a hysterectomy and the patient did not have precancer of the cervix in the previous twenty years, the patient can stop getting Pap smears because these are just tests for cervical cancer.

Some people feel their cervix is an important part of their personal sexual response or ability to achieve orgasm. If this is the case, it's definitely worth discussing the risks and benefits of leaving versus removing the cervix. Sometimes the cervix might also be preserved for surgical safety; for example, prior cesarean sections can cause scarring between the bladder and cervix, and if severe scar tissue is present, a surgeon may decide to leave the cervix in place to decrease the risk of injuring the bladder.

MENOPAUSE-RELATED HEALTH RISKS

Even if the ovaries are preserved, patients who have hysterectomies seem to experience menopausal symptoms a few years earlier on average than people who haven't had them. There's also an increased risk of cardiovascular disease. These effects may be because there are small blood vessels between the uterus and ovaries that are sealed and cut during hysterectomy, and this change in blood flow might alter the function of the ovaries.

There's no definite pattern in risk of pelvic organ prolapse and incontinence except that patients who already had these problems before surgery may have a higher risk of worsening prolapse or incontinence after hysterectomy.

SEXUAL HEALTH

Patients often wonder about long-term sexual health after hysterectomy, and there are myths that a hysterectomy will lead to loss of libido or ability to orgasm. Researchers have looked at several different factors, including hysterectomy type and whether the ovaries or cervix were removed, in many studies about sexual function and satisfaction after hysterectomy. Most studies show no long-term change in sexual function with any type of hysterectomy unless the ovaries were removed, and in several cases, sexual satisfaction actually improved after having a hysterectomy. This is because patients undergoing hysterectomy almost always had severe pain or bleeding issues that were affecting their sexual function or libido, and these problems were eliminated by surgery. There may initially be some discomfort with sex after the recommended postoperative period of pelvic rest, but this usually resolves with time, lubrication, and patience.

It's important to note that if the ovaries are removed, there can be decreasing of libido, vaginal dryness, and pain with sex, similar to what is experienced during nonsurgical menopause.

GENERAL SURGICAL RISKS

Hysterectomies have the same basic risks of any other surgery in the abdomen or pelvis. These surgical risks include infection, bleeding, the need for blood transfusion, development of blood clots in the veins, anesthesia complications including heart or lung issues, and injury to other organs, such as the bowel, bladder, and ureters.

DECIDING ON A HYSTERECTOMY

The decision to have a hysterectomy is a very personal one. If you're considering a hysterectomy, you may be inundated with outside opinions. Friends and family might have strong feelings about hysterectomies based on societal myths. A doctor may say that you must have a hysterectomy even if you don't want one. On the flip side, a doctor may say you shouldn't have a hysterectomy even if you feel you need one—for instance, if you're in your twenties or you haven't had children. Ultimately, the decision is yours—and as always, if you don't feel comfortable with what a doctor is recommending, seek a second opinion to discuss your options.

TAKE-HOME POINTS

- More than four hundred thousand people undergo hysterectomies every year in the United States.
- Hysterectomies involve removal of the uterus, not the ovaries.
- There is a higher long-term risk of cardiovascular disease if someone has a hysterectomy, even if the ovaries remain in place.
- Sexual function usually remains the same or even improves after having a hysterectomy.

Tubal Sterilization

After the fall of *Roe v. Wade* in 2022, many people in the United States rushed to seek permanent sterilization procedures, particularly tubal ligations. I personally saw patients from as far away as Florida come to my practice in Pennsylvania, and in the weeks following the fall of *Roe*, up to fifty people a day called my office to schedule consults for sterilization. Many of these patients had previously tried to get a tubal ligation but had been denied by doctor after doctor, often because they were child-free, in their twenties, or unmarried. Even mothers of multiple children and people in their thirties or forties reported experiencing the same rejection. The conclusions of these stories were always the same: gynecologists refused to do the procedure because they said that the patient might regret it someday.

Frustrated but feeling powerless, people often accepted this status quo—until the reversal of *Roe* suddenly criminalized abortion in several states. Faced with a terrifying and uncertain future where birth control failure could mean being forced to carry an undesired pregnancy or risking jail time for having an abortion, they sought out sterilization consults with newfound urgency. Child-free groups on social media, one of the largest being a child-free subreddit with over one million members, have long published directories of doctors willing to do sterilizations regardless of a patient's age, marital status, or number of children. Post-*Roe*, people desperate to get a sterilization traveled across state lines to see doctors on these lists.

TUBAL STERILIZATION BASICS

If someone with a uterus wants to have a sterilization, it is done by blocking or removing the fallopian tubes so that sperm can't reach the eggs. In colloquial terms, this is called getting your tubes tied, having a tubal ligation, or simply a tubal. It is no longer common to literally tie the tubes, but most people still use these expressions.

Gynecologists now often surgically remove both fallopian tubes entirely for sterilization; this is called a *bilateral salpingectomy*. The benefits are that salpingectomy has the lowest pregnancy risk of any tubal sterilization method, and salpingectomy also decreases the chances of getting ovarian cancer, since many ovarian cancers actually start in the fallopian tube.

A tubal can be done laparoscopically or right after delivering a baby. Postpartum tubal ligations can be performed directly through a C-section incision. With vaginal deliveries, the uterus remains high in the abdomen for a day or so after the baby is born, and the tubes can be reached through a small incision made in the belly button. The tubes can be removed entirely, as above, or a small portion of the tube may be literally tied with dissolvable stitches and the tied-off portion cut out, cauterized, or both.

Laparoscopic tubal sterilization can be performed by using instruments to burn or cut out a smaller portion of the middle of the tube without removing the entire thing. Other techniques for laparoscopic tubal ligation include using small clips or rubber rings to block off the tubes. The clip and ring methods are easier to reverse if patients change their minds later, since only a small portion of the tube is damaged, but they also have the highest risk of pregnancy since the devices can slip off. Clips and rings can also cause some pain after placement. For these reasons, these devices are less common now that salpingectomy has become more popular.

REVERSIBILITY

Salpingectomy is never reversible, since the entire tube is taken out. For the methods that don't involve removing the entire tube, it might be possible for the undamaged parts of the tube to be stitched back together in a *tubal reversal*. Unfortunately, it's never a guarantee that any tubal can be reversed. Heat from cautery may have caused too much damage to the remaining tube; the repaired tube can scar, leading to risk of ectopic pregnancies; and tubal reversal is an expensive surgery that isn't covered by insurance. For all of these reasons, patients should consider any sort of tubal sterilization only if they plan never to be pregnant in the future, or if they'd be willing to do IVF and bypass the tubes entirely if they ever changed their minds.

Between 5 to 25 percent of people who have a tubal will regret having it done, with the highest rate of regret among people who were in their early twenties at the time of surgery. Factors such as having a new partner who wants a child may also contribute to regret. Because expensive, invasive methods such as tubal reversal surgery and IVF would be needed to conceive after a tubal, doctors may worry that patients will hold them liable if they change their minds in the future. However, the vast majority of people who choose to have a tubal are very happy with their choice.

Gynecologists sometimes refuse to perform a sterilization if they feel the woman will regret it in the future, particularly if the patient doesn't have children or is in their twenties. Many people have told me that a doctor said they couldn't have a sterilization until they'd met an arbitrary and often unrealistic goal, such as giving birth to both male and female children, having more than four children, or reaching an advanced age such as forty-five.

While there are no existing studies on how often men versus women are turned down for sterilization, the decision for vasectomy is undoubtably not questioned nearly as often as the decision for tubal ligation. Cultural factors, including gender-role expectations, are at play in the assumption that a person with the physical ability to be a mother will eventually want to be one or will someday want more children, even if they state clearly that they don't. People may regret almost every decision they make in life—undergoing any medical procedure, getting married, deciding to have children. But society isn't allowed to strip adults' rights to make these decisions simply because they may regret them later. Adults with the capacity to make their own medical decisions should have the right to choose sterilization for themselves after being adequately counseled, even if there is a risk of regret.

LEGAL GUIDELINES

There are different restrictions for access to sterilization procedures. These will differ depending on local and national laws as well as the guidelines of each insurance plan. State insurance plans such as Medicaid have a minimum age of twenty-one as well as a mandatory thirty-day waiting period between signing a tubal ligation consent and receiving the surgery.

There is a dark history behind these age restrictions and waiting-period requirements. Between 1909 and 1979, several government-organized eugenics campaigns were carried out in the United States, forcibly sterilizing more than sixty thousand women, primarily women of color, members of poor populations, and people with physical disabilities. Most of these sterilizations were performed on residents of institutions for the "feeble-minded" or "mentally deficient." Now, to protect vulnerable patients from being sterilized without adequate consent, state insurance laws ensure that people getting a tubal sterilization are of an age and mental capacity to consent for this procedure. Medicaid and other public insurance plans also require the month-long waiting period to ensure people have time to think about their decision and change their minds if they wish.

Unfortunately, what sounds like a very reasonable set of rules to protect patients may actually prevent people from getting tubals. For instance, a Medicaid patient starting prenatal care late in pregnancy may not sign the required forms far enough in advance to get a tubal done when they have their baby. They would need to return to have surgery later, which may not be possible due to childcare or work requirements. There needs to be a balance between protecting patients and putting up roadblocks that can obstruct access to care.

SURGICAL RISKS

Every surgery has risks, as I've discussed in prior chapters. For any abdominal surgery, there are risks of infection, bleeding, blood clots in the veins, and injury to the other organs or blood vessels in the abdomen or pelvis, as well as the medical risks of being under anesthesia.

Many people ask if getting their tubes tied or removed will affect hormones or periods. There are rumors that post-tubal syndrome, which doesn't actually exist, supposedly leads to mood problems or period abnormalities. Many studies have looked at hormones and health after tubals and salpingectomies, and there are no significant differences in hormone levels, mood, or periods. Similar to hysterectomies, sexual satisfaction remains the same or even improves after sterilization; this is likely because people feel less stress related to risk of pregnancy, or perhaps because they stop using birth control, which can affect libido. Some people think that the tubes are needed for hormones to travel from the ovaries to the uterus, but this is not true; hormones travel through the bloodstream, not the tube, so periods should be the same even after the tubes are blocked or removed. The surgeon will be careful to avoid harming the ovaries or the ovarian blood vessels during the surgery, because damage to the ovaries can affect hormones.

Stopping hormonal birth control after getting your tubes tied may cause things like acne, irregular or painful periods, and mood swings. This is because hormonal birth control can regulate periods and lighten flow and cramping and can also decrease premenstrual mood swings and hormonal acne. Stopping the birth control after it's no longer needed unmasks symptoms that had been suppressed by the birth control. For these reasons, if patients are happy with the menstrual suppression and other benefits they receive from birth control, they may choose to continue taking it after having a sterilization, even if they no longer need it for pregnancy prevention.

STERILIZATION CONSULTS

During any surgical consult, your doctor will take your medical history and, if needed, do a brief physical exam to assess your safety for surgery. They will discuss the risks and alternatives for the procedure. For a sterilization, that includes the risks of regret and alternatives such as reversible birth control methods. If you have a monogamous, long-term male partner, the option of a vasectomy will be discussed because it is less invasive than a tubal and has lower surgical risks.

Patients who are at all uncertain about the decision will always be encouraged to choose a reversible birth control method until they reach the point that they are absolutely sure. But if you are certain you want a sterilization, are legally able to consent for a surgical procedure, and your doctor has determined that you are able to safely undergo surgery, you should be allowed to proceed. The gynecologist should explain how they perform sterilizations; what to expect before, during, and after the surgery; and review the surgical consent form with you, including any additional forms required for state insurances such as Medicaid.

If you feel uncomfortable with a doctor's recommendations, please try to seek out a second opinion if at all possible. The child-free subreddit and similar surgeon lists may help identify other doctors near you.

TAKE-HOME POINTS

- Bilateral salpingectomy, a sterilization procedure that removes the fallopian tubes completely, lowers the risk of developing ovarian cancer.

cont'd

- State insurance plans such as Medicaid have a minimum age of twenty-one to have a tubal ligation and require a thirty-day wait between signing a tubal ligation consent and getting the surgery.

- Hormones and periods don't change after a tubal ligation.

- Vasectomies are less invasive and have fewer surgical risks than tubal sterilizations.

- If your doctor refuses to perform a tubal ligation, you can seek a second opinion. Child-free social media groups maintain lists of doctors who are willing to perform sterilizations for patients who don't have children.

Abortion

One in four women in the United States will have an abortion in her lifetime. Even if you aren't personally in need of abortion care, you almost certainly know someone who has had an abortion or who will need one someday. The abortion debate ultimately has to do with people's right to bodily autonomy and their ability to make healthcare decisions for themselves. Also, very complex medical and social factors go into the decision to end a pregnancy, and banning or criminalizing abortion can put lives at risk.

ABORTION BASICS

There is an incredible amount of misinformation about abortion, starting with the basic definition of the word. An abortion is simply a medical term referring to the ending of pregnancy. This includes miscarriage. When most people use the word *abortion*, they usually mean a situation where the pregnant person decides to end the pregnancy; this is known as an elective or therapeutic abortion.

A myth perpetuated by the pro-life community is that people get abortions just because they are irresponsible and don't use birth control. The reality is that every birth control method can fail and result in pregnancy, and people can become pregnant as the result of rape or incest. Many carefully planned and much-desired pregnancies also end in abortion for medical reasons. More than half of women who terminate a pregnancy already have children, so they are not simply trying to avoid parental responsibilities.

People may choose to have an elective abortion because they don't want to be pregnant or give birth or cannot have a child because of financial, social, medical, or other circumstances. There are also many situations where there is a medical reason for abortion because the pregnant person's health is at risk. These scenarios include premature rupture of membranes; placental abruption or separation from the uterine wall, which can cause hemorrhaging; severe preeclampsia; severe heart, lung, or kidney issues that are worsened by pregnancy; or if the patient has cancer that cannot be treated while pregnant. There are also fetal anomalies that are either incompatible with life or that would lead to a life of painful medical procedures for the child, and parents may choose to end the pregnancy rather than allow their child to suffer. Contrary to the rhetoric that life is being protected by banning abortion, many cases of abortion are performed with the goal of preserving life: protecting the health of the pregnant person or preventing the suffering of the child.

After the fall of *Roe v. Wade*, several states enacted abortion bans except when necessary for the life of the mother. Unfortunately, these exceptions are not the panacea that many believe they are—and in fact, they may put patients' lives at risk. Because so much of medical care is not black or white, it may not be clear that a patient's life is sufficiently at risk to legally allow for termination of pregnancy until it is too late. Abortion laws provide no clear guidelines as to what constitutes a threat to life, leaving doctors and patients in a dangerous limbo. Because the penalties for performing an abortion in places where it is criminalized include jail time or loss of medical licensure, healthcare providers are forced to err on the side of inaction if there is uncertainty about whether a situation is truly life-threatening.

Since an abortion ban was enacted in Texas, several women have come forward to the press with stories of experiencing premature rupture of membranes early in pregnancy, and although their likelihood of staying pregnant until a viable gestational age was reached was extremely low, because there was no imminent risk to their health, doctors were legally unable to end the pregnancies until the women developed uterine infections and became septic and critically ill. This exact medical scenario led to tragedy in Ireland in 2012, when a woman named Savita Halappanavar broke her water at seventeen weeks' gestation. Because abortion was illegal in Ireland at the time, doctors felt they could not perform an abortion while there was still a fetal heartbeat. They waited until she became critically ill before ending the pregnancy, but by that time it was too late to save her. Savita's death shocked the people of Ireland and contributed to the landslide vote in 2018 that overturned the country's constitutional ban on abortion.

ABORTION AND PUBLIC HEALTH

Banning or criminalizing abortion has never stopped abortions from occurring. In fact, the Guttmacher Institute reports that most countries that restrict abortion actually have higher rates of abortion than those that do not, because contraceptive use also tends to be lower in these countries. The WHO estimates that twenty-five million unsafe abortions occur annually; and in countries where abortion is illegal or difficult to access, unsafe abortion is a significant cause of maternal mortality, resulting in the deaths of tens of thousands of people a year worldwide. Millions more suffer from long-term health complications as a result of unsafe abortions.

In the 1950s and 1960s, prior to the 1973 passage of *Roe v. Wade* by the Supreme Court, which protected the constitutional right to abortion, an estimated 200,000 to 1.2 million illegal abortions were performed per year in the United States. A *New England Journal of Medicine* article on the dangers of illegal abortion prior to *Roe* detailed the horrors witnessed by doctors and medical examiners during this era: women dying of sepsis or air emboli; perforation of organs by objects such as coat hangers, knitting needles, or tree branches used in attempted self-induced abortions. Because such complications were likely highly underreported in the pre-*Roe* era, it is hard to know the exact number of people who suffered. However, the same *New England Journal* article notes that deaths from abortion virtually disappeared in the United States after abortion was legalized in 1973, and similar findings were reported in Romania and South Africa once abortion restrictions were lifted.

Safe, legal abortions performed by trained medical professionals have far lower health risks than pregnancy or childbirth. It's well established that states with the most restrictive abortion laws also have markedly higher maternal mortality, because these states also tend to have higher rates of poverty and less access to healthcare for pregnant people. Data from 2020 showed that states with restrictive abortion laws had 62 percent higher maternal mortality than states where abortion was more accessible. Researchers using this data estimated that a nationwide ban on abortion would increase maternal mortality by 24 percent overall and 39 percent among Black people, who face disproportionately higher risks of death in pregnancy due to multiple factors, including structural racism and implicit biases in healthcare.

Abortion is not only an individual medical decision; it is an important public health and health justice issue. In fact, the WHO considers access to safe abortion to be one of the most important factors in decreasing maternal mortality worldwide. After *Roe v. Wade* was overturned in 2022, every major medical association in the United States dedicated to reproductive and women's health—including the American College of Obstetricians and Gynecologists, the American Society of Reproductive Medicine, the Society of Maternal Fetal Medicine, and the American Medical Association—issued a joint statement denouncing the decision. They emphasized the medical dangers of restricting access to safe abortion care and noted that these risks would particularly harm women in marginalized communities.

COUNSELING AND EVALUATION

In most countries, even if abortion is legal, strict guidelines must be met in order for an abortion to be performed. People seeking an abortion need to discuss the legal regulations in their state or region as well as their particular medical situation with their doctor. Generally, patients must be counseled on the risks of the procedure and offered alternatives such as adoption. The dating of the pregnancy must be estimated as accurately as possible, as most laws have gestational age cutoffs. To determine the gestational age, doctors ask the date of the last menstrual period and whether the person's periods are regular. If someone has irregular cycles or doesn't know the date of the last period, or if there is concern for a possible ectopic pregnancy or miscarriage, an ultrasound may be required. Some states require pelvic ultrasounds to be done on all patients seeking an abortion, although this is medically unnecessary in most first-trimester abortions according to ACOG.

Many people, including lawmakers, don't realize that the gestational age of pregnancy is not the number of weeks since someone finds out that they're pregnant or after a missed period, but rather the number of weeks since the first day of the last period. This means that someone is already several weeks pregnant before a period is missed or a pregnancy test can detect the pregnancy. This is the reason that many people don't know they're expecting until they are at least six to eight weeks pregnant, which is the gestational age cutoff for abortion in some states.

MEDICAL ABORTION

For early pregnancies, medications may be used to end the pregnancy; this is referred to as a medical abortion. In the United States, these pill regimens include a combination of mifepristone (RU-486), an antiprogesterone medication, and misoprostol, a prostaglandin. Since progesterone supports the pregnancy, blocking progesterone can cause the placenta to separate and the pregnancy to detach. Misoprostol causes the cervix to soften and open and the uterus to contract. In the United States, medical abortion with mifepristone is approved by the FDA for use up to ten weeks' gestational age.

Emergency birth control pills are often mistakenly considered abortion pills by the general public, politicians, and the media. This is incorrect, because emergency birth control works like any other birth control pill: by preventing ovulation and pregnancy. It does not cause the abortion of an implanted pregnancy as mifepristone does.

Medical abortions allow a patient to avoid more invasive surgical procedures, and most people needing an abortion early in pregnancy prefer the medical option. Medications may be obtained through tele-medicine consult or mail delivery, which makes it easier to access treatment quickly and helps preserve confidentiality. Several studies have shown the safety of obtaining medical abortion prescriptions remotely, and ACOG and the National Abortion Federation (NAF) support the ability of patients to access medical abortion without requiring an in-person examination.

The limitations of medical abortion are that patients may experience bleeding and pain with passing the pregnancy tissue, and it's possible to need a procedure to remove the rest of the tissue if it doesn't completely pass. There must always be a plan for follow-up to ensure that the abortion is completed safely. But ultimately, medical abortion is usually extremely effective, with 95 to 98 percent of people having complete resolution of the pregnancy with treatment.

SURGICAL ABORTION

Though medical abortion is very effective and allows people the privacy to treat themselves at home, some people either choose or need to have a surgical abortion. This may be because the pregnancy is further along than can be treated with abortion pills, or it may be because the patient doesn't want to experience the bleeding or pain that can be felt with passing a pregnancy at home.

Dilation and curettages (D and Cs) are surgical abortions performed during the first trimester and dilation and evacuations (D and Es) in the second trimester, though sometimes these terms are used interchangeably to refer to a surgical abortion procedure. All surgical abortions are done by gently opening the cervix and using suction or instruments to remove pregnancy tissue from the uterus. These procedures are usually performed with some sort of anesthesia, at a minimum local anesthetic injected into or next to the cervix, with or without sedation. Some first-trimester abortions may be done in the office setting for a patient's comfort and convenience, but many D and Cs and D and Es are performed in an operating room if someone wishes to have anesthesia, or for safety considerations such as risk of bleeding. Surgical abortion procedures have some risks of injury to the cervix or uterus and scar tissue formation in the cavity of the uterus. Both medical and surgical abortions have risks of infection, bleeding, and retained pregnancy tissue that may require additional procedures to completely remove.

SECOND-TRIMESTER ABORTION

It is a myth that there are a large number of late-term abortions being performed. First, because the expression *late-term abortion* is never actually used by medical providers and is extremely misleading, as it implies that abortions are being done close to term when a fetus would be viable outside of the womb. Most states have restrictions on abortion after viability, which, depending on local resources, is around twenty-three to twenty-four weeks of gestation. The vast majority of abortions in the United States, up to 93 percent, are done in the first trimester. Only 6 percent of abortions are done at fourteen to twenty weeks, and only 1 percent after twenty-one weeks. Access to second-trimester abortion is more limited than first-trimester because of legal restrictions, and because there are fewer doctors who have the specialized training required to manage these complex cases. When second-trimester abortions are needed, they are often under very difficult social, emotional, and medical circumstances, and these decisions are never made lightly.

Patients may not have an abortion until the second trimester because of a delay in discovering that they are pregnant, because of barriers to accessing care, or because of medical situations that develop later in pregnancy. Abortions for fetal anomalies usually happen in the second trimester simply because the ultrasound to check anatomy for routine prenatal care is not performed until eighteen to twenty-two weeks. Obstetric complications such as ruptured membranes, pre-eclampsia, or abruptions may occur in the second trimester. Minors are more likely to have a second-trimester abortion than adults for several reasons: children and teenagers may not understand that they are pregnant until there are unmistakable physical signs or an adult notices these changes; they may be scared to report a pregnancy to parents or guardians; or they may not know how to get medical care.

Second-trimester abortions can be performed by D and E or by inducing labor and allowing the fetus to deliver vaginally. Someone may choose to induce labor in order to avoid a surgical procedure, or to be able to hold the fetus in cases of desired pregnancies that are ended for medical reasons. However, experiencing labor may be emotionally and physically painful, which is why D and Es are offered as an alternative. As always, this is a very personal decision that is often made after extensive discussion with medical specialists.

TAKE-HOME POINTS

- One in four women in the United States will have an abortion in her lifetime.
- Banning or criminalizing abortion does not stop abortions from occurring. Most countries that restrict abortion actually have higher rates of abortion than those that do not.
- Mifepristone (RU-486) is the medical abortion pill. This pill is different from emergency birth control, which prevents pregnancy and does not cause an abortion.

- Ninety percent of abortions in the United States are done in the first trimester. Only 1 percent occur after twenty-one weeks.
- Abortions are medical treatments, and like any other medical decision, people should have the autonomy to choose the option that is best for their health and well-being in consultation with their doctors.

Gynecologic Exams and Office Procedures

Whether it's your first visit or your fiftieth, it may be nerve-racking to go to the gynecologist. It's common and normal to feel anxious about pelvic exams or procedures, and past experiences may make someone feel particularly vulnerable. A previous exam may have been painful, healthcare providers may not have explained what was happening or listened to your concerns, or you may have a history of sexual assault or trauma. Transgender men or nonbinary patients can feel especially uncomfortable going to an OB-GYN office because they're worried about being misgendered or experience gender dysphoria during pelvic exams. Whatever background you bring to the visit, you deserve to be respected and supported so that you can get the care that you need.

This chapter will discuss what to expect during a gynecology appointment, including routine exams and office procedures, and strategies for preventing discomfort. I'll also cover how to have an effective dialogue with your healthcare provider about your goals for care, concerns, and questions. I hope these tools will empower you to go into your next gynecologic appointment feeling informed, and make your experience as comfortable and positive as possible.

COMMUNICATION

Your appointment will start with a conversation with the doctor or healthcare provider. An essential part of every medical appointment is learning about you, and providing the information you need to make health decisions. Communication with your providers can be as important or even more important than any exams or procedures, because this is how they will understand what your medical needs are, and what you require in terms of treatment and support.

At the beginning of the visit, a medical assistant, nurse, or doctor will ask about your medical history, any symptoms you may be experiencing, and if you have any particular concerns you want addressed. This is the time when you should bring up specific medical problems or questions about your health. In this initial conversation, please also tell your provider if you have any history of trauma or pain that might make you particularly nervous about pelvic exams or procedures.

Highlight any priorities that you want to focus on during that visit or for your care in general. Telling the provider up front what issues are most pressing or important to you will help make the best use of your appointment time. The same is true for your perspectives on certain categories of treatment, such as whether you want to consider hormonal medications or surgeries. The provider will discuss all of your options, but if they know that you do not want surgery or that you prefer not to take hormones, they can prioritize other treatments.

If you have any questions, you should ask your doctor to clarify. For example, if you don't fully understand why a test is being recommended or what your options are for pain control with a procedure, ask for more information until you feel comfortable. Tell your provider why you are hesitant or confused about a test or treatment. The provider should explain the procedures so that you can make an informed decision.

It may be helpful to bring someone with you to the appointment—a partner, relative, or friend—who can help you take notes, ask questions, remember information, or hold your hand during an exam or procedure. Having a trusted support person there may help to relieve any anxiety you may have.

There may be times when the provider recommends a procedure or treatment you do not want. You can be honest and say, "I'm not comfortable with that option; I'd prefer to do something different." Try to explain why you are concerned, because there might be a solution; for instance, if you're worried about feeling pain with a procedure, pain control options could be offered.

In some circumstances, you may feel that the provider is not listening to you, not giving you the information that you need, or not offering a treatment option that you are interested in. You can explain why the recommendations are not a good fit for you and ask if there are any other possibilities that could better meet your needs. If not, request a referral to another doctor or try to find one on your own through word of mouth or online resources. It's common for doctors not to be experts in every aspect of gynecologic care, and you may need to see a specialist for more options.

ROUTINE GYNECOLOGIC EXAMS AND PROCEDURES

Annual gynecologic exams are preventive-care visits meant to monitor your overall reproductive health. The discussion at the beginning of the appointment will include questions about periods, sexual health, plans for fertility, need for birth control, and any vaginal, urinary, perimenopausal, or menopausal symptoms. The healthcare provider will also check vital signs, discuss general health, and recommend screening for cancers such as breast, cervical, and colon cancer. Testing is offered based on age and risk factors for cancers and STIs.

Once the interview is done, the next part of the appointment may involve an exam of the breasts and pelvis. The doctor or medical assistant will ask you undress fully or from the waist down and will provide you with a gown and sheet to cover yourself. They should step out to give you privacy while you're undressing. This may happen at the very beginning of the appointment or after you've had a discussion with the healthcare provider. If you feel more comfortable speaking with the doctor while dressed, you can request to conduct the interview portion of the visit before undressing.

There are three basic parts to pelvic exams. First, the healthcare provider performs a vulvar inspection to look for any skin changes or irritation. Then, they'll use a speculum to check the vaginal walls and perform a Pap smear or STI testing if necessary, and last, they'll conduct an internal exam to check for uterine or ovarian masses or pain. This internal exam is performed by the doctor inserting one or two fingers into the vagina while pressing on the abdomen to feel the uterus and ovaries.

The entire pelvic exam should take only a minute or two. You'll be asked to place your feet on stirrups and lie back on an examination table. A paper or cloth drape will cover the rest of your body during the exam. A nurse or medical assistant will also be present in the room to assist with the exam and serve as a chaperone. Any exam of the breasts or genitals should be performed with a chaperone present for your comfort and security, no matter the gender of the provider, and you have the right to request a chaperone if one is not present. Also, if you feel more comfortable with a partner or support person there, you can request that.

For most people, the internal portions of a pelvic exam, particularly the speculum insertion, can feel like an intense pressure, menstrual cramping, or stretching or burning discomfort of the vaginal walls. The exam can feel more painful for people who have never had vaginal intercourse or who have vulvovaginal pain or dryness of the vagina from menopause or testosterone use.

To make the pelvic exam as comfortable as possible, fully relax your legs, buttocks, and vaginal muscles before the exam. Tensing your leg and pelvic muscles will tighten the vaginal walls around the speculum or examining fingers, and that can be painful. Because it's common to feel anxious, you can always ask for a few moments to take deep breaths, relax your muscles, and feel ready before the exam. Some techniques to relax the pelvic muscles include letting your knees drop outward to the sides and pretending to sink into the exam table like it is a soft mattress or bed of sand. Some people feel more prepared for the exam if they are shown the speculum and brushes beforehand, whereas others prefer not to see the instruments at all. You can request whichever makes you feel more at ease.

Some people may feel they are not able to undergo pelvic exams due to severe pain or emotional distress associated with vaginal examinations. A healthcare provider should always take these concerns seriously. They should discuss whether the exam is truly essential, if there are risks of skipping it, and whether there are options to make the exam more comfortable. If you experience significant anxiety with pelvic exams, you can ask your provider if they can prescribe a short-acting oral antianxiety medication like alprazolam (Xanax) to be taken before appointments. In some cases, it may be possible for exams or procedures to be done under sedation. Every individual has the right to bodily autonomy and you can always choose which medical procedures you're willing to undergo, though it is important to know that skipping tests such as Pap smears and STI screenings can put your health at risk. Your doctor's role is to give you guidance and care, but ultimately the decisions are up to you.

SPECULUMS AND PAP SMEARS

The most anxiety-provoking part of a routine visit may be the speculum exam and Pap smear. A *speculum* is an instrument made of metal or plastic with narrow arms; it resembles a duck's bill. The speculum is used to gently open the walls of the vagina so that the cervix can be seen by the examiner. Speculums may be used for Pap smears, IUD insertions, colposcopies, and obtaining swabs for certain STI tests.

Many people don't realize that there are several different sizes of speculum. There are very small pediatric sizes for patients who have never been sexually active or who have narrowing of the vagina from menopause or testosterone use, and longer and wider speculums for those with weakening of the vaginal walls from childbirth. Because the speculum insertion can be the most uncomfortable part of the pelvic exam, healthcare providers generally try to use the smallest possible speculum that allows them to see the cervix. If you've had pain or discomfort with even the smallest adult-size speculum in the past, you can request a pediatric speculum before the doctor begins the examination. When the speculum is inserted, if you feel sharp or severe pain, ask the provider to stop and remove it. Since the doctor might not necessarily have used the smallest speculum, you can ask if there is a smaller size available. The drawback of using a pediatric speculum is that the provider may not be able to examine or test the entire cervix, which is why it isn't usually used for adult patients, but a limited view is better than causing severe pain or getting no view at all if someone finds the exam too painful.

Speculum exams are most commonly used to perform Pap smears. Once the speculum has been inserted, a Pap smear can be obtained with either a small brush with soft plastic bristles or a small flat spatula that is used to touch the cervix and pick up cells for inspection. It's a myth that the cervix is scraped during a Pap smear; the brush or spatula is simply rubbed gently across the surface of the cervix, and loose cells are picked up and placed in a vial of liquid. The Pap collection should only take a few seconds. You may feel some cramping during or after the procedure and may have spotting afterward. The cells obtained in a Pap smear are inspected under the microscope in a lab for precancerous or cancerous changes and can also be tested for infections such as HPV, gonorrhea, and chlamydia.

Another misconception is that Pap smears check for abnormalities of all the pelvic organs, including the ovaries and uterus, but this isn't the case—the Pap smear is only meant to be a test of the cervix. Some people also believe that speculum exams and Pap smears are the same, but speculums can be used to check the vaginal walls or cervix without the provider obtaining a Pap smear. This happens commonly in the emergency department, where a speculum exam may be part of an evaluation for heavy bleeding or infection. Pap smears are almost never done in emergency departments, but many patients think that they had a Pap in the ED because a speculum was used. Whenever you get a pelvic exam, the healthcare provider should explain what they're checking for and what tests are being done. If this doesn't happen or you are unsure, ask the provider to clarify.

Another myth is that Pap smears can't be performed while patients are on their period. In the past, doctors performed Pap smears by putting cells directly from the brush onto a microscope slide, so Paps weren't done during periods or after sex because blood, semen, or lubricants could obscure the cervical cells. But in the late 1990s, liquid-based Pap smears were introduced, and with these modern systems, cervical cells can be separated out from blood and semen. Now, a Pap can be done almost anytime except perhaps during a particularly heavy period when there is a large amount of blood in the vagina.

COLPOSCOPY

If your Pap smear shows abnormal cervical cells or tests positive for a strain of HPV that poses a higher risk for cervical precancer and cancer, your doctor will ask you to return a few weeks after the Pap for a colposcopy. A colposcopy is a procedure used to obtain cervical biopsies to test for cervical precancer and cancer. A colposcope is simply a camera with a bright light that magnifies the view of the cervix. During a colposcopy, a speculum is inserted and the cervix is washed with a vinegar solution called acetic acid that highlights abnormal cells and makes them visible as white areas. The acetic acid may feel cold and wet or may cause a mild stinging or burning sensation of the vaginal walls. Your doctor will use the colposcope to closely examine the cervix and take small biopsies of the tissue. Cervical biopsies remove only small pieces of tissue a few millimeters wide. The biopsy can feel like nothing at all, a quick pinch, a cramp, or a sharp pain. To test the cells inside the canal of the cervix, the provider will scrape the area with a narrow instrument or brush; this is called an endocervical curettage. The endocervical curettage usually feels like a strong menstrual cramp.

People may be worried about feeling pain during a colposcopy or they may have previously experienced a painful colposcopy. While studies show that oral pain medications and topical numbing gels are not effective, there is mixed evidence about topical numbing sprays. Local anesthetic—numbing medicine that is injected into the cervix with a needle—isn't usually used during colposcopies because it can disrupt the surface of the cervix and make it difficult for your doctor to see abnormal areas, and insertion of the needle can sometimes be as painful or more painful than the biopsy itself. Distraction techniques such as coughing when biopsies are taken, listening to music, or watching a video during the procedure have been shown to be just as effective as local anesthetic in randomized trials. If you're nervous about the procedure, you can ask your doctor to prescribe an antianxiety medication that can be taken before the colposcopy or you can ask whether there is an option to perform the procedure under sedation in the office or operating room.

LEEP

Most of the time, people undergoing colposcopy won't end up needing any treatment except close monitoring. However, if biopsies show cervical precancer or if results are ambiguous and the doctor is worried about possible precancer, a loop electrosurgical excision procedure (LEEP) may be recommended for treatment. LEEPs are used to remove a small square of tissue from the cervix, typically under local anesthesia in the gynecology office. Oral antianxiety medicine or sedation may be offered in the office if needed.

The entire LEEP process is much faster than most people think. It takes a few minutes for the doctor to evaluate the cervix and administer a local anesthetic, and the LEEP itself is done in under ten seconds. During a LEEP procedure, a speculum is inserted and another quick colposcopy is performed to identify the abnormal area. The cervix is then numbed with several injections of local anesthetic. The first one to two injections may feel like a sharp pinch or burning, but the next injections are not usually felt at all as the cervix becomes numb. The local anesthetic may take a few minutes to start working, and the doctor will test with a needle to ensure that the cervix is fully numb before doing the LEEP.

Once the cervix is numb, the doctor will use a small wire loop called a loop electrode to perform the LEEP. This loop electrode is a very thin semicircular wire one to three centimeters wide that is attached to a long plastic handle. Electrical current is run through the wire loop, allowing it to cut through the tissue and preventing bleeding. Most patients feel nothing at all during the LEEP, though some people may feel warmth because local anesthetic might not fully block temperature sensation. A small piece of cervical tissue a few centimeters wide and a centimeter deep will be removed and sent to a pathologist for evaluation. A medicinal paste is usually placed on the cervix to prevent bleeding, and then the procedure is done. Most people do not need any pain medication besides ibuprofen or acetaminophen after a LEEP. Once the doctor receives the pathology results, a few days to a week after the procedure, they will call or schedule an appointment to discuss the results and explain what follow-up may be needed.

IUD INSERTION

IUDs are some of the most effective contraceptives and may be great options for people who want to minimize the hormonal side effects of birth control. But for some people, fear of pain with IUD insertion can be a deterrent to what might otherwise be an excellent method.

Most people, including teenagers and people who have not had children, can have an IUD inserted in the office. Some patients feel virtually nothing or only mild cramping, whereas others can feel more severe pain. Because the experience is so individual, it is hard to predict what you personally might feel. In general, people who have given birth vaginally will feel the least because their cervices have been dilated before, and the IUD will pass through it more quickly and easily. Those who have severe anxiety with pelvic exams or conditions that make speculum insertion more painful may require sedation for IUD placement, or may choose a different contraceptive method altogether.

Right before you have an IUD inserted, your provider will explain the procedure, including the potential risks or side effects and how the procedure will be done. If the doctor does not explain the process fully or if you are still uncertain about anything, ask any questions you need to clarify before proceeding. Once you're ready, you will be asked to lie down on the exam table; a speculum will be inserted, and your cervix and vagina will be washed with a cleansing solution to prevent infection. A tenaculum may be placed on the cervix—this is a long instrument with two narrow pointed tips that is used to hold the cervix open or to gently straighten a tilted uterus during the procedure. The doctor will then measure how deep your uterus is so they will know how far to insert the IUD. This is called sounding, and it is done by inserting a thin measuring instrument into the uterus. Finally, the IUD device is drawn up into a narrow, hollow plastic tube called an introducer that will deliver the IUD into the uterus. The arms of the IUD are folded up inside this introducer, and it is then inserted through the cervix and into the uterus. The IUD is left inside your uterus when the introducer is removed. The strings attached to the end of the IUD are then trimmed with scissors and tucked beside your cervix so that partners do not feel them.

The entire IUD insertion procedure usually lasts only a minute or two. During the insertion process, you may feel the three steps of placement of the tenaculum, sounding of the uterus, and IUD insertion as anything from a dull cramp to a sharp and intense pain. If the doctor has difficulty inserting the IUD because your cervix is tightly closed or the uterus is tilted at a significant angle, the process might take several minutes longer than usual. In these cases, the doctor may need to use dilators to help open the cervix or an ultrasound to help guide the insertion.

Pain with IUD insertion can be decreased by taking NSAIDs before the appointment or having the doctor perform a local anesthetic paracervical block before the insertion. In a paracervical block, a local anesthetic is injected next to the cervix to numb the nerves of the lower part of the uterus. As mentioned in the LEEP section, the numbing injections themselves can feel like a pinch or a cramping pain, and it might take a few minutes for the anesthesia to take effect. The local anesthetic does not completely eliminate all discomfort felt during an IUD insertion, because different nerves provide sensation to the upper part of the uterus. For these reasons, paracervical blocks are not routinely done for IUD insertions. But if you want to try a block to minimize pain, it is definitely an option worth discussing with your provider. Oral antianxiety medication taken beforehand may also make you more comfortable. Nitrous oxide, or "laughing gas," has not been shown to improve pain with IUD insertion. However, some providers may offer conscious sedation, which is a combination of intravenous sedatives and opioid pain medication (discussed further at the end of this chapter). Finally, if IUD placement is intolerable while the patient is awake, it may be an option to have the IUD inserted under anesthesia in an operating room, although this option may be limited by insurance coverage.

If the opening of your cervix appears very small or tightly closed on a pre-procedure speculum exam and your provider doesn't think that an IUD can be placed easily, a misoprostol tablet may be prescribed for you to insert vaginally the night before your insertion appointment. This is the same medication used to soften and open the cervix for the treatment of miscarriage or a medical abortion, and it may make it easier to insert the IUD. Because misoprostol itself can cause cramping, it is not usually prescribed unless someone has had a failed attempt at IUD before or if your healthcare provider feels the cervix would not allow for insertion of the IUD without additional dilation.

Once the procedure is over and the speculum is removed, the cramping and pain of insertion usually improves quickly. Some cramping may continue for a few days or even weeks, though this can usually be controlled with over-the-counter nonsteroidal anti-inflammatory medications such as ibuprofen or naproxen. You may have light bleeding that lasts for a few days to weeks; some people have more persistent bleeding that lasts for several months, but there are treatments that can be given to control or stop the bleeding. You should not have persistent severe pain or heavy bleeding after the IUD is inserted. If you do, your doctor will order an ultrasound and examine you to ensure that the IUD is not out of place and that there is not a uterine infection.

IUD REMOVAL

Having an IUD removed is far quicker and less uncomfortable than the process for insertion. During a removal, your provider will simply insert a speculum, grasp the strings with an instrument, and pull on them to take the IUD out of your uterus. Removal is usually extremely fast, just a second or two. Most people will feel cramping when the IUD comes out and perhaps for a few hours afterward, but this is usually mild or very easily managed with NSAIDs. Sometimes the strings of the IUD may not be visible because they have been pushed up into the cervix with intercourse. In these situations, your doctor may use a narrow instrument to grasp the strings inside the canal of the cervix or she may perform a hysteroscopy to find and remove the IUD.

ENDOMETRIAL BIOPSY

Endometrial biopsies are tests to obtain a sample of the tissue in the cavity of the uterus. This test is usually performed as part of an evaluation for abnormal bleeding in order to rule out uterine precancer or cancer. They're also sometimes used for fertility testing or as part of IVF cycles. There are no needles or cutting involved with an endometrial biopsy. A speculum is inserted, and a very narrow straw, called a *pipelle*, is inserted through the cervix to pick up some loose tissue from inside the cavity of the uterus. The process feels very similar to the first steps of an IUD insertion. If the pipelle cannot easily pass through the cervix, a tenaculum may be used for this procedure. The biopsy can feel like a sharp cramp or pain like an IUD insertion, but it is usually quicker than an IUD, lasting only a few seconds. Because endometrial biopsies are so fast, they are not usually done with anesthesia, but studies have shown improvement in pain with topical anesthesia sprays, local anesthetic gel inserted into the uterus, paracervical blocks, and NSAIDs.

HYSTEROSCOPY

If the doctor needs to get a more detailed assessment of the endometrium or the cavity of the uterus, a hysteroscopy may be recommended. A hysteroscope is a long, narrow camera just a few millimeters wide that is inserted through the vagina and cervix to inspect the cavity of the uterus. The camera is connected by cords to a light source and a video monitor that the doctor watches during the procedure. Saline or other fluid is usually run through the hysteroscope to open up the cavity of the uterus. Hysteroscopes can be used to obtain biopsies of the endometrial tissue, remove polyps, fibroids, a uterine septum, or scar tissue, or to take out IUDs when the strings are not visible. There are different instruments that can be inserted through a hysteroscope, including scissors or graspers, and there are also hysteroscopes that use tiny rotating blades or cutting loops to remove polyps or fibroids.

Hysteroscopies to quickly assess the cavity of the uterus, remove an IUD, obtain a biopsy of tissue, or remove small polyps can usually be done in the office with local anesthetic and NSAIDs, and most patients will feel mild cramping or pressure. The procedure can sometimes be done without a speculum to minimize discomfort. This is called a *vaginoscopic* hysteroscopy—rather than using the speculum to see the cervix, the camera is inserted into the vagina and used to find and enter the canal of the cervix.

Just like with IUD insertion, conscious sedation can be used if available for those who prefer more significant pain management. Longer procedures, such as removal of larger fibroids or polyps, are usually done in the operating room under anesthesia because these can be more painful. In general, if a hysteroscopy is recommended but you feel uncomfortable with the idea of having the procedure while awake, you should ask for deeper sedation or anesthesia in the operating room.

ANESTHETIC METHODS

When you discuss office procedures with your doctor, part of the counseling should include a review of what you can expect to feel and available options for pain control, including oral pain medications, antianxiety medications, local anesthetics, and sedation. This conversation should cover both the effectiveness of these methods and their potential risks. If there were no risks, every patient could be offered anesthesia for every pelvic exam and procedure. However, because all pain control and anesthesia methods have limitations and potential risks, these must be weighed against the possible pain of the exam so that you can make the decision that is best for you.

Paracervical blocks can make IUD insertions and endometrial biopsies less painful but may themselves cause some pain when performed. There is also a small risk of mild side effects, such as temporary facial numbness, dizziness, allergic reactions, and more dangerous complications, such as seizures or heart arrhythmias, though these complications are rare.

Nitrous oxide is an inhaled anesthetic that provides some pain relief and also has antianxiety properties. It's a weak anesthetic, so it is usually paired with another option, such as local anesthesia injections. Nitrous oxide is generally very safe, but it does have some risks, such as vomiting, closure of the airway, cardiac and lung complications, and low blood pressure. Therefore, nitrous oxide can be offered only in offices where the staff is adequately trained to monitor patients carefully during and after use.

Conscious sedation is a combination of a sedative and an anesthetic.

These medications are usually given through an IV or via injection into a muscle. People receiving conscious sedation will feel drowsy and may even fall asleep but they still breathe on their own and will not be completely unconscious. Because breathing may slow and blood pressure may drop, the office staff and doctor must monitor vital signs very carefully. Not many gynecology offices can offer conscious sedation because of the staffing and resuscitation requirements that are needed to ensure patient safety, so it is more commonly given in operating rooms by anesthesia professionals.

Monitored anesthesia care in the OR is the safest method for sedation, since anesthesiologists and nurse anesthetists are specifically trained in managing respiratory and cardiac emergencies, and they have access to resuscitation equipment and medications that are not usually available in an office setting. The potential drawbacks are that OR-level care usually adds significant expense that may not be covered by insurance, and it requires several hours of monitoring before, during, and after the procedure, even if the procedure itself takes less than a minute to perform. This is why sedation in an operating room is usually reserved for procedures like complicated hysteroscopies or for people who cannot tolerate pelvic exams or procedures while awake. For those with severe anxiety or vulvovaginal pain with pelvic exams, monitored sedation in the OR can provide the most comfortable method for getting necessary gynecologic procedures done.

TAKE-HOME POINTS

- There are different sizes of speculum, including very small pediatric speculums that can be used if people have pain with vaginal exams.
- Pap smears and speculum exams are not the same. A speculum exam can be done to check the vagina or cervix without a Pap smear being performed.
- Local anesthetic injected next to the cervix (a paracervical block) can help minimize pain when someone is having an

IUD insertion. The injection itself can be painful, so it is not used for every IUD insertion.

- If you are confused or uncertain about any test or procedure, ask your healthcare providers to clarify before they proceed.

- It may be helpful to bring a partner, relative, or friend for support if you are anxious about a gynecology appointment.

Weighing Your Options

In medicine, there are rarely definitive right or wrong choices for treatment—only what is best for an individual person. With cancer treatment and prevention, there are algorithms that suggest the best course based on test results. However, when people are dealing with general gynecologic problems, there aren't any fixed treatment pathways. In fact, people with the exact same symptoms can have completely different healthcare goals and may choose very different treatment plans. The only common theme is that generally everyone wants to be healthy and have a good quality of life.

You are the only one who can decide what quality of life means for you and what will best help you achieve it. Sometimes after hearing all of the options, you may decide that you don't actually need or want treatment at all because your quality of life would be best without any interventions—and that is a valid choice.

To help you solidify your personal healthcare goals, I've listed some questions for you to consider as well as some sample responses to give you a jumping-off point for reflection. Once you've thought about your own answers to these questions, you may want to jot down them down and bring the notes to your next medical appointment. Then, sit down with your doctor so that you can discuss which options would be the best fit for your particular wishes and circumstances.

Which statements best describe your goals for treatment?

☐ I want to eliminate pain, abnormal bleeding, or other bothersome symptoms.

☐ I want to resume activities such as exercise, work, and sex.

☐ I want to relieve gender dysphoria.

☐ I want to get pregnant, either now or someday in the future.

☐ What other goals do you have?

Do any of these statements reflect your thoughts regarding medications?

☐ I've experienced bothersome side effects with medications before, and I am worried about the possible side effects of medicines.

☐ I have concerns about remembering to take daily medications.

☐ I would prefer to use medications rather than undergo procedures or surgeries.

What are your preferences in terms of surgery?

☐ I want to avoid surgery or any invasive procedures if possible.

☐ I am interested in surgery but want to try to minimize the risk of complications by being more conservative in the surgical approach.

☐ I want to be as aggressive surgically as possible if more conservative methods could fail. (An example of this would be choosing a hysterectomy for fibroids rather than a method that preserves the uterus.)

What is the rest of your medical history?

☐ I have medical conditions that could increase the risks of certain medications or surgeries (these include high blood pressure, diabetes, and chronic heart, lung, kidney, or liver problems).

☐ I have had prior abdominal surgeries or pelvic or abdominal infections. (If so, please try to obtain operative reports and pathology reports for your doctor to review, because prior surgeries or infections may affect your risks in future surgeries.)

☐ I have a strong family history of cancer or other medical issues, such as problems with anesthesia or excessive bleeding or blood clots.

What are your thoughts regarding fertility?

☐ I want to try to conceive now, in the near future, or several years from now.

☐ I'm not actively planning to become pregnant, but I'm not ruling it out for the future.

☐ I am certain that I will never desire future fertility and would be interested in treatments such as sterilization or hysterectomy.

What would influence your decision to pursue one treatment versus another?

☐ I want medications or treatment methods that are easy to use.

☐ I want to avoid disruption to my daily life, including work and hobbies.

☐ I am concerned about the cost of medications or procedures, including whether they are covered by insurance.

☐ I wish to minimize potential risks or side effects.

☐ I want to preserve or optimize my fertility.

☐ I want to reduce my risk of cancer or other serious medical conditions.

☐ What other factors would make you more or less likely to choose a certain treatment?

How do you want your healthcare provider to discuss treatment options with you?

☐ I want the provider to directly explain what treatments are recommended for my situation, because I am not sure how to decide.

☐ I want the provider to offer information and guidance but allow me full autonomy to decide for myself.

☐ I want the provider to direct me to reading material or resources to learn more so I can research options further before deciding.

Are there any other factors that are important to you and that you want your healthcare team to know?

Conclusion

Every gynecologic condition is linked by a common thread: a gross lack of information. Eighty percent of Black women will develop fibroids in their lifetime, yet no one knows why they occur, so there is no way to treat the root cause or prevent them from returning. Imagine if there was a condition that affected 80 percent of white men and caused hemorrhaging, debilitating pain, severe bloating, constipation, frequent urination, and infertility. I'd wager that scientists would have long ago discovered the exact biological cause, and there would be a range of effective treatment options available and covered by insurance.

Other common medical conditions such as diabetes and hypertension receive a constant flow of research and funding, and new treatments come on the market all the time. In contrast, over the decades that I've been studying and then practicing medicine, I've seen virtually no new research breakthroughs or treatments for conditions such as endometriosis, fibroids, PCOS, PMDD, miscarriage, and menopause. Virtually 100 percent of women will deal with one or more of these conditions at some point, and they can cause debilitating physical and emotional stress. How is it possible that there is so little funding, research, and attention given to these problems? How are gynecologic health issues so abysmally under-researched, underfunded, and undertreated?

Layers of ingrained misogyny, racism, and assumptions about women and the female body have brought us to this point. All too often, medical problems that primarily affect women are simply expected to be tolerated. They aren't perceived to be legitimate medical diseases and don't receive the research funding, education, and attention they deserve. As a result, people assigned female at birth are condemned to patterns of ever worsening pain and suffering.

The more symptoms a patient has, the more likely it is that frustrated healthcare providers will simply throw up their hands and say, "This woman's tests are all normal, but she's complaining about *everything*— she's hysterical." Against a backdrop of misogyny that has been embedded in our society, politics, and history, gynecologic health issues have become stigmatized to a harmful extent, and it must stop now.

I wrote this book to break the cycle of misinformation and suffering. It's time for women and people assigned female at birth to be able to make sense of their own bodies. If you've been experiencing gynecologic health problems, schedule that consult, discuss that surgery, or ask about treatment options; advocate for yourself if you're not getting answers, and seek out second opinions when necessary. You deserve to reclaim your own health and well-being.

I have a burning hope that this book will spark a movement to finally change these injustices. Why should women, trans men, intersex, and nonbinary people be forced to fight so hard just to get good medical care? Why should we simply shake our heads in outrage and be forced to accept the lack of answers? Why must people struggle alone, not realizing that millions across the world share the same experiences and pain?

It's time to change the status quo. Talk with your friends and community. Share your story, and break the stigma surrounding periods, sex, fertility, pain, pregnancy loss, menopause—all of these seemingly taboo topics that affect us all. Join support groups and make connections. Raise funds for research or, better yet, lobby for organizations and governments to commit more funding for research, education, and awareness. If you work in medicine or health-related industries, put your time and energy into reproductive health research or advocacy.

I believe that we can achieve this vision together. We're leaving the concept of "hysteria" in the past where it belongs, and the future is bright.

ACKNOWLEDGMENTS

When you think of an author, you may imagine someone sitting alone in front of a computer with a stack of papers. In the course of writing this book, I learned that it takes an entire strike force of people to bring an author's dream to life—and I'll never be able to adequately thank the publishing and medical experts who supported me throughout this process.

My literary agents, Sarah Passick, Mia Vitale, and Anna Petkovich at Park & Fine, understood my vision for a "gynecology revolution" from the very beginning. This book is in your hands because they championed it with such passion. They also came up with the title, *It's Not Hysteria*—and when they suggested it, I may have yelled, "Holy !@#$, that's an amazing title!" Thank you also to Kat Toolan and Ben Kaslow-Zieve at Park & Fine for your kindness and support.

My editor, Samantha Zukergood, has the patience of twenty saints. Whenever I started shifting the focus to myself or sounding too much like a medical textbook, she repeatedly reminded me that this book is for *you*, the reader. This book has more humanism and heart (and infinitely less mind-numbing medical jargon) because of her.

When I was deciding between publishers, I knew that Flatiron was the right home for this project because of Sam Zukergood and Malati Chavali. They shared my goal of not just putting out a book, but of starting a movement to transform how the world understands and cares for gynecologic health. Thank you also to Julie Will and Keith Hayes, who created this absolutely extraordinary cover, and Erin Kibby, Joanne Raymond, Marlena Bittner, Drew Kilman, Emma West, Frances Sayers, Elishia Merricks, and the sales teams, who all worked so tirelessly to get the book into the hands of everyone who needs it. My copy editor, Tracy Roe, MD, is also an emergency medicine physician! She made sure that my grammar *and* my medical facts were flawless. The Flatiron crew is like the 1990s Chicago Bulls of publishing, and I'm just a rookie who's honored to be part of the team.

I also had the most ludicrously overqualified people helping me to organize references and endnotes. Allegra Caldera, you're a lifesaver, and I bow before your expertise in Chicago style. Thank you also to Bethany Dus, MD, who managed to help me while finishing medical school.

Stephanie Winter was the first publishing professional to see the potential for a book in the educational content I was creating on social media. I will always be grateful to her for nudging me to take that first step.

In order to ensure that this book was as up-to-date, accurate, and sensitive as possible, I called upon an elite group of reproductive health experts and advocates who were gracious enough to read chapters of the book and provide their invaluable feedback. Thank you so much to Lora Shahine, MD; Annette Lee, MD; Gina Cunningham, DPT; Jocelyn Fitzgerald, MD; Suzanne Gilberg-Lenz, MD; Karla Maguire, MD; Alexandra Milspaw, PhD, MEd; Nkem Osian, MPH; Kate Debiec, MD; Ilene Wong, MD; Dane Menkin, CRNP; Jenneh Rishe, BSN, RN; and Alicia Roth Weigel.

I'm also grateful to William Li, MD; Kimmery Martin, MD; Lydia Kang, MD and Nina Shapiro, MD—experienced physician authors who took the time to answer my questions about publishing, and encouraged me along the way.

How do you thank your parents for everything that they've done? My mom and dad always encouraged me to do my best, but when things didn't exactly go according to plan, they also reassured me that it would all work out somehow. They provided childcare during the pandemic, and still make dinner for us at least twice a week (complete with cut-up fruit). Absolute best parents of all time.

To my kids, Evelyn, Lily, and Raymond. You're much smarter and more talented than I am, and I'm so honored to be your mom. I'm sorry that I took so many nights and weekends away from you to write this book. Hopefully, seeing your mother achieve this crazy goal will encourage you to shoot for your own dreams, whether that's becoming a brilliant artist, a speed-cubing engineer, or a ninja (or whatever Raymond ends up doing). Many huggies and smooches. I love you so much.

My husband, Ray, is the best human being I know. No matter what absolutely ludicrous plan I've thrown out there ("I'm going to start making TikToks," "I'm going to write a book," "I'm going to quit my job and start my own practice from scratch") he has supported me 100 percent and done everything possible to help me reach those goals. He believes in me much more than I believe in myself, and reminds me to think about how my work can serve others. Everyone needs a Ray in their lives, but I have the best one. I love and appreciate you more than I can say.

Finally, to you the reader: Thank you from the bottom of my heart for picking up this book and joining me in this movement. I wish you all the best in your journey toward health, happiness, and freedom from suffering.

NOTES

CHAPTER 1: THE HISTORY OF HYSTERIA

10–11 **Healers recommended treatments such as:** Laurence Totelin, "Old Recipes, New Practice? The Latin Adaptations of the Hippocratic *Gynaecological Treatises*," *Social History of Medicine* 24, no. 1 (April 2011): 74–91, https://doi.org/10.1093/shm/hkq103.

11 **"And in women again":** Plato, *Timaeus*, trans. W. R. M. Lamb, in *Plato in Twelve Volumes*, vol. 9 (Cambridge, MA: Harvard University Press, 1925), 91c, Perseus Digital Library, http://data.perseus.org/citations /urn:cts:greekLit:tlg0059.tlg031.perseus-eng1:91c.

12 **A Briefe Discourse of a Disease:** Edward Jorden, *A Briefe Discourse of a Disease Called the Suffocation of the Mother* (London, 1603), British Library Online, https://www.bl.uk/collection-items/first-english-book-on -hysteria-1603.

13 **He recommended clitoridectomy:** Isaac Baker Brown, *On the Curability of Certain Forms of Insanity, Epilepsy, Catalepsy, and Hysteria in Females* (London: Robert Hardwicke, 1866), 7, Wellcome Collection Online, https://wellcomecollection.org/works/e2gtcp9u.

13 **removal of the ovaries for cases:** Robert Battey, *Extirpation of the Functionally Active Ovaries for the Remedy of Otherwise Incurable Diseases* (Rome, GA: 1876), 2, National Library of Medicine Digital Collections, https://wellcomecollection.org/works/e2gtcp9u.

13 **thousands of oophorectomies:** Thomas Schlich, "Cutting the Body to Cure the Mind," *Lancet: Psychiatry* 2, no. 5 (May 2015): 390–92, https:// doi.org/10.1016/S2215–0366(15)00188–1.

14 *phantom limb syndrome*: S. Weir Mitchell, "Phantom Limbs," *Lippin-cott's Magazine,* December 1871, 563–69, National Library of Medicine Digital Collections, https://collections.nlm.nih.gov/catalog/nlm:nlmuid -101661195-bk.

14 **even worse "mental agony"**: Charlotte Perkins Gilman, *The Living of Charlotte Perkins Gilman: An Autobiography* (New York: D. Appleton-Century, 1935; Madison: University of Wisconsin Press, 1990), 102.

15–16 **hysteria was the physical manifestation**: Sigmund Freud and Josef Breuer, *Studies in Hysteria,* trans. A. A. Brill (New York: Nervous and Mental Disease Publishing, 1936), 4, Wellcome Collection Online, https:// wellcomecollection.org/works/cfstr64q.

16 **ten-to-one female-to-male ratio**: Stuart L. Kurlansik and Mario S. Maf-fei, "Somatic Symptom Disorder," *American Family Physician* 93, no. 1 (January 2016): 49–54, https://pubmed.ncbi.nlm.nih.gov/26760840/.

17 **"Recognizing that race is a social"**: "Joint Statement: Collective Action Addressing Racism," Advocacy and Health Policy, American College of Obstetricians and Gynecologists, August 27, 2020, https://www.acog.org /news/news-articles/2020/08/joint-statement-obstetrics-and-gynecology -collective-action-addressing-racism.

17 **bending a pewter spoon**: J. Marion Sims, *The Story of My Life* (New York: D. Appleton, 1884), 234, Library of Congress Online, https://lccn.loc.gov /13017881.

18 **women suffered terribly during these operations**: Sims, *Story of My Life*, 238.

18 **less likely to be offered minimally**: Eve Zaritsky et al., "Minimally Inva-sive Myomectomy: Practice Trends and Differences Between Black and Non-Black Women Within a Large Integrated Healthcare System," *American Journal of Obstetrics and Gynecology* 226, no. 6 (January 2022): 826. e1–826.e11, https://doi.org/10.1016/j.ajog.2022.01.022.

18 **2016 study showed that half**: Kelly M. Hoffman et al., "Racial Bias in Pain Assessment and Treatment Recommendations, and False Beliefs About Biological Differences Between Blacks and Whites," *Proceedings of the National Academy of Sciences of the United States of America* 113, no. 16 (April 2016): 4296–4301, https://doi.org/10.1073/pnas.1516047113.

18 **three times more likely**: Emily E. Petersen et al., "Vital Signs: Pregnancy-Related Deaths, United States, 2011–2015, and Strategies for Prevention, 13 States, 2013–2017," *Morbidity and Mortality Weekly Report* 68, no. 18 (May 2019): 423–29, https://doi.org/10.15585/mmwr.mm6818e1.

18 **four times more likely**: House of Commons Women and Equalities

Committee, "Black Maternal Health, 2022–2023," March 29, 2023, https://committees.parliament.uk/publications/38989/documents/191706/default/.

18 **maternal mortality rate for the richest:** Kate Kennedy-Moulton et al., "Maternal and Infant Health Inequality: New Evidence from Linked Administrative Data" (NBER Working Paper Series, National Bureau of Economic Research, Cambridge, MA, November 2022), http://doi.org/10.3386/w30693.

19 **weathering of the body:** Allana T. Forde et al., "The Weathering Hypothesis as an Explanation for Racial Disparities in Health: A Systematic Review," *Annals of Epidemiology* 33 (May 2019): 1–18.e3, https://doi.org/10.1016/j.annepidem.2019.02.011.

19 **Black people experience more social stressors:** David R. Williams, "Stress and the Mental Health of Populations of Color: Advancing Our Understanding of Race-Related Stressors," *Journal of Health and Social Behavior* 59, no. 4 (December 2019): 466–85, https://doi.org/10.1177/0022146518814251.

19 **study by Duke University:** Christy Zhou Koval and Ashleigh Shelby Rosette, "The Natural Hair Bias in Job Recruitment," *Social Psychological and Personality Science* 12, no. 5 (August 2020): 741–50, https://doi.org/10.1177/1948550620937937.

20 **that President Clinton signed:** Anna C. Mastroianni, Ruth Faden, and Daniel Federman, eds., *Women and Health Research: Ethical and Legal Issues of Including Women in Clinical Studies*, vol. 1 (Washington, DC: National Academy Press, 1994), 233–36, https://www.ncbi.nlm.nih.gov/books/NBK236531/.

20 **Food and Drug Administration (FDA) finally eliminated:** "Study and Evaluation of Gender Differences in the Clinical Evaluation of Drugs," Guidance Document, U.S. Food and Drug Administration, July 1993, https://www.fda.gov/regulatory-information/search-fda-guidance-documents/study-and-evaluation-gender-differences-clinical-evaluation-drugs.

20 **late 1980s, less than 15 percent:** Ruth L. Kirschstein, "Research on Women's Health," *American Journal of Public Health* 81, no. 3 (March 1991): 291–93, https://doi.org/10.2105/ajph.81.3.291.

20 **2022, the NIH allocated $37 million:** "Estimates of Funding for Various Research, Condition, and Disease Categories (RCDC)," National Institutes of Health, March 31, 2023, https://report.nih.gov/funding/categorical-spending#/.

20 **Crohn's disease, which affects 0.21 percent:** Mahesh Gajendran et al.,

"A Comprehensive Review and Update on Crohn's Disease," *Disease-a-Month* 64, no. 2 (February 2018): 20–57, https://doi.org/10.1016/j.disamonth.2017.07.001.

20 **70 percent of white women:** Donna Day Baird et al., "High Cumulative Incidence of Uterine Leiomyoma in Black and White Women: Ultrasound Evidence," *American Journal of Obstetrics and Gynecology* 188, no. 1 (January 2003): 100–107, https://doi.org/10.1067/mob.2003.99.

22 **biopsies of the uterus or vulva:** M. F. Benoit, J. F. Ma, and B. A. Upperman, "Comparison of 2015 Medicare Relative Value Units for Gender-Specific Procedures: Gynecologic and Gynecologic-Oncologic Versus Urologic CPT Coding. Has Time Healed Gender-Worth?," *Gynecologic Oncology* 144, no. 2 (February 2017): 336–42, https://doi.org/10.1016/j.ygyno.2016.12.006.

22 **40 to 75 percent of OB-GYN physicians:** "Why Ob-Gyns Are Burning Out," American College of Obstetricians and Gynecologists, October 28, 2019, https://www.acog.org/en/news/news-articles/2019/10/why-ob-gyns-are-burning-out.

CHAPTER 2: ANATOMY AND SEX ED

24 **90 percent of college students:** "College Resources and Sexual Health," Maternal and Child Health Bureau, Health Resources and Services Administration (HRSA), last updated December 2022, https://mchb.hrsa.gov/research/project_info.asp?ID=145.

26 **one to two million eggs:** *Merck Manual* Consumer Version, "How Many Eggs?," accessed June 23, 2023, https://www.merckmanuals.com/home/multimedia/table/how-many-eggs.

28 **fertile window during which an egg:** "Fertility Awareness–Based Methods of Family Planning," FAQs, American College of Obstetricians and Gynecologists, January 2019, https://www.acog.org/womens-health/faqs/fertility-awareness-based-methods-of-family-planning.

28 **remaining tube can pick up:** Jackie A. Ross et al., "Ovum Transmigration After Salpingectomy for Ectopic Pregnancy," *Human Reproduction* 28, no. 4 (April 2013): 937–41, https://doi.org/10.1093/humrep/det012.

30 **majority of women polled reported:** Pedro Vieira-Baptista et al., "G-spot: Fact or Fiction?: A Systematic Review," *Sexual Medicine* 9, no. 5 (October 2021): 1, https://doi.org/10.1016/j.esxm.2021.100435.

32 **Severe endometriosis can scar or block:** Claudio Ponticelli, Giorgio Graziani, and Emanuele Montanari, "Ureteral Endometriosis: A Rare and

Underdiagnosed Cause of Kidney Dysfunction," *Nephron Clinical Practice* 114, no. 2 (2010): c89–c94, https://doi.org/10.1159/000254380.

33   **endometriosis can actually grow into:** Working group of ESGE, ESHRE, and WES, Joerg Keckstein et al., "Recommendations for the Surgical Treatment of Endometriosis. Part 2: Deep Endometriosis," *Human Reproduction Open* 2020, no. 1 (2020): hoaa002, https://doi.org/10.1093/hropen/hoaa002.

35   **up to four inches along:** Helen E. O'Connell, Kalavampara V. Sanjeevan, and John M. Hutson, "Anatomy of the Clitoris," *Journal of Urology* 174, no. 4 (October 2005): 1189–95, https://doi.org/10.1097/01.ju.0000173639.38898.cd.

37   **average cycle is twenty-eight days:** Beverly G. Reed and Bruce R. Carr, "The Normal Menstrual Cycle and the Control of Ovulation" in *Endotext*, ed. Kenneth R. Feingold et al. (South Dartmouth, MA: MDText.com), last updated August 5, 2018, https://www.ncbi.nlm.nih.gov/books/NBK279054/.

38   **live up to five days:** "Fertility Awareness–Based Methods."

CHAPTER 4: FIBROIDS

49   **80 percent of Black women:** Donna Day Baird et al., "High Cumulative Incidence of Uterine Leiomyoma in Black and White Women: Ultrasound Evidence," *American Journal of Obstetrics and Gynecology* 188, no. 1 (January 2003): 100–107, https://doi.org/10.1067/mob.2003.99.

53   **rare cancerous uterine tumors called *leiomyosarcomas*:** Lingxiang Wang et al., "Prevalence and Occult Rates of Uterine Leiomyosarcoma," *Medicine* 99, no. 33 (August 2020): e21766, https://doi.org/10.1097/MD.0000000000021766.

55   **three times higher for Black patients:** Lynn M. Marshall et al., "Variation in the Incidence of Uterine Leiomyoma Among Premenopausal Women by Age and Race," *Obstetrics and Gynecology* 90, no. 6 (December 1997): 967–73, https://doi.org/10.1016/s0029-7844(97)00534-6.

55   **two times higher for Hispanic patients:** William H. Catherino, Heba M. Eltoukhi, and Ayman Al-Hendy, "Racial and Ethnic Differences in the Pathogenesis and Clinical Manifestations of Uterine Leiomyoma," *Seminars in Reproductive Medicine* 31, no. 5 (2013): 370–79, https://doi.org/10.1055/s-0033-1348896.

55   **ten to fifteen years earlier:** Quaker E. Harmon, Ky'Era V. Actkins, and Donna D. Baird, "Fibroid Prevalence—Still So Much to Learn," *JAMA*

Network Open 6, no. 5 (May 2023): e2312682, https://doi.org/10.1001/jamanetworkopen.2023.12682.

56 **adequate levels of vitamin D:** Michał Ciebiera et al., "Vitamin D and Uterine Fibroids—Review of the Literature and Novel Concepts," *International Journal of Molecular Sciences* 19, no. 7 (July 2018): 2051, https://doi.org/10.3390/ijms19072051.

56 **inhibit the growth of tumor cells:** Chakradhari Sharan et al., "Vitamin D Inhibits Proliferation of Human Uterine Leiomyoma Cells Via Catechol-O-Methyltransferase," *Fertility and Sterility* 95, no. 1 (January 2011): 247–53, https://doi.org/10.1016/j.fertnstert.2010.07.1041.

56 **vitamin D supplementation may slightly:** Maryam Hajhashemi et al., "The Effect of Vitamin D Supplementation on the Size of Uterine Leiomyoma in Women with Vitamin D Deficiency," *Caspian Journal of Internal Medicine* 10, no. 2 (Spring 2019): 125–31, https://doi.org/10.22088/cjim.10.2.125.

57 **Increased chronic stress is associated:** Hao Qin et al., "The Association Between Chronic Psychological Stress and Uterine Fibroids Risk: A Meta-Analysis of Observational Studies," *Stress and Health* 35, no. 5 (2019): 585–94, https://doi.org/10.1002/smi.2895.

57 **phthalates and bisphenol A (BPA) may:** Philippa D. Darbre, "Chemical Components of Plastics as Endocrine Disruptors: Overview and Commentary," *Birth Defects Research* 112, no. 17 (2020): 1300–1307, https://doi.org/10.1002/bdr2.1778.

57 **products such as hair relaxers:** Lauren A. Wise et al., "Hair Relaxer Use and Risk of Uterine Leiomyomata in African-American Women," *American Journal of Epidemiology* 175, no. 5 (2012): 432–40, https://doi.org/10.1093/aje/kwr351; Che-Jung Chang et al., "Use of Straighteners and Other Hair Products and Incident Uterine Cancer," *Journal of the National Cancer Institute* 114, no. 12 (2022): 1636–45, https://doi.org/10.1093/jnci/djac165.

59 **fibroids may increase slightly in size:** "Uterine Fibroids," FAQs, American College of Obstetricians and Gynecologists, last updated July 2022, https://www.acog.org/womens-health/faqs/uterine-fibroids.

59 **risk of fibroid development or progression:** Ron K. Ross et al., "Risk Factors for Uterine Fibroids: Reduced Risk Associated with Oral Contraceptives," *BMJ* 293 (August 1986): 359–62, https://doi.org/10.1136/bmj.293.6543.359.

60 **decrease fibroid volume about 50 percent:** Piotr Czuczwar et al., "Predicting the Results of Uterine Artery Embolization: Correlation Between Initial Intramural Fibroid Volume and Percentage Volume Decrease," *Menopause Review/Przegląd Menopauzalny* 13, no. 4 (September 2014): 247–52, https://doi.org/10.5114/pm.2014.45001.

65 **vitamin D supplementation for women:** Hajhashemi, "The Effect of Vitamin D."

66 **several servings of fruits and vegetables:** Lauren A. Wise et al., "Intake of Fruit, Vegetables, and Carotenoids in Relation to Risk of Uterine Leiomyomata," *American Journal of Clinical Nutrition* 94, no. 6 (2011): 1620–1631, https://doi.org/10.3945/ajcn.111.016600.

CHAPTER 5: ENDOMETRIOSIS AND ADENOMYOSIS

67 **it takes seven years on average:** Parveen Parasar, Pinar Ozcan, and Kathryn L. Terry, "Endometriosis: Epidemiology, Diagnosis and Clinical Management," *Current Obstetrics and Gynecology Reports* 6 (2017): 34–41, https://doi.org/10.1007/s13669-017-0187-1.

69 **at least one in ten women:** A. L. Shafrir et al., "Risk for and Consequences of Endometriosis: A Critical Epidemiologic Review," *Best Practice and Research Clinical Obstetrics and Gynaecology* 51 (August 2018): 1–15, https://doi.org/10.1016/j.bpobgyn.2018.06.001.

69 **half of women who experience infertility:** B. S. Verkauf, "Incidence, Symptoms, and Signs of Endometriosis in Fertile and Infertile Women," *Journal of the Florida Medical Association* 74, no. 9 (1987): 671–75, https://pubmed.ncbi.nlm.nih.gov/2961844/.

69 **a third of hysterectomy specimens:** P. Vercellini et al., "Adenomyosis at Hysterectomy: A Study on Frequency Distribution and Patient Characteristics," *Human Reproduction* 10, no. 5 (May 1995): 1160–62, https://doi.org/10.1093/oxfordjournals.humrep.a136111.

69 **uterus in early embryologic development:** Christina Rei, Thomas Williams, and Michael Feloney, "Endometriosis in a Man as a Rare Source of Abdominal Pain: A Case Report and Review of the Literature," *Case Reports in Obstetrics and Gynecology* 2018 (January 2018): https://doi.org/10.1155/2018/2083121.

70 **Sampson's theory of retrograde menstruation:** John A. Sampson, "Heterotopic or Misplaced Endometrial Tissue," *American Journal of Obstetrics and Gynecology* 10, no. 5 (November 1925): 649–64, https://doi.org/10.1016/S0002-9378(25)90629-1.

70 **Cisgender men can even get endometriosis:** Rei, Williams, and Feloney, "Endometriosis in a Man."

75 **hydrosalpinx decreases embryo implantation rates:** Hoda Maaly Harb et al., "Hydrosalpinx and Pregnancy Loss: A Systematic Review and Meta-Analysis," *Reproductive Biomedicine Online* 38, no. 3 (March 2019): 427–41, https://doi.org/10.1016/j.rbmo.2018.12.020.

75   **decreased implantation rates with IVF:** Mukhri Hamdan et al., "Influence of Endometriosis on Assisted Reproductive Technology Outcomes: A Systematic Review and Meta-Analysis," *Obstetrics and Gynecology* 125, no. 1 (January 2015): 79–88, https://doi.org/10.1097/AOG .0000000000000592.

75   **higher risks of preterm labor:** Hiroshi Kobayashi et al., "A Relationship Between Endometriosis and Obstetric Complications," *Reproductive Sciences* 27 (2020): 771–778, https://doi.org/10.1007/s43032-019-00118-0.

79   **For mild disease, there may be:** Channing Burks et al., "Excision Versus Ablation for Management of Minimal to Mild Endometriosis: A Systematic Review and Meta-Analysis," *Journal of Minimally Invasive Gynecology* 28, no. 3 (March 2021): 587–97, https://doi.org/10.1016/j.jmig.2020.11.028.

80   **intravenous fluorescent dye:** John R. Lue, Adam Pyrzak, and Jennifer Allen, "Improving Accuracy of Intraoperative Diagnosis of Endometriosis: Role of Firefly in Minimal Access Robotic Surgery," *Journal of Minimal Access Surgery* 12, no. 2 (April/June 2016): 186–89, https://doi.org/10 .4103/0972–9941.158969.

80   **studies have not shown robotic:** Stefano Restaino et al., "Robotic Surgery vs. Laparoscopic Surgery in Patients with Diagnosis of Endometriosis: A Systematic Review and Meta-Analysis," *Journal of Robotic Surgery* 14, no. 5 (October 2020): 687–94, https://doi.org/10.1007/s11701-020-01061-y.

80   **stage doesn't determine symptom severity:** Mauricio S. Abrao et al., "AAGL 2021 Endometriosis Classification: An Anatomy-Based Surgical Complexity Score," *Journal of Minimally Invasive Gynecology* 28, no. 11 (November 2021): 1941–50.e1, https://doi.org/10.1016/j.jmig.2021.09.709.

82   *presacral neurectomy*, **involves:** E. D. Biggerstaff III and Susan N. Foster, "Laparoscopic Presacral Neurectomy for Treatment of Midline Pelvic Pain," *Journal of the American Association of Gynecologic Laparoscopists* 2, no. 1 (November 1994): 31–35, https://doi.org/10.1016 /s1074–3804(05)80828-x.

84   **prescribed for six to twenty-four months:** "Full Prescribing Information," Orilissa, RxAbbVie, revised June 2023, https://www.rxabbvie.com /pdf/orilissa_pi.pdf.

85   **nutritional changes might improve endometriosis symptoms:** Martina Helbig et al., "Does Nutrition Affect Endometriosis?," *Geburtshilfe Frauenheilkd* 81, no. 2 (February 2021): 191–99, https://doi.org/10.1055 /a-1207–0557.

85   **Vitamin D supplementation was shown:** Fariba Almassinokiani et al., "Effects of Vitamin D on Endometriosis-Related Pain: A Double-Blind

Clinical Trial," *Medical Science Monitor* 22 (December 2016): 4960–66, https://doi.org/10.12659/MSM.901838.

85 **curcumin, the main active agent:** Javad Sharifi-Rad et al., "Turmeric and Its Major Compound Curcumin on Health: Bioactive Effects and Safety Profiles for Food, Pharmaceutical, Biotechnological and Medicinal Applications," *Frontiers in Pharmacology* 11 (September 2020): 01021, https://doi.org/10.3389/fphar.2020.01021.

86 **pain and symptoms with medical marijuana:** Justin Sinclair et al., "Effects of Cannabis Ingestion on Endometriosis-Associated Pelvic Pain and Related Symptoms," *PLoS One* 16, no. 10 (2021): e0258940, https://doi.org/10.1371/journal.pone.0258940.

CHAPTER 6: POLYCYSTIC OVARIAN SYNDROME

88 **PCOS affects 10 percent or more:** Gurkan Bozdag et al., "The Prevalence and Phenotypic Features of Polycystic Ovary Syndrome: A Systematic Review and Meta-Analysis," *Human Reproduction* 31, no. 12 (2016): 2841–55, https://doi.org/10.1093/humrep/dew218.

89 **ethnic and regional differences:** Helena J. Teede et al., "Recommendations from the International Evidence-Based Guideline for the Assessment and Management of Polycystic Ovary Syndrome," *Human Reproduction* 33, no. 9 (September 2018): 1602–18, https://doi.org/10.1093/humrep/dey256.

89 **2003, experts from the European Society:** Rotterdam ESHRE/ASRM-Sponsored PCOS Consensus Workshop Group, "Revised 2003 Consensus on Diagnostic Criteria and Long-Term Health Risks Related to Polycystic Ovary Syndrome," *Fertility and Sterility* 81, no. 1 (January 2004): 19–25, https://doi.org/10.1016/j.fertnstert.2003.10.004.

92 **lean PCOS, meaning they have normal:** Sehar Toosy, Ravinder Sodi, and Joseph M. Pappachan, "Lean Polycystic Ovary Syndrome (PCOS): An Evidence-Based Practical Approach," *Journal of Diabetes and Metabolic Disorders* 17, no. 2 (2018): 277–85,https://doi.org/10.1007/s40200-018-0371–5.

92 **70 percent of patients with PCOS will:** John C. Marshall and Andrea Dunaif, "Should All Women with PCOS Be Treated for Insulin Resistance?," *Fertility and Sterility* 97, no. 1 (January 2012): 18–22, https://doi.org/10.1016/j.fertnstert.2011.11.036.

93 **higher risk of metabolic syndrome:** Toosy, Sodi, and Pappachan, "Lean Polycystic Ovary Syndrome."

94 **80 percent of people with PCOS:** Anderson Sanches Melo, Rui Alberto

Ferriani, and Paula Andrea Navarro, "Treatment of Infertility in Women with Polycystic Ovary Syndrome: Approach to Clinical Practice," *Clinics* 70, no. 11. (November 2015): 765–69, https://doi.org/10.6061/clinics/2015(11)09.

96 **Letrozole has been shown to be:** Sebastian Franik et al., "Aromatase Inhibitors (Letrozole) for Subfertile Women with Polycystic Ovary Syndrome," *Cochrane Database of Systematic Reviews* 5, no. 5 (2018): CD010287, https://doi.org/10.1002/14651858.CD010287.pub3.

96 **Inositol may be involved:** Bharti Kalra, Sanjay Kalra, and J. B. Sharma, "The Inositols and Polycystic Ovary Syndrome," *Indian Journal of Endocrinology and Metabolism* 20, no. 5 (September/October 2016): 720–24, https://doi.org/10.4103/2230–8210.189231.

97 **Ovarian drilling can restore ovulation:** H. Gjønnaess, "Late Endocrine Effects of Ovarian Electrocautery in Women with Polycystic Ovary Syndrome," *Fertility and Sterility* 69, no. 4 (1998): 697–701, https://doi.org/10.1016/s0015–0282(98)00006–5.

98 **loss of 5 to 10 percent of body weight:** Chan-Hee Kim and Seon-Heui Lee, "Effectiveness of Lifestyle Modification in Polycystic Ovary Syndrome Patients with Obesity: A Systematic Review and Meta-Analysis," *Life* 12, no. 2 (2022): 308, https://doi.org/10.3390/life12020308.

98 **Regular exercise, sleep, and stress:** David Scott et al., "Exploring Factors Related to Changes in Body Composition, Insulin Sensitivity and Aerobic Capacity in Response to a 12-Week Exercise Intervention in Overweight and Obese Women with and Without Polycystic Ovary Syndrome," *PloS One* 12, no. 8 (August 2017): e0182412, https://doi.org/10.1371/journal.pone.0182412; Chenzhao Ding et al., "Sleep and Obesity," *Journal of Obesity and Metabolic Syndrome* 27, no. 1 (2018): 4–24, https://doi.org/10.7570/jomes.2018.27.1.4.

98 **stress hormones like cortisol:** Lauren Thau, Jayashree Gandhi, and Sandeep Sharma, "Physiology, Cortisol," in *StatPearls* (Treasure Island, FL: StatPearls Publishing), last updated August 29, 2022, https://www.ncbi.nlm.nih.gov/books/NBK538239/.

CHAPTER 7: OVARIAN CYSTS

101 **Dermoids develop from germ cells:** "Ovarian Cysts," FAQs, American College of Obstetricians and Gynecologists, last updated November 2021, https://www.acog.org/womens-health/faqs/ovarian-cysts.

104 **experts don't recommend checking CA-125:** Committee on Gynecologic Practice, Society of Gynecologic Oncologists, "ACOG Committee

Opinion Number 280: The Role of the Generalist Obstetrician-Gynecologist in the Early Detection of Ovarian Cancer," *Obstetrics and Gynecology* 100, no. 6 (December 2002): 1413–16, https://doi.org/10.1016/s0029-7844(02)02630-3.

106 **cystectomy can decrease the pool:** Roa Alammari, Michelle Lightfoot, and Hye-Chun Hur, "Impact of Cystectomy on Ovarian Reserve: Review of the Literature," *Journal of Minimally Invasive Gynecology* 24, no. 2 (2017): 247–57, https://doi.org/10.1016/j.jmig.2016.12.010.

107 **higher risks of cardiovascular disease:** Maria C. Cusimano et al., "Association of Bilateral Salpingo-Oophorectomy with All Cause and Cause Specific Mortality: Population Based Cohort Study," *BMJ* 375, no. 8318 (December 2021): e067528, https://doi.org/10.1136/bmj-2021-067528.

107 **important for cardiac and other health:** Cathleen M. Rivera et al., "Increased Cardiovascular Mortality After Early Bilateral Oophorectomy," *Menopause* 16, no. 1 (2009): 15–23, https://doi.org/10.1097/gme.0b013e31818888f7.

CHAPTER 8: PELVIC FLOOR DYSFUNCTION

108 **European countries, such as France:** Bonnie Rochman, "Why France Pays for Postpartum Women to 'Re-Educate' Their Vagina," *Time*, February 22, 2012, https://healthland.time.com/2012/02/22/why-france-pays-for-postpartum-women-to-re-educate-their-vagina/.

111 **hovering over public toilets:** K. H. Moore et al., "Crouching Over the Toilet Seat: Prevalence Among British Gynaecological Outpatients and Its Effect upon Micturition," *British Journal of Obstetrics and Gynaecology* 98, no. 6 (June 1991): 569–72, https://doi.org/10.1111/j.1471-0528.1991.tb10372.x.

115 **amitriptyline, can actually improve pain:** Amit Thour and Raman Marwaha, "Amitriptyline," in *Stat Pearls* (Treasure Island, FL: StatPearls Publishing), last updated February 16, 2023, https://www.ncbi.nlm.nih.gov/books/NBK537225/.

116 **vaginal diazepam has a significant effect:** Rebecca H. Stone et al., "A Systematic Review of Intravaginal Diazepam for the Treatment of Pelvic Floor Hypertonic Disorder," *Journal of Clinical Pharmacology* 60, no. S2 (December 2020): S110–20, https://doi.org/10.1002/jcph.1775.

116 **Pelvic floor botulinum toxin (Botox):** Fei-Chi Chuang, Tsai-Hwa Yang, and Hann-Chorng Kuo, "Botulinum Toxin A Injection in the Treatment of Chronic Pelvic Pain with Hypertonic Pelvic Floor in Women: Treatment Techniques and Results," *Lower Urinary Tract Symptoms* 13, no. 1 (January 2021): 5–12, https://doi.org/10.1111/luts.12334.

CHAPTER 9: PELVIC ORGAN PROLAPSE

118 **two hundred thousand surgical procedures to treat pelvic:** Sarah Hamilton Boyles, Anne M. Weber, and Leslie Meyn, "Procedures for Pelvic Organ Prolapse in the United States, 1979–1997," *American Journal of Obstetrics and Gynecology* 188, no. 1 (2003): 108–15, https://doi.org/10.1067/mob.2003.101.

121 **pelvic PT reduces the prolapse:** Julija Makajeva, Carolina Watters, and Panos Safioleas, "Cystocele," in *StatPearls* (Treasure Island, FL: StatPearls Publishing), last updated October 17, 2022, https://www.ncbi.nlm.nih.gov/books/NBK564303/; Chunbo Li, Yuping Gong, and Bei Wang, "The Efficacy of Pelvic Floor Muscle Training for Pelvic Organ Prolapse: A Systematic Review and Meta-Analysis," *International Urogynecology Journal* 27, no. 7 (2016): 981–92, https://doi.org/10.1007/s00192-015-2846-y.

122 **2019 the U.S. Food and Drug Administration:** "Pelvic Organ Prolapse (POP): Surgical Mesh Considerations and Recommendations," U.S. Food and Drug Administration, last updated August 16, 2021, https://www.fda.gov/medical-devices/urogynecologic-surgical-mesh-implants/pelvic-organ-prolapse-pop-surgical-mesh-considerations-and-recommendations.

123 **colpocleisis is less invasive:** Shameem Abbasy and Kimberly Kenton, "Obliterative Procedures for Pelvic Organ Prolapse," *Clinical Obstetrics and Gynecology* 53, no. 1 (March 2010): 86–98, https://doi.org/10.1097/GRF.0b013e3181cd4252.

CHAPTER 10: URINARY INCONTINENCE

124 ***Urinary incontinence,* or loss of bladder:** I. Milsom and M. Gyhagen, "The Prevalence of Urinary Incontinence," *Climacteric: The Journal of the International Menopause Society* 22, no. 3 (2019): 217–22, https://doi.org/10.1080/13697137.2018.1543263.

128 **Obesity is a risk factor:** William Sheridan et al., "Weight Loss with Bariatric Surgery or Behaviour Modification and the Impact on Female Obesity-Related Urine Incontinence: A Comprehensive Systematic Review and Meta-Analysis," *Clinical Obesity* 11, no. 4 (August 2021): e12450, https://doi.org/10.1111/cob.12450.

128 **Kegel exercises to strengthen:** Nicola Adanna Okeahialam et al., "Pelvic Floor Muscle Training: A Practical Guide," *BMJ* 378, no. 8352 (September 2022): e070186, https://doi.org/10.1136/bmj-2022-070186.

129 **considered a first-line treatment:** Monica M. Christmas et al., "Menopause Hormone Therapy and Urinary Symptoms: A Systematic Review,"

Menopause 30, no. 6 (June 2023): 672–85, https://doi.org/10.1097/GME
.0000000000002187.

130 **older category of medication called anticholinergics:** David R. Staskin
and Scott A. MacDiarmid, "Using Anticholinergics to Treat Overactive
Bladder: The Issue of Treatment Tolerability," in "Overactive Bladder: Issues and Management," ed. John P. Lavelle and Mickey Karram, supplement
1, *American Journal of Medicine* 119, no. 3 (March 2006): 9–15, https://
doi.org/10.1016/j.amjmed.2005.12.011.

130 **Botulinum toxin can be injected:** Michael K. Flynn et al., "Outcome of
a Randomized, Double-Blind, Placebo Controlled Trial of Botulinum A
Toxin for Refractory Overactive Bladder," *Journal of Urology* 181, no. 6
(June 2009): 2608–15, https://doi.org/10.1016/j.juro.2009.01.117.

130 **Stimulating the nerves:** Paul D. M. Pettit and Anita Chen, "Implantable
Neuromodulation for Urinary Urge Incontinence and Fecal Incontinence:
A Urogynecology Perspective," *Urologic Clinics of North America* 39, no. 3
(August 2012): 397–404, https://doi.org/10.1016/j.ucl.2012.06.004.

131 **studied extensively for over twenty years:** Ferdinando Fusco et al., "Updated Systematic Review and Meta-Analysis of the Comparative Data on
Colposuspensions, Pubovaginal Slings, and Midurethral Tapes in the Surgical Treatment of Female Stress Urinary Incontinence," *European Urology* 72, no. 4 (October 2017): 567–91, https://doi.org/10.1016/j.eururo
.2017.04.026.

132 **World Health Organization estimates:** "Obstetric Fistula," World Health
Organization, February 19, 2018, https://www.who.int/news-room/facts
-in-pictures/detail/10-facts-on-obstetric-fistula.

CHAPTER 11: SEXUAL DYSFUNCTION

135 **20 percent of women in the United States:** Muhammad Tayyeb and Vi-
kas Gupta, "Dyspareunia," in *StatPearls* (Treasure Island, FL: StatPearls
Publishing), last updated June 11, 2022, https://www.ncbi.nlm.nih.gov
/books/NBK562159/.

135 **40 percent experience other problems of sexual:** Ronald W. Lewis et al.,
"Epidemiology/Risk Factors of Sexual Dysfunction," *Journal of Sexual
Medicine* 1, no. 1 (July 2004): 35–39, https://doi.org/10.1111/j.1743–6109
.2004.10106.x.

140 **Low libido is the most common:** Jan L. Shifren et al., "Sexual Problems and
Distress in United States Women: Prevalence and Correlates," *Obstetrics and
Gynecology* 112, no. 5 (November 2008): 970–78, https://doi.org/10.1097
/AOG.0b013e3181898cdb.

140   **coronavirus (COVID-19) infection:** Anna Fuchs et al., "The Impact of COVID-19 on Female Sexual Health," *International Journal of Environmental Research and Public Health* 17, no. 19 (2020): 7152, https://doi.org/10.3390/ijerph17197152.

142   **men and women with neurologic conditions:** Marcalee Alexander et al., "Randomized Trial of Clitoral Vacuum Suction Versus Vibratory Stimulation in Neurogenic Female Orgasmic Dysfunction," *Archives of Physical Medicine and Rehabilitation* 99, no. 2 (February 2018): 299–305, https://doi.org/10.1016/j.apmr.2017.09.001; J. Denil, D. A. Ohl, and C. Smythe, "Vacuum Erection Device in Spinal Cord Injured Men: Patient and Partner Satisfaction," *Archives of Physical Medicine and Rehabilitation* 77, no. 8 (August 1996): 750–53, https://doi.org/10.1016/s0003–9993(96)90252-x.

143   **safe to use with latex condoms:** "How to Choose Lubricants and Vaginal Moisturizers for Pleasure and Safety," Our Bodies Ourselves Today, Suffolk University, last modified July 2022, https://ourbodiesourselves.org/health-info/how-to-choose-lubricants-and-vaginal-moisturizers-for-pleasure-and-safety/.

144   **Women's Health Initiative (WHI):** Jennifer Hays et al., "Effects of Estrogen plus Progestin on Health-Related Quality of Life," *New England Journal of Medicine* 348, no. 19 (May 2003): 1839–54, https://doi.org/10.1056/NEJMoa030311.

144   **have shown some potential benefit:** Marcela González et al., "Sexual Function, Menopause and Hormone Replacement Therapy (HRT)," *Maturitas* 48, no. 4 (August 2004): 411–20, https://doi.org/10.1016/j.maturitas.2003.10.005.

144   **Vaginal estrogen can significantly improve dryness:** David D. Rahn et al., "Vaginal Estrogen for Genitourinary Syndrome of Menopause: A Systematic Review," *Obstetrics and Gynecology* 124, no. 6 (December 2014): 1147–56, https://doi.org/10.1097/AOG.0000000000000526.

144   **testosterone supplementation can improve desire, arousal:** Susan R. Davis et al., "Global Consensus Position Statement on the Use of Testosterone Therapy for Women," *Journal of Clinical Endocrinology and Metabolism* 104, no. 10 (October 2019): 4660–66, https://doi.org/10.1210/jc.2019–01603.

145   **Flibanserin (Addyi), which was the first:** Rashmi Baid and Rakesh Agarwal, "Flibanserin: A Controversial Drug for Female Hypoactive Sexual Desire Disorder," *Industrial Psychiatry Journal* 27, no. 1 (January/June 2018): 154–57, https://doi.org/10.4103/ipj.ipj_20_16.

145   **Bupropion (Wellbutrin) is an antidepressant:** Robert Taylor Segraves et al., "Bupropion Sustained Release for the Treatment of Hypoactive Sexual Desire Disorder in Premenopausal Women," *Journal of Clinical Psy-*

chopharmacology 24, no. 3 (June 2004): 339–42, https://doi.org/10.1097 /01.jcp.0000125686.20338.c1.

146   **bremelanotide (Vyleesi) received FDA approval:** Danielle Mayer and Sarah E. Lynch, "Bremelanotide: New Drug Approved for Treating Hypoactive Sexual Desire Disorder," *The Annals of Pharmacotherapy* 54, no. 7 (July 2020): 684–690, https://doi.org/10.1177/1060028019899152.

146   **Randomized studies in women have not:** Rosemary Basson et al., "Efficacy and Safety of Sildenafil Citrate in Women with Sexual Dysfunction Associated with Female Sexual Arousal Disorder," *Journal of Women's Health and Gender-Based Medicine* 11, no. 4 (May 2002): 367–77, https:// doi.org/10.1089/152460902317586001.

146   **women experiencing sexual dysfunction from SSRI:** H. George Nurnberg et al., "Sildenafil Treatment of Women with Antidepressant-Associated Sexual Dysfunction: A Randomized Controlled Trial," *JAMA* 300, no. 4 (2008): 395–404, https://doi.org/10.1001/jama.300.4.395.

146   **those with nerve-related issues:** M. S. Alexander et al., "Sildenafil in Women with Sexual Arousal Disorder Following Spinal Cord Injury," *Spinal Cord* 49, no. 2 (February 2011): 273–79, https://doi.org/10.1038/sc.2010.107.

CHAPTER 12: VULVOVAGINAL CONDITIONS

149   **Three out of four women will:** "Vaginal Yeast Infection (Thrush): Overview," InformedHealth.org (Cologne, Germany: Institute for Quality and Efficiency in Health Care), last updated June 19, 2019, https://www.ncbi .nlm.nih.gov/books/NBK543220/.

149   **Candida can be found in up to 20 percent:** Jack D. Sobel, "Vulvovaginal Candidosis," *Lancet* 369, no. 9577 (June 2007): 1961–71, https://doi.org /10.1016/S0140–6736(07)60917–9.

151   **most common cause of discharge:** Makella S. Coudray and Purnima Madhivanan, "Bacterial Vaginosis—A Brief Synopsis of the Literature," *European Journal of Obstetrics and Gynecology and Reproductive Biology* 245 (February 2020): 143–48, https://doi.org/10.1016/j.ejogrb.2019.12.035.

152   **one in twenty sexually active teens:** "Chlamydia—CDC Detailed Fact Sheet," Centers for Disease Control and Prevention, last updated April 11, 2023, https://www.cdc.gov/std/chlamydia/stdfact-chlamydia-detailed .htm.

153   **Trichomonas is the most common nonviral:** "Sexually Transmitted Infections (STIs)," Fact Sheets, World Health Organization, August 22, 2022, https://www.who.int/news-room/fact-sheets/detail/sexually-transmitted -infections-(stis).

155 **Herpes is extremely common, affecting 12 percent:** "Genital Herpes—CDC Detailed Fact Sheet," Centers for Disease Control and Prevention, last updated July 22, 2021, https://www.cdc.gov/std/herpes/stdfact-herpes-detailed.htm.

158 **Vulvar cancer is very rare:** Anthony Capria, Nayha Tahir, and Mary Fatehi, "Vulva Cancer," in *StatPearls* (Treasure Island, FL: StatPearls Publishing), last updated January 9, 2023, https://www.ncbi.nlm.nih.gov/books/NBK567798/.

159 **treatment of vulvodynia is very complex:** Andrew T. Goldstein et al., "Vulvodynia: Assessment and Treatment," *Journal of Sexual Medicine* 13, no. 4 (April 2016): 572–90, https://doi.org/10.1016/j.jsxm.2016.01.020.

159 **Vaginal estrogen is generally the most effective:** Rahn et al., "Vaginal Estrogen for Genitourinary Syndrome of Menopause."

160 **FDA published a warning that laser:** "Statement from FDA Commissioner Scott Gottlieb, M.D., on Efforts to Safeguard Women's Health from Deceptive Health Claims and Significant Risks Related to Devices Marketed for Use in Medical Procedures for 'Vaginal Rejuvenation,'" FDA News Release, U.S. Food and Drug Administration, last updated August 2, 2018, https://www.fda.gov/news-events/press-announcements/statement-fda-commissioner-scott-gottlieb-md-efforts-safeguard-womens-health-deceptive-health-claims.

160 **American Urogynecologic Society have both issued:** Jonia Alshiek et al., "AUGS Clinical Consensus Statement: Vaginal Energy-Based Devices," *Female Pelvic Medicine and Reconstructive Surgery* 26, no. 5 (May 2020): 287–98, https://doi.org/10.1097/SPV.0000000000000872

161 **contribute to bacteria or yeast growth:** Divya A. Patel et al., "Risk Factors for Recurrent Vulvovaginal Candidiasis in Women Receiving Maintenance Antifungal Therapy: Results of a Prospective Cohort Study," *American Journal of Obstetrics and Gynecology* 190, no. 3 (March 2004): 644–53, https://doi.org/10.1016/j.ajog.2003.11.027.

CHAPTER 13: PREMENSTRUAL SYNDROME AND PREMENSTRUAL DYSPHORIC DISORDER

162 **Up to 75 percent of women suffer:** Meir Steiner, "Premenstrual Syndrome and Premenstrual Dysphoric Disorder: Guidelines for Management," *Journal of Psychiatry and Neuroscience* 25, no. 5 (2000): 459–68, https://www.ncbi.nlm.nih.gov/pmc/articles/PMC1408015/.

163 **medical criteria for diagnosing PMS:** Patrick Michael Shaughn O'Brien et al., "Towards a Consensus on Diagnostic Criteria, Measurement and

Trial Design of the Premenstrual Disorders: The ISPMD Montreal Consensus," *Archives of Women's Mental Health* 14, no. 1 (2011): 13–21, https://doi.org/10.1007/s00737-010-0201-3.

164   **Serotonin may also be:** Steiner, "Premenstrual Syndrome."

164   **antidepressants such as selective serotonin:** Sara V. Carlini and Kristina M. Deligiannidis, "Evidence-Based Treatment of Premenstrual Dysphoric Disorder: A Concise Review," *Journal of Clinical Psychiatry* 81, no. 2 (March/April 2020): 19ac13071, https://doi.org/10.4088/JCP.19ac13071.

166   **oral contraceptive pill that is:** "YAZ Full Prescribing Information," U.S. Food and Drug Administration, last revised March 2011, https://www.accessdata.fda.gov/drugsatfda_docs/label/2011/021676s008lbl.pdf.

166   **only during the luteal phase:** Uriel Halbreich et al., "Efficacy of Intermittent, Luteal Phase Sertraline Treatment of Premenstrual Dysphoric Disorder," *Obstetrics and Gynecology* 100, no. 6 (December 2002): 1219–29, https://doi.org/10.1016/s0029-7844(02)02326-8.

167   **surgical removal of the ovaries:** P. Casson et al., "Lasting Response to Ovariectomy in Severe Intractable Premenstrual Syndrome," *American Journal of Obstetrics and Gynecology* 162, no. 1 (January 1990): 99–105, https://doi.org/10.1016/0002-9378(90)90830-z.

167   **diet rich in complex carbohydrates:** Rodica Siminiuc and Dinu Țurcanu, "Impact of Nutritional Diet Therapy on Premenstrual Syndrome," *Frontiers in Nutrition* 10 (2023): 1079417, https://doi.org/10.3389/fnut.2023.1079417.

CHAPTER 14: PERIMENOPAUSE AND MENOPAUSE

170   **twelve months in a row without:** "Menopause 101: A Primer for the Perimenopausal," North American Menopause Society, accessed June 20, 2023, https://www.menopause.org/for-women/menopauseflashes/menopause-symptoms-and-treatments/menopause-101-a-primer-for-the-perimenopausal.

170   **average age of menopause:** "Menopause 101," North American Menopause Society.

170   **Removing both ovaries has serious:** Elisabeth A. Erekson, Deanna K. Martin, and Elena S. Ratner, "Oophorectomy: The Debate Between Ovarian Conservation and Elective Oophorectomy," *Menopause* 20, no. 1 (January 2013): 110–14, https://doi.org/10.1097/gme.0b013e31825a27ab.

173   **Decreasing estrogen levels can cause:** Sindhu Prabakaran, Arielle Schwartz, and Gina Lundberg, "Cardiovascular Risk in Menopausal Women and Our Evolving Understanding of Menopausal Hormone

Therapy: Risks, Benefits, and Current Guidelines for Use," *Therapeutic Advances in Endocrinology and Metabolism* 12 (2021), https://doi.org/10.1177/20420188211013917.

173 **Loss of bone mass actually starts before:** Arun S. Karlamangla, Sherri-Ann M. Burnett-Bowie, and Carolyn J. Crandall, "Bone Health During the Menopause Transition and Beyond," *Obstetrics and Gynecology Clinics of North America* 45 no. 4 (December 2018): 695–708, https://doi.org/10.1016/j.ogc.2018.07.012.

174 **Estrogen-containing** *menopausal hormone therapy* **(MHT):** John Paciuc, "Hormone Therapy in Menopause," *Advances in Experimental Medicine and Biology* 1242 (2020): 89–120, https://doi.org/10.1007/978-3-030-38474-6_6.

175 **gynecologists will recommend transdermal patches rather:** Committee on Gynecologic Practice, "ACOG Committee Opinion No. 556: Postmenopausal Estrogen Therapy; Route of Administration and Risk of Venous Thromboembolism," *Obstetrics and Gynecology* 121, no. 4 (2013): 887–90, https://doi.org/10.1097/01.AOG.0000428645.90795.d9.

175 **Women's Health Initiative (WHI) showed that:** JoAnn E. Manson et al., "Estrogen Plus Progestin and the Risk of Coronary Heart Disease," *New England Journal of Medicine* 349, no. 6 (August 2003); 523–34, https://doi.org/10.1056/NEJMoa030808.

176 **cardiovascular and cancer risks of MHT:** Paola Villa et al., "Cardiovascular Risk/Benefit Profile of MHT," *Medicina* 55, no. 9 (2019): 571, https://doi.org/10.3390/medicina55090571.

177 **vaginal estrogen doesn't increase:** Shilpa N. Bhupathiraju et al., "Vaginal Estrogen Use and Chronic Disease Risk in the Nurses' Health Study," *Menopause* 26, no. 6 (June 2019): 603–10, https://doi.org/10.1097/GME.0000000000001284.

177 **Depo-Provera birth control injection:** R. A. Lobo et al., "Depo-Medroxyprogesterone Acetate Compared with Conjugated Estrogens for the Treatment of Postmenopausal Women," *Obstetrics and Gynecology* 63, no. 1 (January 1984): 1–5, https://pubmed.ncbi.nlm.nih.gov/6318170/.

177 **commercial MHT estrogen is actually:** Morris Notelovitz, "Clinical Opinion: The Biologic and Pharmacologic Principles of Estrogen Therapy for Symptomatic Menopause," *MedGenMed: Medscape General Medicine* 8, no. 1 (2006): 85, https://www.ncbi.nlm.nih.gov/pmc/articles/PMC1682006/.

178 **recommend against using compounded hormones:** Committee on Gynecologic Practice and the American Society for Reproductive Medicine

Practice Committee, "ACOG Committee Opinion 532: Compounded Bi-oidentical Menopausal Hormone Therapy," *Obstetrics and Gynecology* 120 (August 2012): 411–15, http://doi.org/10.1097/AOG.0b013e318268049e; NAMS 2022 Hormone Therapy Position Statement Advisory Panel, "The 2022 Hormone Therapy Position Statement of the North American Menopause Society," *Menopause* 29, no. 7 (2022): 767–94, https://doi.org/10.1097/GME.0000000000002028.

178   **hormone testing is not necessary to guide:** Committee on Practice Bulletins—Gynecology and Clarisa Gracia, "ACOG Practice Bulletin No. 141: Management of Menopausal Symptoms," *Obstetrics and Gynecology* 123, no. 1 (January 2014): 202–16, https://doi.org/10.1097/01.AOG.0000441353.20693.78.

178   **most effective alternatives to estrogen:** Heidi D. Nelson et al., "Non-hormonal Therapies for Menopausal Hot Flashes: Systematic Review and Meta-Analysis," *JAMA* 295, no. 17 (May 2006): 2057–71, https://doi.org/10.1001/jama.295.17.2057.

179   **In 2023, the FDA approved a medication:** "FDA Approves Novel Drug to Treat Moderate to Severe Hot Flashes Caused by Menopause," FDA News Release, U.S. Food and Drug Administration, May 12, 2023, https://www.fda.gov/news-events/press-announcements/fda-approves-novel-drug-treat-moderate-severe-hot-flashes-caused-menopause.

179   **Taken daily, fezolinetant was shown:** Samuel Lederman et al., "Fezolin-etant for Treatment of Moderate-to-Severe Vasomotor Symptoms associated with Menopause (SKYLIGHT 1): A Phase 3 Randomised Controlled Study," *Lancet* 401, no. 10382 (April 2023): 1091–1102, https://doi.org/10.1016/S0140-6736(23)00085-5; "Veozah Full Prescribing Information," Astellas Pharma, May 2023, https://www.astellas.com/us/system/files/veozah_uspi.pdf.

180   **data on soy and black cohosh:** Oscar H. Franco et al., "Use of Plant-Based Therapies and Menopausal Symptoms: A Systematic Review and Meta-analysis," *JAMA* 315, no. 23 (June 2016): 2554–63, https://doi.org/10.1001/jama.2016.8012.

180   **differences between acupuncture and placebo:** Nancy E. Avis et al., "A Randomized, Controlled Pilot Study of Acupuncture Treatment for Menopausal Hot Flashes," *Menopause* 15, no. 6 (December 2008): 1070–78, https://doi.org/10.1097/gme.0b013e31816d5b03.

181   **weight loss in overweight or obese:** Allison J. Huang et al., "An Intensive Behavioral Weight Loss Intervention and Hot Flushes in Women," *Archives of Internal Medicine* 170, no. 13 (July 2010): 1161–67, https://doi.org/10.1001/archinternmed.2010.162.

181   **Cognitive behavioral therapy may improve:** "Nonhormonal Management of Menopause-Associated Vasomotor Symptoms: 2015 Position Statement of the North American Menopause Society," *Menopause* 22, no. 11 (November 2015): 1155–74, https://doi.org/10.1097/GME .0000000000000546.

CHAPTER 15: INFERTILITY

183   **186 million people globally live:** Shea O. Rutstein and Iqbal H. Shah, "Infecundity, Infertility, and Childlessness in Developing Countries—DHS Comparative Reports No. 9," World Health Organization, September 29, 2004, https://www.who.int/publications/m/item/infecundity-infertility -and-childlessness-in-developing-countries—dhs-comparative-reports -no.-9.

184   **Fertility testing should be considered after:** American College of Obstetricians and Gynecologists Committee on Gynecologic Practice, "Committee Opinion No. 589: Female Age-Related Fertility Decline," *Fertility and Sterility* 101, no. 3 (March 2014): 633–34, https://doi.org/10.1016/j .fertnstert.2013.12.032.

185   **10 percent of a person's original egg:** W. Hamish B. Wallace and Thomas W. Kelsey, "Human Ovarian Reserve from Conception to the Menopause," *PLoS One* 5, no. 1 (January 2010): e8772, https://doi.org/10.1371 /journal.pone.0008772.

185   **cancer treatments such as chemotherapy:** "Primary Ovarian Insufficiency," Diseases and Conditions, Mayo Clinic, October 27, 2021, https:// www.mayoclinic.org/diseases-conditions/premature-ovarian-failure /symptoms-causes/syc-20354683.

186   **fluid inside a hydrosalpinx is inflammatory:** Hoda Maaly Harb et al., "Hydrosalpinx and Pregnancy Loss: A Systematic Review and Meta-Analysis," *Reproductive Biomedicine Online* 38, no. 3 (March 2019): 427–41, https://doi.org/10.1016/j.rbmo.2018.12.020.

187   **8 percent of cases were due to:** WHO Scientific Group, "Recent Advances in Medically Assisted Conception," *WHO Technical Report Series* 820 (Geneva: World Health Organization, 1992), https://apps.who.int/iris /handle/10665/38679.

187   **a third of cases are due:** Ashok Agarwal et al., "A Unique View on Male Infertility Around the Globe," *Reproductive Biology and Endocrinology* 13, no. 37 (2015): https://doi.org/10.1186/s12958-015-0032-1.

187   **Almost a third of infertility cases:** The Practice Committee of the American Society for Reproductive Medicine, "Effectiveness and Treatment

for Unexplained Infertility," *Fertility and Sterility* 86 no. 5, supplement 1 (November 2006): S111–14, https://doi.org/10.1016/j.fertnstert.2006.07 .1475.

187–188   **likelihood of getting pregnant is 25 percent:** Alison Taylor, "ABC of Subfertility: Extent of the Problem," *BMJ* 327, no. 7412 (2003): 434–36, https://doi.org/10.1136/bmj.327.7412.434; S. J. Chua et al., "Age-Related Natural Fertility Outcomes in Women Over 35 Years: A Systematic Review and Individual Participant Data Meta-Analysis," *Human Reproduction* 35, no. 8 (August 2020): 1808–20, https://doi.org/10.1093/humrep /deaa129.

190   **multiple-gestation pregnancies:** "ART and Multiple Births," Assisted Reproductive Technology (ART), Centers for Disease and Control and Prevention, last modified April 1, 2016, https://www.cdc.gov/art/key -findings/multiple-births.html.

191   **risk of *ovarian hyperstimulation syndrome*:** Annick Delvigne and Serge Rozenberg, "Epidemiology and Prevention of Ovarian Hyperstimulation Syndrome (OHSS): A Review," *Human Reproduction Update* 8, no. 6 (November 2002): 559–77, https://doi.org/10.1093/humupd/8.6.559.

192   **IVF is the most effective form:** Audrey J. Gaskins et al., "Predicted Probabilities of Live Birth Following Assisted Reproductive Technology Using United States National Surveillance Data from 2016 to 2018," *American Journal of Obstetrics and Gynecology* 228, no. 5 (May 2023): 557.e1–e10, https://doi.org/10.1016/j.ajog.2023.01.014.

193   **only a single embryo is transferred:** Practice Committee of the American Society for Reproductive Medicine and the Practice Committee for the Society for Assisted Reproductive Technologies, "Guidance on the Limits to the Number of Embryos to Transfer: A Committee Opinion," *Fertility and Sterility* 116 no. 3 (September 2021): 651–54, https://doi.org /10.1016/j.fertnstert.2021.06.050.

193–194   **eight million babies born through IVF:** David Adamson et al., "ICMART Preliminary World Report 2015" (ESHRE, Vienna, Austria, June 25, 2019), https://www.icmartivf.org/wp-content/uploads/ICMART -ESHRE-WR2015-FINAL-20200901.pdf.

194   **up to 10 percent of pregnancies:** Alice Goisis et al., "The Demographics of Assisted Reproductive Technology Births in a Nordic Country," *Human Reproduction* 35, no. 6 (May 2020): 1441–50, https://doi.org/10.1093 /humrep/deaa055; Daphna Birenbaum-Carmeli, "Thirty-Five Years of Assisted Reproductive Technologies in Israel," *Reproductive Biomedicine and Society Online* 2 (June 2016): 16–23, https://doi.org/10.1016/j.rbms .2016.05.004.

194   **improved if vitamin D levels are normal:** Jing Zhao et al., "Whether Vitamin D Was Associated with Clinical Outcome After IVF/ICSI: A Systematic Review and Meta-Analysis," *Reproductive Biology and Endocrinology* 16, no. 1 (2018): 13, https://doi.org/10.1186/s12958-018 -0324-3.

194   **randomized study of vitamin D supplementation:** Edgardo Somigliana et al., "Single Oral Dose of Vitamin D_3 Supplementation Prior to In Vitro Fertilization and Embryo Transfer in Normal Weight Women: The SUNDRO Randomized Controlled Trial," *American Journal of Obstetrics and Gynecology* 225, no. 3 (April 2021): 283.e1–e10, https://doi.org/10.1016/j .ajog.2021.04.234.

194   **CoQ10 supplementation during fertility treatment:** Panagiota Florou et al., "Does Coenzyme Q_{10} Supplementation Improve Fertility Outcomes in Women Undergoing Assisted Reproductive Technology Procedures? A Systematic Review and Meta-Analysis of Randomized-Controlled Trials," *Journal of Assisted Reproduction and Genetics* 37, no. 10 (October 2020): 2377–87, https://doi.org/10.1007/s10815-020-01906-3.

194   *Dehydroepiandrosterone* **(DHEA) is a testosterone hormone:** Lin Xu et al., "The Effect of Dehydroepiandrosterone (DHEA) Supplementation on IVF or ICSI: A Meta-Analysis of Randomized Controlled Trials," *Geburtshilfe und Frauenheilkunde* 79, no. 7 (July 2019): 705–12, https://doi .org/10.1055/a-0882-3791.

195   **Acupuncture is thought to potentially improve:** Dong-mei Huang et al., "Acupuncture for Infertility: Is It an Effective Therapy?," *Chinese Journal of Integrative Medicine* 17, no. 5 (2011): 386–95, https://doi.org/10.1007 /s11655-011-0611-8.

CHAPTER 16: MISCARRIAGE

197   **Up to 25 percent of recognized pregnancies:** A. García-Enguídanos et al., "Risk Factors in Miscarriage: A Review," *European Journal of Obstetrics, Gynecology, and Reproductive Biology* 102, no. 2 (May 2002): 111–19, https://doi.org/10.1016/s0301–2115(01)00613-3.

197   **up to 70 percent of fertilized eggs:** D. K. Edmonds et al., "Early Embryonic Mortality in Women," *Fertility and Sterility* 38, no. 4 (October 1982): 447–53, https://pubmed.ncbi.nlm.nih.gov/7117572/.

198   **Most miscarriages occur within the first:** Carla Dugas and Valori H. Slane, "Miscarriage," in *StatPearls* (Treasure Island, FL: StatPearls Publishing), last updated June 27, 2022, https://www.ncbi.nlm.nih.gov /books/NBK532992/.

200 **occurring in less than 1 percent of pregnancies:** Andrea Altieri et al., "Epidemiology and Aetiology of Gestational Trophoblastic Diseases," *Lancet: Oncology* 4, no. 11 (November 2003): 670–78, https://doi.org/10.1016/s1470–2045(03)01245–2.

201 **molar pregnancy can even become cancerous:** Kevin M. Elias, Ross S. Berkowitz, and Neil S. Horowitz, "State-of-the-Art Workup and Initial Management of Newly Diagnosed Molar Pregnancy and Postmolar Gestational Trophoblastic Neoplasia," *Journal of the National Comprehensive Cancer Network* 17, no. 11 (November 2019): 1396–1401, https://doi.org/10.6004/jnccn.2019.7364.

202 **80 percent of first-trimester miscarriages:** Ciro Luise et al., "Outcome of Expectant Management of Spontaneous First Trimester Miscarriage: Observational Study," *BMJ* 324, no. 7342 (April 2002): 873–75, https://doi.org/10.1136/bmj.324.7342.873.

203 **mifepristone and misoprostol is more effective:** Sarita Sonalkar et al., "Management of Early Pregnancy Loss with Mifepristone and Misoprostol: Clinical Predictors of Treatment Success from a Randomized Trial," *American Journal of Obstetrics and Gynecology* 223, no. 4 (October 2020): 551.e1–e7, https://doi.org/10.1016/j.ajog.2020.04.006.

204 **More than half of miscarriages:** Joe Leigh Simpson and Sandra Ann Carson, "Genetic and Nongenetic Causes of Pregnancy Loss," *Global Library of Women's Medicine*, last updated January 2013, https://doi.org/10.3843/GLOWM.10319.

204 **risk of miscarriage is 10 percent:** Maria C. Magnus et al., "Role of Maternal Age and Pregnancy History in Risk of Miscarriage: Prospective Register Based Study," *BMJ* 364, no. l869 (March 2019), https://doi.org/10.1136/bmj.l869.

205 **COVID-19 infection in pregnancy:** Seyyedeh Neda Kazemi et al., "COVID-19 and Cause of Pregnancy Loss During the Pandemic: A Systematic Review," *PloS One* 16, no. 8 (August 2021): e0255994, https://doi.org/10.1371/journal.pone.0255994.

206 **supplemental progesterone has not been shown:** Adam J. Devall et al., "Progestogens for Preventing Miscarriage: A Network Meta-Analysis," *Cochrane Database of Systematic Reviews* 4, no. 4 (2021): CD013792, https://doi.org/10.1002/14651858.CD013792.pub2.

207 **50 percent of patients experiencing recurrent:** Leela Sharath Pillarisetty and Heba Mahdy, "Recurrent Pregnancy Loss," in *StatPearls* (Treasure Island, FL: StatPearls Publishing), last updated September 6, 2022, https://www.ncbi.nlm.nih.gov/books/NBK554460/.

207 **77 percent of people with a history:** Kirsten Duckitt and Aysha Qureshi, "Recurrent miscarriage," *BMJ Clinical Evidence* 2015, no. 2015 (October 2015): 1409, https://www.ncbi.nlm.nih.gov/pmc/articles/PMC4610348/.

CHAPTER 17: GENDER DIVERSITY

209 **1.6 million transgender people ages thirteen:** "How Many Adults and Youth Identify as Transgender in the United States," Williams Institute, UCLA Law, last updated June 2022, https://williamsinstitute.law.ucla.edu /publications/trans-adults-united-states/.

210 **2018 study, the American Academy:** Russell B. Toomey, Amy K. Syvertsen, and Maura Shramko, "Transgender Adolescent Suicide Behavior," *Pediatrics* 142, no. 4 (October 2018): e20174218, https://doi.org/10.1542 /peds.2017–4218.

210 **significantly improve depression and anxiety:** Diana M. Tordoff et al., "Mental Health Outcomes in Transgender and Nonbinary Youths Receiving Gender-Affirming Care," *JAMA Network Open* 5, no. 2 (February 2022): e220978, https://doi.org/10.1001/jamanetworkopen.2022.0978.

210 **WHO defines *gender* as:** "Gender and Health," Health Topics, World Health Organization, accessed July 7, 2023, https://www.who.int/health -topics/gender#tab=tab_1.

211 **Pew Research Center showed that 5 percent:** Anna Brown, "About 5% of Young Adults in the U.S. Say Their Gender Is Different from Their Sex Assigned at Birth," Pew Research Center, June 7, 2022, https://pewrsr.ch /3Qi2Ejd.

212 **every major medical society:** Jason Rafferty et al., "Policy Statement, American Academy of Pediatrics: Ensuring Comprehensive Care and Support for Transgender and Gender-Diverse Children and Adolescents," *Pediatrics* 142, no. 4 (October 2018): e20182162, https://doi.org/10.1542 /peds.2018–2162; Committee on Gynecologic Practice and Committee on Health Care for Underserved Women, "ACOG Committee Opinion 832: Health Care for Transgender and Gender Diverse Individuals," *Obstetrics and Gynecology* 137, no. 3 (March 2021): e75–88, https://doi.org /10.1097/AOG.0000000000004294.

211–212 **more than half the states:** "Attacks on Gender-Affirming and Transgender Health Care," American College of Physicians, April 24, 2023, https:// www.acponline.org/advocacy/state-health-policy/attacks-on-gender -affirming-and-transgender-health-care.

213 **70 percent reduction in suicidality:** Tordoff et al., "Mental Health Outcomes."

213 **Gender-affirming treatment in minors:** "Transgender Health Position Statement," Pediatric Endocrine Society, December 2020, https://www.endocrine.org/-/media/endocrine/files/advocacy/position-statement/position_statement_transgender_health_pes.pdf.

213 **98 percent of transgender adolescents:** Maria Anna Theodora Catharina van der Loos et al., "Continuation of Gender-Affirming Hormones in Transgender People Starting Puberty Suppression in Adolescence: A Cohort Study in the Netherlands," *Lancet: Child and Adolescent Health* 6, no. 12 (December 2022): 869–75, https://doi.org/10.1016/S2352-4642(22)00254-1.

215 **normal pubertal development usually resumes:** Caroline Salas-Humara et al., "Gender Affirming Medical Care of Transgender Youth," *Current Problems in Pediatric and Adolescent Health Care* 49, no. 9 (September 2019): 100683, https://doi.org/10.1016/j.cppeds.2019.100683.

216 **Genital surgeries and surgeries to remove:** E. Coleman et al., "Standards of Care for the Health of Transgender and Gender Diverse People, Version 8," *International Journal of Transgender Health* 23, suppl. 1 (September 2022): S1–259, https://doi.org/10.1080/26895269.2022.2100644.

CHAPTER 18: INTERSEX

222 **Starting in the 1950s:** J. Money, J. G. Hampson, and J. L. Hampson, "Hermaphroditism: Recommendations Concerning Assignment of Sex, Change of Sex and Psychologic Management," *Bulletin of the Johns Hopkins Hospital* 97, no. 4 (October 1955): 284–300, https://pubmed.ncbi.nlm.nih.gov/13260819/.

223 **compared to the color spectrum:** "What Is Intersex?," Intersex Society of North America, last modified 2008, https://isna.org/faq/what_is_intersex/.

224 **Up to 1.7 percent:** "Intersex People: OHCHR and the Human Rights of LGBTI People," United Nations Human Rights, Office of the High Commissioner, accessed June 30, 2023, https://www.ohchr.org/en/sexual-orientation-and-gender-identity/intersex-people.

224 **one in 1,000 to 4,500 infants:** Melanie Blackless et al., "How Sexually Dimorphic Are We? Review and Synthesis," *American Journal of Human Biology* 12, no. 2 (March/April 2000): 151–66, https://doi.org/10.1002/(SICI)1520-6300(200003/04)12:2<151::AID-AJHB1>3.0.CO;2-F; Ieuan A. Hughes et al., "Consequences of the ESPE/LWPES Guidelines for Diagnosis and Treatment of Disorders of Sex Development." *Best Practice and Research Clinical Endocrinology and Metabolism* 21, no. 3 (September 2007): 351–65, https://doi.org/10.1016/j.beem.2007.06.003.

224   **both XX and XY chromosomes:** A. S. Freiberg et al., "XX/XY Chimerism Encountered During Prenatal Diagnosis," *Prenatal Diagnosis* 8, no. 6 (July 1988): 423–26, https://doi.org/10.1002/pd.1970080606.

226   **risk of early cancer:** Peter A. Lee et al., "Global Disorders of Sex Development Update Since 2006: Perceptions, Approach and Care," *Hormone Research in Paediatrics* 85, no. 3 (April 2016): 158–80, https://doi.org/10.1159/000442975.

CHAPTER 19: CANCER

231   **More than 99 percent of cases:** Jan M. M. Walboomers et al., "Human Papillomavirus Is a Necessary Cause of Invasive Cervical Cancer Worldwide," *Journal of Pathology* 189, no. 1 (September 1999): 12–19, https://doi.org/10.1002/(SICI)1096–9896(199909)189:1<12::AID-PATH431>3.0.CO;2-F.

231   **90 percent of cervical cancer deaths:** David Viveros-Carreño, Andreina Fernandes, and Rene Pareja, "Updates on Cervical Cancer Prevention," *International Journal of Gynecological Cancer* 33, no. 3 (March 2023): 394–402, https://doi.org/10.1136/ijgc-2022–003703.

231   **2020, the WHO adopted:** "Cervical Cancer Elimination Initiative," World Health Organization, accessed June 30, 2023, https://www.who.int/initiatives/cervical-cancer-elimination-initiative#cms.

232   **DES was given to mothers:** Anthony A. Bamigboye and Jonathan Morris, "Oestrogen Supplementation, Mainly Diethylstilbestrol, for Preventing Miscarriages and Other Adverse Pregnancy Outcomes," *Cochrane Database of Systematic Reviews* 2003, no. 3 (July 2003): CD004353, https://doi.org/10.1002/14651858.CD004353.

232   **80 percent, will contract a strain:** Harrell W. Chesson et al., "The Estimated Lifetime Probability of Acquiring Human Papillomavirus in the United States," *Sexually Transmitted Diseases* 41, no. 11 (November 2014): 660–64, https://doi.org/10.1097/OLQ.0000000000000193.

232   **70 percent of cervical cancers:** Silvia de Sanjose et al., "Human Papillomavirus Genotype Attribution in Invasive Cervical Cancer: A Retrospective Cross-Sectional Worldwide Study," *Lancet: Oncology* 11, no. 11 (November 2010): 1048–56, https://doi.org/10.1016/S1470–2045(10)70230–8.

233   **98 to 99 percent of cervical precancers and cancers:** "Efficacy of Gardasil 9," Merck Vaccines, accessed June 30, 2023, https://www.merckvaccines.com/gardasil9/efficacy/.

233   **women and men through age forty-five:** "Gardasil 9," U.S. Food and Drug Administration, last updated April 28, 2023, https://www.fda.gov/vaccines-blood-biologics/vaccines/gardasil-9.

233 **hundreds of millions of doses:** "Safety of HPV Vaccines," Global Advisory on Vaccine Safety, World Health Organization, July 15, 2017, https://www.who.int/groups/global-advisory-committee-on-vaccine-safety/topics/human-papillomavirus-vaccines/safety.

234 **recommended starting at age twenty-one:** "Updated Cervical Cancer Screening Guidelines," Practice Advisory, American College of Obstetricians and Gynecologists, April 2021, https://www.acog.org/clinical/clinical-guidance/practice-advisory/articles/2021/04/updated-cervical-cancer-screening-guidelines.

235 **American Cancer Society (ACS), recommend HPV screening:** "The American Cancer Society Guidelines for the Prevention and Early Detection of Cervical Cancer," American Cancer Society, last revised April 22, 2021, https://www.cancer.org/cancer/types/cervical-cancer/detection-diagnosis-staging/cervical-cancer-screening-guidelines.html.

237 **90 percent of postmenopausal women:** Megan A. Clarke et al., "Association of Endometrial Cancer Risk with Postmenopausal Bleeding in Women: A Systematic Review and Meta-Analysis," *JAMA Internal Medicine* 178, no. 9 (September 2018): 1210–22, https://doi.org/10.1001/jamainternmed.2018.2820.

238 **10 percent of women with postmenopausal bleeding:** J. Carugno, "Clinical Management of Vaginal Bleeding in Postmenopausal Women," *Climacteric: The Journal of the International Menopause Society* 23, no. 4 (2020): 343–49, https://doi.org/10.1080/13697137.2020.1739642.

241 **Only about a thousand women:** "Vaginal and Vulvar Cancers Statistics," Division of Cancer Prevention and Control, Centers for Disease Control and Prevention, last updated June 8, 2023, https://www.cdc.gov/cancer/vagvulv/statistics/index.htm.

242 **one in eight women:** Kristin Rojas and Ashley Stuckey, "Breast Cancer Epidemiology and Risk Factors," *Clinical Obstetrics and Gynecology* 59, no. 4 (December 2016): 651–72, https://doi.org/10.1097/GRF.0000000000000239.

243 **hormonal birth control methods may pose:** Collaborative Group on Hormonal Factors in Breast Cancer, "Breast Cancer and Hormonal Contraceptives: Collaborative Reanalysis of Individual Data on 53,297 Women with Breast Cancer and 100,239 Women Without Breast Cancer from 54 Epidemiological Studies," *Lancet* 347, no. 9017 (June 1996): 1713–27, https://doi.org/10.1016/s0140–6736(96)90806–5/.

243 **Postmenopausal hormone replacement therapy:** Yana Vinogradova, Carol Coupland, and Julia Hippisley-Cox, "Use of Hormone Replacement Therapy and Risk of Breast Cancer: Nested Case-Control Studies

Using the QResearch and CPRD Databases," *BMJ* 2020, no. 371 (October 2020): m3873, https://doi.org/10.1136/bmj.m3873.

243   **85 percent lifetime risk of:** D. Ford et al., "Risks of Cancer in BRCA1-Mutation Carriers," *Lancet* 43, no. 8899 (1984): 692–95, https://doi.org/10.1016/S0140-6736(94)91578-4.

243   **More than a third of all:** Mara Y. Roth et al., "Self-Detection Remains a Key Method of Breast Cancer Detection for U.S. Women," *Journal of Women's Health* 20, no. 8 (August 2011): 1135–39, https://doi.org/10.1089/jwh.2010.2493.

244   **routine screening mammograms should begin:** Committee on Practice Bulletins—Gynecology, "Practice Bulletin 179: Breast Cancer Risk Assessment and Screening in Average-Risk Women," *Obstetrics and Gynecology* 130, no. 1 (July 2017): e1–16, https://doi.org/10.1097/AOG.0000000000002158.

244   **ACOG now recommends that women:** Committee on Practice Bulletins, "Practice Bulletin 179."

245   **WHO notes that clinical exams:** World Health Organization, "WHO Position Paper on Mammography Screening: Summary of Recommendations," last modified 2014, https://paho.org/hq/dmdocuments/2015/WHO-ENG-Mammography-Factsheet.pdf.

245   **FDA issued a safety communication:** "Breast Cancer Screening: Thermogram No Substitute for Mammogram," FDA Consumer Updates, U.S. Food and Drug Administration, last modified January 13, 2021, https://www.fda.gov/consumers/consumer-updates/breast-cancer-screening-thermogram-no-substitute-mammogram.

245   **five-year survival rate of 90 percent:** "Cancer Stat Facts: Female Breast Cancer," Surveillance, Epidemiology, and End Results Program, National Cancer Institute, accessed June 30, 2023, https://seer.cancer.gov/statfacts/html/breast.html.

CHAPTER 20: BIRTH CONTROL

251   **far less than 1 percent:** Marcos de Bastos et al., "Combined Oral Contraceptives: Venous Thrombosis," *Cochrane Database of Systematic Reviews* 3 (2014): CD010813, https://doi.org/10.1002/14651858.CD010813.pub2.

251   **increased fivefold in pregnancy:** Paola Devis and M. Grace Knuttinen, "Deep Venous Thrombosis in Pregnancy: Incidence, Pathogenesis and Endovascular Management," *Cardiovascular Diagnosis and Therapy* 7, supplement 3 (December 2017): S309–19, https://doi.org/10.21037/cdt.2017.10.08.

254 **effectiveness is 93 percent with combined pills:** "Contraception," Centers for Disease Control and Prevention, U.S. Department of Health and Human Services, last updated May 1, 2023, https://www.cdc.gov/reproductivehealth/contraception/index.htm.

254 **91 percent with progesterone-only pills:** "Birth Control Methods," Office on Women's Health, U.S. Department of Health and Human Services, last modified December 29, 2022, https://www.womenshealth.gov/a-z-topics/birth-control-methods.

254 **same effectiveness as pills:** "Contraception," Centers for Disease Control.

255 **body mass index (BMI) higher than thirty:** "Xulane Prescribing Information," Daily Med, National Library of Medicine, National Institutes of Health, last modified March 2022, https://dailymed.nlm.nih.gov/dailymed/fda/fdaDrugXsl.cfm?type=display&setid=f7848550–086a-43d8–8ae5–047f4b9e4382.

255–256 **loss of bone density is only temporary:** Andrew M. Kaunitz, Raquel Arias, and Michael McClung, "Bone Density Recovery After Depot Medroxyprogesterone Acetate Injectable Contraception Use," *Contraception* 77, no. 2 (February 2008): 67–76, https://doi.org/10.1016/j.contraception.2007.10.005.

256 **96 percent with typical use:** "Contraception," Centers for Disease Control.

257 **highest effectiveness rates: more than 99 percent:** "Contraception," Centers for Disease Control.

257 **studies performed in the 1970s:** M. E. Ortiz and H. B. Croxatto, "The Mode of Action of IUDs," *Contraception* 36, no. 1 (July 1987): 37–53, https://doi.org/10.1016/0010–7824(87)90060–6; F. Alvarez et al., "New Insights on the Mode of Action of Intrauterine Contraceptive Devices in Women," *Fertility and Sterility* 49, no. 5 (May 1988): 768–73, https://pubmed.ncbi.nlm.nih.gov/3360166/.

258 **won't have periods while the IUD:** Margarete Hidalgo et al., "Bleeding Patterns and Clinical Performance of the Levonorgestrel-Releasing Intrauterine System (Mirena) up to Two Years," *Contraception* 65, no. 2 (February 2002): 129–32, https://doi.org/10.1016/s0010–7824(01)00302-x.

259 **99 percent effective when placed correctly:** "Contraception," Centers for Disease Control.

260 **Ulipristal is more effective than:** Anna F. Glasier et al., "Ulipristal Acetate Versus Levonorgestrel for Emergency Contraception: A Randomised Non-inferiority Trial and Meta-Analysis," *Lancet* 375, no. 9714 (February 2010): 555–62, https://doi.org/10.1016/S0140–6736(10)60101–8.

260 **85 to 97 percent effective up to three days:** Task Force on Postovulatory Methods of Fertility Regulation, "Randomised Controlled Trial of Levonorgestrel Versus the Yuzpe Regimen of Combined Oral Contraceptives for Emergency Contraception," *Lancet* 352, no. 9126 (1998): 428–33, https://pubmed.ncbi.nlm.nih.gov/9708750/; Glasier, "Ulipristal Acetate Versus Levonorgestrel," 555–62, https://pubmed.ncbi.nlm.nih.gov/20116841/.

261 **99 percent effectiveness rate when inserted:** Kelly Cleland et al., "The Efficacy of Intrauterine Devices for Emergency Contraception: A Systematic Review of 35 Years of Experience," *Human Reproduction* 27, no. 7 (July 2012): 1994–2000, https://doi.org/10.1093/humrep/des140.

261 **ulipristal is the next best:** Tara C. Jatlaoui and Kathryn M. Curtis, "Safety and Effectiveness Data for Emergency Contraceptive Pills Among Women with Obesity: A Systematic Review," *Contraception* 94, no. 6 (December 2016); 605–11, https://doi.org/10.1016/j.contraception.2016.05.002.

262 **can prevent up to 98 percent of pregnancies:** World Health Organization Department of Reproductive Health and Research and Johns Hopkins Bloomberg School of Public Health/Center for Communication Programs, *Family Planning: A Global Handbook for Providers*, 2018 Edition (Baltimore and Geneva: CCP and WHO, 2018).

262 **lower than male condoms, 79 percent:** "Contraception," Centers for Disease Control.

263 **inserted up to twenty-four hours before:** "Today Sponge: Consumer Information Leaflet," Mayer Laboratories, accessed June 30, 2023, https://www.todaysponge.com/pdf/todaysponge-pi2.pdf.

263 **86 percent for people who have never:** "Contraception," Centers for Disease Control.

264 **lasts for one hour, and must be:** "Phexxi Full Prescribing Information," U.S. Food and Drug Administration, May 2020, https://www.accessdata.fda.gov/drugsatfda_docs/label/2020/208352s000lbl.pdf.

264 **vaginal gel has a typical-use effectiveness:** Michael A. Thomas et al., "A Novel Vaginal pH Regulator: Results from the Phase 3 AMPOWER Contraception Clinical Trial," *Contraception: X* 2 (2020): 100031, https://doi.org/10.1016/j.conx.2020.100031.

264 **effectiveness of the cervical cap is 71 percent:** "How Effective Are Cervical Caps?," Planned Parenthood, accessed June 30, 2023, https://www.plannedparenthood.org/learn/birth-control/cervical-cap/how-effective-are-cervical-caps.

264 **effectiveness of the diaphragm is 87 percent:** W. Bounds et al., "The Diaphragm with and Without Spermicide: A Randomized, Comparative

Efficacy Trial," *Journal of Reproductive Medicine* 40, no. 11 (November 1995): 764–74, https://pubmed.ncbi.nlm.nih.gov/8592310/.

265   **typical-use effectiveness is 80 percent:** "Pull Out Method," Cleveland Clinic, last updated September 15, 2022, https://my.clevelandclinic.org /health/articles/24174-pull-out-method.

266   **effectiveness rate of about 75 percent:** "Natural Family Planning as a Means of Preventing Pregnancy," Kaiser Family Foundation, May 15, 2018, https://www.kff.org/womens-health-policy/fact-sheet/natural-family -planning-as-a-means-of-preventing-pregnancy.

267   **effectiveness of fertility-awareness methods is 77 to 98 percent:** R. A. Hatcher et al., eds., "Table 26–1: Percentage of Women Experiencing an Unintended Pregnancy During the First Year of Typical Use and the First Year of Perfect Use of Contraception and the Percentage of Continuing Use," in *Contraceptive Technology,* 21st ed. (New York: Ayer Company, 2018), 844.

CHAPTER 21: HYSTERECTOMY

270   **four hundred thousand people undergo hysterectomies:** "Health Services Research on Hysterectomy and Alternatives," Agency for Healthcare Research and Quality, U.S. Department of Health and Human Services, last modified August 1998, https://archive.ahrq.gov/research/hysterec.htm.

271   **50 percent of women undergoing hysterectomies:** Vanessa L. Jacoby et al., "Factors Associated with Undergoing Bilateral Salpingo-Oophorectomy at the Time of Hysterectomy for Benign Conditions," *Obstetrics and Gynecology* 113, no. 6 (June 2009): 1259–67, https://doi.org/10.1097/AOG .0b013e3181a66c42.

271   **2008, ACOG recommended:** American College of Obstetricians and Gynecologists, "Practice Bulletin No. 89: Elective and Risk-Reducing Salpingo-Oophorectomy," *Obstetrics and Gynecology* 111, no. 1 (January 2008): 231–41, https://doi.org/10.1097/01.AOG.0000291580.39618.cb.

275   **no difference in sexual satisfaction:** Anne Lethaby, Asima Mukhopadhyay, and Raj Naik, "Total Versus Subtotal Hysterectomy for Benign Gynaecological Conditions," *Cochrane Database of Systematic Reviews* 4 (April 2012): CD004993, https://doi.org/10.1002/14651858.CD004993 .pub3.

275   **menopausal symptoms a few years earlier:** C. Y. Deng et al., "Effect of Premenopausal Hysterectomy on Ovarian Function," *Acta Academiae Medicinae Sinicae* 24, no. 6 (December 2002): 639–42, https://europepmc .org/article/med/12905696.

276 **increased risk of cardiovascular disease:** Erik Ingelsson et al., "Hysterectomy and Risk of Cardiovascular Disease: A Population-Based Cohort Study," *European Heart Journal* 32, no. 6 (March 2011): 745–50, https://doi.org/10.1093/eurheartj/ehq477.

276 **sexual satisfaction actually improved:** Jan-Paul W. R. Roovers et al., "Hysterectomy and Sexual Wellbeing: Prospective Observational Study of Vaginal Hysterectomy, Subtotal Abdominal Hysterectomy, and Total Abdominal Hysterectomy," *BMJ* 327, no. 7418 (2003): 774–78, https://doi.org/10.1136/bmj.327.7418.774; Julia C. Rhodes et al., "Hysterectomy and Sexual Functioning," *JAMA* 282, no. 20 (November 1999): 1934–41, https://doi.org/10.1001/jama.282.20.1934.

CHAPTER 22: TUBAL STERILIZATION

278 **child-free subreddit:** "The Childfree Friendly Doctors List," Childfree Forum, Reddit, accessed July 1, 2023, https://www.reddit.com/r/childfree/wiki/doctors/.

279 **decreases the chances of getting ovarian:** Henrik Falconer et al., "Ovarian Cancer Risk After Salpingectomy: A Nationwide Population-Based Study," *Journal of the National Cancer Institute* 107, no. 2 (January 2015): dju410, https://doi.org/10.1093/jnci/dju410.

280 **5 to 25 percent of people who have:** Susan D. Hillis et al., "Poststerilization Regret: Findings from the United States Collaborative Review of Sterilization," *Obstetrics and Gynecology* 93, no. 6 (June 1999): 889–95, https://doi.org/10.1016/s0029-7844(98)00539-0.

281 **Medicaid have a minimum age:** Sonya Borrero et al., "Medicaid Policy on Sterilization—Anachronistic or Still Relevant?," *New England Journal of Medicine* 370, no. 2 (January 2014): 102–4, https://doi.org/10.1056/NEJMp1313325.

281 **1909 and 1979, several government-organized:** Alexandra Minna Stern, "Sterilized in the Name of Public Health: Race, Immigration, and Reproductive Control in Modern California," *American Journal of Public Health* 95, no. 7 (July 2005): 1128–38, https://doi.org/10.2105/AJPH.2004.041608.

282 **no significant differences in hormone levels:** Gwen P. Gentile et al., "Hormone Levels Before and After Tubal Sterilization," *Contraception* 73, no. 5 (May 2006): 507–11, https://doi.org/10.1016/j.contraception.2005.12.002.

282 **sexual satisfaction remains the same:** Caroline Costello et al., "Effect of Interval Tubal Sterilization on Sexual Interest and Pleasure," *Obstetrics and Gynecology* 100, no. 3 (September 2002): 511–17, https://doi.org/10.1016/s0029-7844(02)02042-2.

CHAPTER 23: ABORTION

285   **One in four women:** R. K. Jones and J. Jerman, "Population Group Abortion Rates and Lifetime Incidence of Abortion: United States, 2008–2014," *American Journal of Public Health* 112, no. 9 (September 2022): 1284–96, https://doi.org/10.2105/AJPH.2017.304042.

286   **More than half of women:** Katherine Kortsmit et al., "Abortion Surveillance—United States, 2019," *Morbidity and Mortality Weekly Report: Surveillance Summaries* 70, no. SS-9 (November 2021): 1–29, http://dx.doi.org/10.15585/mmwr.ss7009a1.

286–287   **several women have come forward:** Kate Zernike, "Five Women Sue Texas over the State's Abortion Ban," *New York Times*, March 6, 2023, https://www.nytimes.com/2023/03/06/us/texas-abortion-ban-suit.html.

287   **Ireland in 2012:** Megan Specia, "How Savita Halappanavar's Death Spurred Ireland's Abortion Rights Campaign," *New York Times*, May 27, 2018, https://www.nytimes.com/2018/05/27/world/europe/savita-halappanavar-ireland-abortion.html.

287   **Guttmacher Institute reports that most countries:** Jonathan Bearak et al., "Unintended Pregnancy and Abortion by Income, Region, and the Legal Status of Abortion: Estimates from a Comprehensive Model for 1990–2019," *Lancet: Global Health* 8, no. 9 (September 2020): e1152–61, https://doi.org/10.1016/S2214-109X(20)30315-6.

287   **WHO estimates that twenty-five million unsafe:** Bella Ganatra et al., "Global, Regional, and Subregional Classification of Abortions by Safety, 2010–14: Estimates from a Bayesian Hierarchical Model," *Lancet* 390, no. 10110 (November 2017): 2372–81, https://doi.org/10.1016/S0140-6736(17)31794-4.

287   **deaths of tens of thousands:** Iqbal Shah and Elisabeth Ahman, "Unsafe Abortion: Global and Regional Incidence, Trends, Consequences, and Challenges," *Journal of Obstetrics and Gynaecology Canada* 31, no. 12 (December 2009): 1149–58, https://pubmed.ncbi.nlm.nih.gov/20085681/.

287   **200,000 to 1.2 million illegal abortions:** Rachel Benson Gold, "Lessons from Before *Roe*: Will Past Be Prologue?," *Guttmacher Report on Public Policy* 6, no. 1 (March 2003): https://www.guttmacher.org/sites/default/files/article_files/gr060108.pdf.

287   ***New England Journal of Medicine* article:** Lisa Rosenbaum, "Perilous Politics—Morbidity and Mortality in the Pre-*Roe* Era," *New England Journal of Medicine* 381, no. 10 (September 2019): 893–95, https://doi.org/10.1056/NEJMp1910010.

288   **Romania and South Africa:** Janie Benson, Kathryn Andersen, and

Ghazaleh Samandari, "Reductions in Abortion-Related Mortality Following Policy Reform: Evidence from Romania, South Africa and Bangladesh," *Reproductive Health* 8 (December 2011): 39, https://doi.org/10.1186/1742-4755-8-39.

288   **62 percent higher maternal mortality:** Eugene Declercq et al., "The U.S. Maternal Health Divide: The Limited Maternal Health Services and Worse Outcomes of States Proposing New Abortion Restrictions," Issue Briefs, *Commonwealth Fund*, December 14, 2022, https://doi.org/10.26099/z7dz-8211.

288   **24 percent overall, and 39 percent among Black:** Amanda Jean Stevenson, Leslie Root, and Jane Menken, "The Maternal Mortality Consequences of Losing Abortion Access," *SocArXiv* (June 2022), https://doi.org/10.31235/osf.io/7g29k.

288   **WHO considers access to safe abortion:** "Abortion," Fact Sheets, World Health Organization, last modified November 25, 2021, https://www.who.int/news-room/fact-sheets/detail/abortion.

288   **every major medical association:** "More Than 75 Health Care Organizations Release Joint Statement in Opposition to Legislative Interference," News Release, American College of Obstetricians and Gynecologists, July 7, 2022, https://www.acog.org/news/news-releases/2022/07/more-than-75-health-care-organizations-release-joint-statement-in-opposition-to-legislative-interference.

289   **unnecessary in most first-trimester abortions:** Committee on Practice Bulletins—Gynecology and the Society of Family Planning, "Practice Bulletin Number 255: Medication Abortion up to 70 Days of Gestation," *Obstetrics and Gynecology* 136, no. 4 (October 2020): e31–47, https://doi.org/10.1097/AOG.0000000000002158.

290   **mifepristone is approved by the FDA:** "Information About Mifepristone for Medical Termination of Pregnancy Through Ten Weeks Gestation," U.S. Food and Drug Administration, last updated March 23, 2023, https://www.fda.gov/drugs/postmarket-drug-safety-information-patients-and-providers/information-about-mifepristone-medical-termination-pregnancy-through-ten-weeks-gestation.

290   **ACOG and the National Abortion Federation:** Committee on Practice Bulletins, "Practice Bulletin 255."

290   **95 to 98 percent of people:** Dustin Costescu et al., "Clinical Practice Guideline: Medical Abortion," *Journal of Obstetrics and Gynaecology Canada* 38, no. 4 (2016): 366–89, https://doi.org/10.1016/j.jogc.2016.01.002.

291   **93 percent, are done in the first:** Kortsmit et al., "Abortion Surveillance."

CHAPTER 24: GYNECOLOGIC EXAMS AND OFFICE PROCEDURES

301   **oral pain medications and topical numbing:** Lili Church et al., "Analgesia for Colposcopy: Double-Masked, Randomized Comparison of Ibuprofen and Benzocaine Gel," *Obstetrics and Gynecology* 97, no. 1 (January 2001): 5–10, https://doi.org/10.1016/s0029–7844(00)01084-x.

301   **just as effective as local anesthetic:** Bernd C. Schmid et al., "Forced Coughing Versus Local Anesthesia and Pain Associated with Cervical Biopsy: A Randomized Trial," *American Journal of Obstetrics and Gynecology* 199, no. 6 (December 2008): 641.E1–E3, https://doi.org/10.1016/j.ajog.2008.07.017.

303   **Pain with IUD insertion:** Laureen M. Lopez et al., "Interventions for Pain with Intrauterine Device Insertion," *Cochrane Database of Systematic Reviews* 2015, no. 7 (July 2015): CD007373, https://doi.org/10.1002/14651858.CD007373.pub3.

306   **topical anesthesia sprays, local anesthetic gel:** Ahmed M. Abbas et al., "Medications for Pain Relief in Outpatient Endometrial Sampling or Biopsy: A Systematic Review and Network Meta-Analysis," *Fertility and Sterility* 112, no. 1 (July 2019): 140–48, https://doi.org/10.1016/j.fertnstert.2019.03.028.

INDEX

ABOUT THE AUTHOR

Karen Tang, MD, MPH, is a board-certified gynecologist and minimally invasive gynecologic surgeon who is an internationally recognized leader in reproductive health. She received her medical degree and master's in public health at Columbia University, and trained in obstetrics and gynecology at Beth Israel Deaconess Medical Center / Harvard Medical School. As @KarenTangMD on TikTok, Instagram, and YouTube, she reaches millions of viewers each month with her educational videos about period health, pelvic pain, and reproductive rights. Dr. Tang has been featured in the *Washington Post*, *Self*, *Glamour*, NBCNews.com, and NPR, among other media outlets. She lives outside of Philadelphia with her husband and three children.